I Sold the Moon!

A True Story

Silver Street
Publishing

First Edition
2163 Meeker Avenue, Suite 101
Richmond, CA 94804
(510) 219-5900

Cover and interior design by Yvette Mangual
Interior type set in Chaparral Pro

ISBN: 978-0-9793673-9-7

Library of Congress Control Number: 2007901347

Front and back cover photograph courtesy of Paula Saed.
Front cover and interior full moon photograph provided by bigstockphoto.
p. 16 Berkeley Daily Gazette (1973), p.28 The Newsrecord-University of Cincinnati
(1975), p. 86 Sacramento Bee (1975), p. 116 Chico Enterprise Record (1977),
p. 148 Riverside Daily Enterprise (1974), p. 156 University Times-Los Angeles (1976),
p. 156 Daily Trojan-Los Angeles (1976), p. 162 (left) San Bernardino News (1975),
p. 162 (right) Irish Press, Ireland (1973), p. 170 (top) The Irish Press, Ireland (1973),
p. 170 (bottom) San Franciso Chronicle (1975), p. 178 Irish Press, Ireland (1973),
p. 224 The Wisconsin State Journal (1975), p. 232 After Dark, Honolulu (1979),
p. 244 (top) The Daily Forty-Niner, Long Beach (1976), p. 244 (bottom) Redlands Daily
Facts (1974), p. 260 Photograph by Michael Kienitz

Some names have been changed to protect privacy.

Special thanks to David Riker for his friendship, guidance and editorial insistence.

www.isoldthemoon.com

I Sold the Moon!

A True Story

By

Barry McArdle

Dedicated to Paula and Sheri
For Paula who lived the story...
For Sheri whose loving support allowed me to write it.

Think Cosmically—Act Globally

"It is the very error of the moon,
She comes more near the earth than she was wont,
And makes men mad."

—William Shakespeare (Othello)

MOONSTRUCK

It was hard to tell where the cold gray haze ended and the cold gray Pacific started. The ocean at Stinson Beach on Northern California's coastline, on the afternoon of July 20th, 1969, looked like a giant lake of mercury shrouded in mist and fog. I was there with my best friend from high school, David Barclay. Having arrived at the beach, our objectives were simple and time-honored for young men our age: we hoped to meet some girls and find someone willing to buy us some beer.

I don't know who saw it first, the faint white glow of mysterious flickering light shining through the low hanging fog. With the beach deserted, our natural instinct drew us to this strange rectangle of phosphorescent energy. As we came closer, we were able to make out, through a temporary clearing in the fog, a small camper trailer and one grizzled old man staring intently at a small, not so mysterious, television.

The faint black and white image was a bit grainy, but that was understandable. It was coming from over 220,000 miles away. It was coming from the surface of the moon. It was now 1:15 PM. In two minutes, the first human in history, would climb down a small ladder and set foot on a body in space other than the earth. The three of us stared transfixed, knowing we were sharing a moment in world history that would forever be remembered.

Later that night the fog cleared away and I stared, with new eyes, at earth's satellite. I thought how special it was to be alive during the time man had first arrived on the moon. I wondered if America would lay claim, or assume sovereignty now that we had planted our flag there.

Would the government ever consider selling moon property? Who really owns the moon? Would anybody consider buying it? What would it sell for? Why hadn't anybody tried selling it before? Why couldn't I sell it?

Sleep was hard to come by that night. I was mesmerized by the moon's light on the sea, on the sand and on my mind. Had moon property ever been sold in the past? Could it ever be sold in the future?

These were questions I would need to think about. These were questions I did think about.

CHAPTER 1

SELLING PIE IN THE SKY

I HAD TO LAUGH AT MYSELF. OF COURSE, I KNEW I WASN'T THE ONLY one who found my appearance comical. But I could handle the stares and snickers of my fellow pedestrians as I made my way to my "office." Looking like a low-rent comic book Super Hero come to life, I was eager to get started. I was also excited knowing I'd be making money —perhaps lots of money. This pleasure, I realized, was fueled less from the money itself, and more from the satisfaction I felt sharing it with Paula, the woman I loved, and the woman who loved me.

Like most everyone who survives childhood, I felt different from the person I once was. Yet my reflection, in the storefront window, reminded me that I still liked playing dress up, I still liked wearing a cape, and I was still in search of an audience.

✳ ✳ ✳

It was 1975. I'd been making my living for the past four years by selling "land" on the moon, and I was just getting started. I was back in Berkeley, California—the place I considered Moon Man Headquarters. In Berkeley, one street was custom made for my brand of lunacy. It was Telegraph Avenue. "The Ave," as it was called, was the commercial and social Mecca for tourists, street people and the 30,000 undergraduate students attending the University of California at Berkeley.

At the corner of Telegraph and Bancroft, on the University side of the street, there was, and still is, a three-foot high by six-foot square brick planter. A two-foot ledge framed the structure on top. That would be my stage. If you were out on The Ave or on campus for any length of time, there was a good chance you would pass by this corner, and when you did, I was going to be impossible to miss.

Although the competition for my share of the street's disposable income was considerable, my product, my dress and especially my presentation, would prove unique enough to insure my fair share of the consumer pie.

Besides the normal college-town retail stores, coffee bars and head shops, there were over a hundred street vendors. They gave The Ave its unique pulse and wonderfully energized sense of madness.

For eight blocks leading up to the campus, Telegraph Avenue was lined on both sides with shops and vendors. They sold jewelry, pottery, tie-dyed clothing, macramé, incense, crystals, pot-smoking paraphernalia, photography, paintings, decoupage, musical instruments, kites, carved masks, soaps, wind chimes, ceramic hobbit characters, political bumper stickers, tattoo's, glass beads, wooden toys, and on, and on.

Intermingled with the vendor stalls were card tables covered with shimmering material in scarlet, gold, and indigo blue. Incense burned and crystal balls or glass pyramids sat atop decks of tarot cards waiting for the next devotee to lay down $5.00 for a reading. Those more inclined to divine the future through palmistry or astrology were catered to equally.

The daily throng included pedestrians of every nationality, every social and economic stratum, and every religious, political, and sexually oriented persuasion. It was as if cities and towns all across America had sent their outcasts, misfits, and disenfranchised to Berkeley. However, along with the disproportionate number of dropouts, runaways, and burned-out druggies, these same communities would also contribute their most brilliant minds, musical prodigies, and gifted athletes.

Walking The Ave was a multi-dimensional kaleidoscope of sights, accompanied by a cacophony of sounds, political debate, and pungent aroma. The air was sweet with the smell of marijuana, and on most corners, bags of pot could be negotiated without a word spoken. Make eye contact, flash a ten-dollar bill, and the exchange would be made before the light turned green. I never understood the value in asking, "Is this good shit?" Sometimes it was, and sometimes it wasn't—and on occasion, it turned out to be oregano.

Into this circus of entrepreneurial commerce, drugs, and street theatre, the Moon Man would hold court. The fact that someone selling the moon would be in Berkeley somehow seemed normal. People came to Berkeley expecting to find someone like me. They came to see for themselves what this counterculture really looked like. They wanted their picture taken with a flower child, or in front of a "Make Love Not War" poster. If they got lucky they might get to tell their bowling buddies back in Iowa that they talked to some "real hippies." If that didn't work out, a Moon Man was not a bad second choice.

From where I stood, I could see down Telegraph Avenue, up Bancroft, and across most of Sproul Plaza. And best of all, everybody in my line of sight could see me. I felt confident as I stood above the bustling pedestrians wearing my new, internationally-designed costume. I cleared my throat and began.

"Ladies and gentlemen, mention the name Berkeley, California anywhere in the world and most people have a preconceived idea of what it's like here. Today I offer you a chance to prove them right! Today I offer you a chance to take a little bit of Berkeley home with you. You would be crazier than people think I am if you came to Berkeley and didn't at least consider buying what I'm selling. One dollar, one acre! How wrong can you go? Move in a little closer please. It looks like it's going to be another standing room only crowd. People come from everywhere to see Berkeley's very own Moon Man. But don't believe everything you may have heard. I am not a living brain donor. I am, however, a living example of why not to take LSD. Remember this is not radio, this is not television, and this is not a movie. What you are witnessing at this very moment is live, and that has value, that is what makes it special. You alone, however, will decide if that value is worth the asking price of one dollar. Exactly what I'm selling for one dollar some of you already know, the rest of you are to be spared no longer. I must caution you now, and do so on the advice of legal counsel. If any of you are on medication—I'm talking about legal drugs only—or have a weak heart, it may be advisable for you to leave the area now while your exposure level is still low. Be advised there are no medical personnel standing by during this performance. Anyone who stays does so at his or her own risk."

This preliminary mumbo-jumbo was used to gather the beginnings of a crowd. As I had discovered, once even a small crowd forms, it becomes the attraction and like a magnet, draws more and more curiosity seekers. And in Berkeley, almost everyone is curious.

"For those of you joining us late, you missed the appearance of the Invisible Man. To the parents of students here at Berkeley, I just want to assure you your money is well spent. I mean, look at me—I'm a living example of what a college degree can do for your kids."

This line would usually get a good laugh—proving that the truth is at least as funny as fiction.

"I did try to get work after graduating, but I discovered all the drop-outs already had the jobs."

Next, I would bring out my "Moon Book." In this binder, covered with silver fabric, I had my copyright certificate and all my newspaper clippings, which now numbered about 10. In time, I would amass over 100. My reasons for showing these clippings were threefold: They gave me some credibility. They provided "comfort in numbers" for prospective buyers, and they promoted an aura of celebrity. I opened the book now.

"*The Berkeley Daily Gazette* on December 19, 1973 ran this front-page story. Please notice the big picture that accompanied the article." (Quoting from the article):

"**ONLY IN BERKELEY**—'Moonman' Barry McArdle, just back from Dublin, Ireland where he was fined three pounds for selling without a license..."

"Yes, it's true I am just back from the Old Sod where moon land sold for a pound an acre. Those of you who buy one today will be paying less than half that price. The real story is not that I didn't have a license—which I didn't—but my contention is that no city, state, or country has the power to grant me that license. The simple fact is I am the first person in history ever to lay claim to the moon. My claim was made in 1971. I draw your attention to this copyright granting me the sole right to print these documents. However, you should be forewarned that the United States Government is considering taking me to court for fraud. Anyone considering buying an acre should know that my legal case does not look good at this time. In fact, it looks a little...shaky. However, I will be countersuing the government on two charges. Number one—trespassing. They didn't even have the courtesy to ask my permission. They just went. And number two— littering. We have a bad enough litter problem here on earth, and now the government is trashing my property on the moon—and I have pictures to prove it! One dollar one acre! This is the only place in the world where you can buy land on the moon!"

By this time, there would usually be a crowd of people facing me in a loosely formed semicircle. I could not expect to hold the crowd too long. It was time for the close.

"You may be in Berkeley today partly because you wanted to see if what you've been hearing and reading about is true. Is Berkeley really different? Is Berkeley really weird? My answer to that would be where else can you find someone selling the moon? Thank God for Berkeley, California. As long as someone like me can stand in a public forum dressed like this, and have the liberty to express a rather radical interpretation of real estate law, I have to believe freedom of expression is alive and well in America. You would never have seen someone like me in Nazi Germany, or today in Russia, China, Czechoslovakia...Chicago."

I really was proud to be an American knowing that a place existed where freedom of speech seemed to be valued above the bureaucratic imperative of demanding that my "papers" be in order.

"If you believe in the majority of one, freedom of speech, freedom of assembly, the birthright of all citizens of earth to have unfettered access to planetary habitation throughout our solar system...or if you're just looking for a wacky cheapo gift for Uncle Larry, consider a Moon Acre. One dollar, one acre! I challenge you to find anything as original or creative, with the potential of becoming one of history's greatest collector's items, as is this document I'm selling today. When you get home, do you want to admit that you saw someone selling land on the moon and you didn't buy one? And why not? Because it cost a whole dollar? My friends, there is a lot to see and do here in the Bay Area. By all means visit San Francisco, have a shrimp cocktail on Fisherman's Wharf, eat some sourdough bread, drive across the Golden Gate Bridge, but most of all take home land on the moon!

I Sold *the* Moon!

This is not swampland in Florida. You'll need to talk to my cousin for that. And don't forget every parcel I sell comes with a picturesque view of earth and I still have a number of lots available right on...Moon River. I'm not here to trick you, to con you, or to make promises I know I can't keep. If I were, I would most likely be wearing a business suit with an American flag pin in my lapel. This insanity happens in the open, not behind locked committee doors in Washington, D.C. Help keep lunacy public where it belongs. Support originality and creativity. Remember, buying moon acres keeps me off welfare. Is there a better gift anywhere in the world? You may know someone in real estate. You may know someone who has just had a frontal lobotomy. Have some fun. Do something really different today. One dollar, one acre —land boom on the moon!"

But I'm getting ahead of myself... How I came to be the Moon Man was still hard for me to figure out. After all, college had not prepared me for my current occupation. There were no classes in how to sell the moon. There were no degrees offered in Lunar Real Estate. In fact, I almost didn't graduate at all.

CHAPTER 2

CHICO DAZE

EARNING MY FOUR YEAR DEGREE SEEMED MIRACULOUS CONSIDERING all the parties, all the beer, and, more than anything, living up to the "no hold'em-smoke'em," battle cry of my generation. Yes, I'm talking about God's sweet herb, the peace pipe combustible of choice and every black light distributor's best friend…marijuana. Like the song says, it was a time when you smoked two joints before you smoked two joints and then you smoked two more. When you hear about "Sex, Drugs and Rock & Roll," you need look no further for the source than my Chico State College graduating class of 1971. Fortunately, the liberated women of the era were into the bong pipe and sex as much as their male counterparts. We, of course, had no problem with the revolutionary statement expressed by the burning of their bras. I, for one, always carried a book of matches with me. No doubt a carry-over from my Boy Scout training to "be prepared."

I majored in Mass Communications, partly because you got to see lots of movies and my best friend and roommate, David Barclay, was in the program. Barclay knew how to dress, with the studied indifference of a lead singer in a rock band. He stood a bit over six feet tall and was svelte at 160 pounds. With rakishly good looks, he was often told he looked like Cary Grant—although with darker, longer hair. Women were attracted to his mega-watt smile, boyish charm and highly developed sense of humor.

Like me, David tended to look for the humor in life, and would do almost anything for a laugh. He was at his best when he turned his intellect inward and allowed himself and those around him to laugh at his insecurities and self-deprecating humor.

When the magic of Barry and David was in top form, or when the pot was especially good, we could have a room full of people laughing so hard they would cry. Laughter was the drug David and I liked best, and we were both hopelessly addicted.

Life was wonderful and the future was before us. One troubling thing about the future though—everyone I talked to always mentioned something about work, something about the real world.

As fate would have it our department head—everybody called him Mr. Weed—was also David's and my counselor. Five weeks before we were due to graduate, he came out of the ether to inform both of us that we somehow had missed taking a required course: "Mass Communications and the Law" and therefore, unfortunately, we would not be graduating with our class. He recommended summer school, adding "Look on the bright side. You'll be in town June, July and August and that's harvest time."

Well, we had other plans, big plans. What they were exactly, or even vaguely, needed to be worked out. We just knew whatever they were they did not include being left behind in sweltering Chico, California for the summer, taking some boring class about our chosen profession and the law. Besides, that would put into jeopardy our immediate plan to spend the summer in sweltering Sacramento, California mooching free room and board, perhaps for the last time, from our respective families.

The embarrassment of not graduating on time motivated us to inquire as to whether there was any other option available to us.

It was the first time either of us heard the term "Challenge the Course." Mr. W. explained it was a seldom-used procedure to get credit without actually having to take the class.

"We don't often suggest it because very few students ever pass the exam. In fact," he said, "'Mass Communication and the Law' has never been successfully challenged in my 18 years at this College."

He not too subtlety let us know that he felt
of failures would be safe from the intellectual
would be bringing to the endeavor.

We had no choice. We also had very litt'
paper work submitted for graduation we wo‿
Challenge in two weeks time.

Neither David nor I could be considered gifted students.
Although we didn't think life owed us a living, we had yet to buy off
on the concept that we owed life our best effort.

Together we decided to apply ourselves, perhaps for the first
time in our lives, as never before. That meant no beer, television
or pot until after the test. Explaining our situation, we were given
dispensation to miss our current classes for the next two weeks.
Then, we borrowed notes from three students who had aced the
course the previous semester. That afternoon, we began reading
the first of four books covered in that class. I called Paula, and then
disconnected the phone.

I had fallen in love with Paula long before she distracted me from the
flow of the game with the cartwheels, flips and splits she performed
as Del Campo High School's head varsity cheerleader. And even
though the gold panties she wore were part of her cheerleader's
costume and not the real thing, win or lose, seeing them was always
the highlight of the night.

Her voluptuous 5'4" frame radiated spontaneity and sensuality.
Her hair was golden brown and her eyes a brilliant emerald green.
With her Norwegian pearl-like skin, she had a body that would be
very much at home on the pages of *Playboy* magazine. Her physical
proportionality and exuberance were in the classic cheerleader mold,
however, she was *not* your stereotypical cheerleader.

When I met her, she was a Maoist, and for a time wore the
red star of China pin. She studied astrology and the I Ching and
read Tarot Cards. Paula wrote poetry, was a woman's liberationist
long before it became popular, read Baba Ram Dass and the Yogi
Paramahansa Yogananda. She baked homemade bread and was
the first person I ever knew who had taken LSD. She was also a
virgin. Her experimental nature, at that time, did not extend to sex.

ve dated for a full year before she let me kiss her. But that was when I discovered some things in life are worth the wait....

I knew something was different from the moment I picked her up. She always looked good but tonight she was radiant. She wore a short halter dress that blended with her body like cream being stirred into a cup of coffee. Her hair was alive in hundreds of loose bouncing curls.

We both had seen "Gone With The Wind" before, but this time it seemed more poignant. I felt a kinship with Rhett Butler in his long pursuit of Scarlett O'Hara. For the first time Paula held my hand during a movie, even returning a squeeze from me with one of her own.

After the show, we were back in the family car—a 1965 Chrysler station wagon. My older sister Dourene was up front with her boy friend Carl McWilliams, who was driving. I had my arm around Paula's shoulder and half my face buried in her curls and her delicious smell. This was a new experience. I started to differentiate between the smell of her perfume and the more stimulating scent of her body. My lips brushed her skin and I kissed the small hollow at the base of her neck, where the collarbone starts its run to the shoulder. She turned her head up and towards me.

It's funny what one remembers. Why do some everyday occurrences remain vivid one's whole life? What is it that happens in the brain to lock in a memory forever that in and of itself has no significance whatsoever? I have such a memory. As I lifted my head back to give room for Paula to face me, I saw a billboard advertising a company called Carpeteria. Their celebrity spokesperson was Dale Robertson. His picture was the last thing I saw as we sped by, moments before my life changed forever.

Paula's face was now turned fully toward me, and just inches away. I could feel the sweet, warm breath coming in irregular bursts from her mouth. I had never felt like this before. I put my hands on either side of her upturned face and in slow motion pulled her towards me. Flashes of colored light were exploding all around me as I ascended on cushions of air. I had forgotten to breathe, and was becoming light-headed, but more than the awareness that I needed oxygen was the all-enveloping realization that I was in love.

The following day, in a quiet ceremony, Paula and I tied three bands of leather around my left wrist. We considered these cords of rawhide a talisman— never to be taken off. They would serve as a reminder that Paula and I would be together forever.

✳ ✳ ✳

Paula was currently attending the University of California at Berkeley on a Dramatic Arts scholarship, and we were managing to conduct a long-distance romance. She agreed to help us cram for the test on one condition: promise to follow her study schedule to the letter. We did.

She arrived the following afternoon, after hitchhiking the 150-odd miles north to Chico and immediately informed me there would be no sex until after the test, and not then if I failed. She then taped our study schedule to the refrigerator:

7:00–8:00 Shower/Push-Ups/Breakfast
8:00–11:00 Read/Create 20 questions
11:00–12:00 Q & A
12:00–1:00 Lunch—Review missed questions
1:00–4:00 Read/Question development
4:00–5:00 Free time (She encouraged us to jog or take a cold shower.)
5:00–8:00 Read/Question development
8:00–9:00 Dinner/Review
9:00–11:00 Q & A
11:15–7:00 Bed (Alone)

Our study coach was a strong believer in reinforcing a right answer. Paula kept saying, "You'll need lots of right answers to pass." By the third day she had written hundreds of flash cards, each with one question and its answer on the back. By late in the second week both David and I had completed the reading, and were spending the entire day working off Paula's flash cards, which now numbered over 1,200.

The Challenge was set for Monday morning. When we got up on Saturday, Paula informed us we were changing locations. She had rented a cheap hotel room and told us we were not leaving until Monday morning. We arrived with a change of underwear, a toothbrush and a suitcase full of books, papers and flash cards. For two days, we did nothing but answer questions over and over and over again.

11

A strange and wondrous thing happened in that room over those two days. I had never before wanted to take a test, felt ready to take a test, or, God forbid, looked forward to taking a test, and now I did.

We were the first in line to be issued our test packets. Each of the 12 students taking the test was assigned a test monitor. Nobody was going to cheat on this exam. We were instructed that we would have 6 hours to complete the test. If we needed to visit the bathroom, our monitor would go with us. Anyone talking or observed looking at another's desk would be asked to leave and their test would be confiscated.

I thought my mind would explode. My stomach heaved and suddenly everything went blank. The panic express train was gaining momentum and my leg felt caught under the rail. From out of the fog, I heard the words: "Good luck. You may begin."

I flipped to the last page in the test. There were "only" 362 questions. I had been answering 1200 questions a day for four days and hearing David answer just as many. My leg suddenly had wiggle room.

After two hours and twenty minutes, I was finished.

Everyone else except David was still working. He was in the hall, having finished five minutes earlier. "Let's get a drink," he said, "I'm buying."

At The Wildcat, "Home of the Two-Dollar Pitcher of Beer," Paula was worried.

"Did you rush? Were there questions we didn't cover? When would we know?"

"Paula, do you really think I would forfeit sleeping with you forever?" I asked.

The results would be posted on Mr. Weed's door at 7 PM. At 6:45, three drunken friends were letting the wall support them in front of an office door that suddenly took on a great importance. When Mr. W. finally posted the results, it was Paula who ran to check. In those few moments before I could confirm what I believed to be true, my confidence evaporated and I wondered if in fact I had been relying on liquid courage. Paula's face, as she turned from the sheet, told me everything I needed to know and her kiss was prelude to one of those nights of bliss that can only be appreciated by those who earn them.

We were going to graduate! Word spread fast that we had done the impossible, and for the remainder of the year the other students in our department called us the "Einstein Boys." It was a moniker I rather enjoyed.

There is one thing I would have changed. David and I made a regrettable decision on the morning of our Graduation Day. Actually, this bonehead scheme had been agreed upon months earlier. For three or four months prior to "G" day we had been saving out a pinch or two of the best pot we came in contact with. This "super stash" had been rolled up and put aside.

Bidwell Creek meandered its way through the center of campus. Our favorite place on the stream was thickly shaded by a variety of trees and 14-foot tall bamboo stalks. It was a typically hot June day in Chico and we were both wearing shorts and tee shirts. (David was in his favorite Rolling Stones shirt, showing a big red tongue displayed on the front. I was in my well-worn "Hell No We Won't Go—Stop the War Now" shirt.) In our arms, we carried our long black graduation robes and accompanying mortarboards with tassels. We also had in our possession 6 of the fattest, most potent, American flag-designed, and banana-flavored papered "Killer" joints. I remember very clearly smoking that first celebratory rocket. I'm not quite as clear about what went on during the partaking of joint number two. I do know we thought the water in the creek was very funny. Half way through big bomber number three it looked like the tongue on David's shirt was starting to move and curl. Then through the haze of laughter and smoke we heard a very authoritarian voice yell, "Campus security! Get your butts up here."

This was now a classic case of where the term "bummer" could be accurately applied. Was our day of glory going to be ruined by a rent-a-cop? We ran. Stoned we may have been, but not so blitzed that we forgot the cardinal rule when faced with capture, while in possession of any illegal substance...you eat it. No evidence—no crime. We made our way through running water, tree branches and mud. Scrambling up the opposite bank we emerged under the cover of low hanging growth, some 150 yards downstream from where we had started. Our unseen pursuer had given up early in the chase, having felt he had done his duty, and kept his uniform clean and dry in the process. Besides, busting someone for smoking pot on a California college campus in 1971 was not going to get your name in the paper, or do much to advance your career.

Have you ever wondered what everyone is looking at only to discover they're all looking at you? It took us about two minutes to figure out that all the clean, crisp, freshly scrubbed graduates, in their nicely pressed robes attended to by their equally clean, crisp, freshly scrubbed parents and friends, were all wide-eyed and unabashedly staring directly at us. It was then that I took a good look at my companion. David was covered in a mixture of sweat, twigs and mud. His robe was trailing on the ground and looked like an old beach towel you might find being used as a sleeping mat for someone's German shepherd. I stared, along with everyone else, and then started to laugh.

David finally understood the scene, and in typical defensive rhetoric pointed at me and announced, "Hey, screw you. You don't exactly look like the valedictorian yourself." He was right. I too looked like something that had just crawled through a drainpipe. Although our robes now covered our sweaty, dirty bodies, they didn't make us look anything like the picture of the graduate shown on the cover of the box they had come so neatly folded in.

David's parents and family friends were sitting just below my large family group along the 40-yard line in the school's football stadium. They started waving to us as we walked in somber columns toward our chairs lined up on the playing field. They all seemed to have powerful binoculars trained on us. Everyone around us looked like poster models of the perfect graduate. We looked like two unmade beds in a Motel 6 the morning after a fraternity initiation party. That was the good news. The bad news was we were starting to feel the additional dizzying effects brought on by the recently consumed marijuana. I have never had what one might call an iron stomach. In fact, being a Virgo, Paula had informed me, adds to my weak intestinal fortitude. In any event, be it astrological inheritance, or just the hot sun and excitement of the day, I started to barf. Unfortunately, there is no polite, and in my case quiet, way to vomit. I remember the guy behind me saying, "Come on dude the speech isn't that bad." I bent over as far as I could without losing contact with my chair. I was trying to use my body to shield those binoculars I felt bore into the back of my head.

I later found out my 12-year-old sister, Thea, was using them at the time, and announced to everyone around her, "Gross, Barry is throwing up on everybody."

David's moment of embarrassment was imminent. After ascending to the stage, and accepting his diploma, he went to move his tassel to the other side of his mortarboard only to be confused by not finding one. Everyone in the stadium could see that he didn't have a tassel on. David unfortunately concluded that if he just felt for it long enough he would find it.

The world and all its promise suddenly seemed open to me and I felt I had an infinite amount of time in which to explore and live out those possibilities. But what now seems even stranger than believing that time would stand still is the uncomfortable feeling that even if I knew then what I know now about the fleeting nature of time, about the transitory quality of dreams, could I, would I, have done anything differently?

I don't remember much of what was said during the graduation ceremony, but I do remember hearing, more than once, those three frightening words..."The Real World."

ONLY IN BERKELEY — "Moonman"
rry McArdle, 24, has been on the
iversity of California campus here
s week selling acreage on the moon
$1 per acre (or $1 for each of the

said he has been in the moon la
business for a couple of years off a
on. "It's lunacy," he admitted. But j
whom he meant by that statem

HOLLYWOOD CALLS

Dᴀᴠɪᴅ ᴀɴᴅ I ᴡᴇʀᴇ ꜰᴇᴇʟɪɴɢ ꜱᴍᴜɢ. Wᴇ ꜱᴜᴅᴅᴇɴʟʏ ʜᴀᴅ ᴀ ᴘʟᴀɴ to keep the real world at bay. A family friend was a producer with CBS television. After pleading and pointing out that we had in fact won the American River Junior College's talent show, an audition was arranged. It so happened the network was casting for a new comedy series called *The Newcomers*.

It was not surprising that word got around that Barry and David were headed to Hollywood to become stars. One person in our extended family who heard the news was Big Eddie Fergus. I had known Eddie, and his family, all my life. He was three years older than me and always big—well, OK, fat—for his age and as a kid always pushy—well, OK, a bully. I still held a grudge against him, remembering how 11 years earlier Big Eddie had taken a huge knife and...

I was nine at the time and spending another summer with the Fergus family. They had just gotten a new cherry-red swing set. One of the neighborhood kids was shouting "I'm the man in the flying trapeze," as he went higher and higher in the swing.

I Sold *the* Moon!

The idea came to me in a flash of illogical greed. I stood in the center of the yard and yelled. "Attention everyone...may I have your attention? Tomorrow I will walk across the top bar of this swing set," I announced as I pointed to the cross bar now suddenly looming much higher than it had a moment ago.

The kids started cheering.

"Why don't you just do it now if you think you're so brave?" Eddie Fergus challenged.

"Well, just like in the circus," I continued, "it will cost you to see me do it."

A chorus of, "No way," "Drop dead," and from Eddie Fergus, "Fuck off."

"Wait. I'm not finished. If I should fail to make it to the end, if I fall... everyone will get to watch me...KILL MYSELF!"

This last statement had them cheering and clapping again. The only two questions left to settle was how much I was going to charge, and what method I would use to fulfill my promise should I fail to cross what Eddie was now calling "Barry's Bar of Death."

I wanted to charge a quarter, but that was shouted down as too much and impossible to get on such short notice. The mob wanted to pay a nickel, but when I told them I would be stabbing myself with the hunting knife that Eddie was happy enough to pass around for inspection, they agreed to show up the next day at noon, with the admission price now fixed at ten cents.

It was hard falling to sleep that night. Jimmy Fergus, who was two years younger than me, kept asking where exactly would I be stabbing myself. He also wanted to know if he should sharpen the knife.

"It might not hurt so much if it's sharp," he said.

I thought it would hurt more, so I told him, "No, don't, but it would be OK to wash it."

I skipped breakfast thinking I could use the time to practice. Using a ladder, I was able to climb up high enough so that I needed only to step down a few inches onto the top bar. I would be attempting the crossing barefoot, after Jimmy told me my toes would help my grip. One drawback to this method was the searing heat the aluminum cross bar transferred to the soles of my feet. However, Jimmy was quick to point out the advantages of burned feet over a cold dead body.

My rehearsals were not going well. My feet were starting to blister, I had already taken one hard fall, and I had yet to make it even halfway across.

By noon the backyard was full of excited kids all chanting: "We want a show...We want a show..." Jimmy came into the bedroom to tell me he had collected over three dollars. Some of the big kids, Eddie and all of his friends, *had refused to pay, but nevertheless Jimmy had collected more than we thought possible. Any second thoughts I may have had vanished when he opened the cigar box, and I let my hands plunge into all those dimes.*

Jimmy's sister Marjorie had decorated the swing set with yellow and orange crepe paper. She also loaned me a red taffeta cape—part of her Snow White Halloween costume.

The appointed hour was upon me. I emerged from the bedroom wearing my bathing suit, pink sunglasses, and what I now thought of as my magic cape.

Maybe it was the way things looked through the sunglasses that gave the clapping kids and the softly blowing strips of colored crepe paper a dreamlike quality. I reluctantly made my way up the ladder.

As I stepped off the top rung I felt the scorching heat of the bar find its way into the most tender, blistered patches of skin. It was now deathly silent, not only in my mind, but in the audience as well. I made it half way across—further than I had ever gone in rehearsal. I was thankful that there was very little breeze, only enough to flutter the bottom of my magic cape as I inched my way closer to deliverance.

The soles of my feet actually hurt less now than when I had first stepped on the bar. The end was in sight, my goal a mere four steps away.

Suddenly my concentration was broken by two simultaneous events. At that moment, a dog started barking as it charged the swing set. This in turn got all of the other dogs in the yard excited and they joined in, barking and running wildly directly below me.

This unsettling turn of events made me feel wobbly, but I only had three steps to go and was convinced I could make it. Before I could take another small step, however, I was momentarily blinded by a flash of silver light that, sunglasses or not, left me seeing black spots and rings of color. I tried to steady myself, and was relieved to find this disorientation passed quickly. Rather than forging ahead, I made the mistake of looking out in the direction of where I thought the flash had originated.

Scanning the crowd, I picked up a small glint of silver light and focused my attention on what turned out to be Eddie Fergus holding the big hunting knife lengthwise between his hands. The jolt of fear I got seeing the knife was almost enough to knock me off the bar. But when he angled the long blade into the sun and then guided the reflected light back into my eyes for the second time, I lost any chance I might have had to complete my historical journey.

I Sold *the* Moon!

My wobbling was quickly turning into more of teetering and that led to an all out flailing motion. The sweet sound of a young girl pleading, "Don't fall," was the last thing I remembered hearing on my quick and embarassing fall from grace, and into a quickly closing circle of yelping dogs.

An unsettling hush descended on the gathered rabble now hungry for my blood. A couple of the younger girls started crying and left running from the yard. Big Eddie dramatically handed me the knife.

"You promised to kill yourself if you fell, so now you have to do it," he demanded

I took the knife in my hands. What would Davy Crockett do in this situation I thought?

"I won't do it until all of you guys that didn't pay get out of here."

"Yeah," Jimmy said, jumping in to help, "and I know exactly who didn't pay."

What followed was general yelling and arguing with the liberal use of the words "Liar," "Cheater" and "Chicken."

Finally my combined argument that not everybody had paid, and that I'd been blinded by Big Eddie (I showed everybody how the sun reflected off the knife by shining the glare in each of their eyes), started to soften the call for my immediate death.

I'm not sure how 30 some kids, none older than 12, came to a workable compromise that day. It was finally decided that I would be allowed to live, but I would need to cut myself and let fall 32 drops of blood—one for each kid. (Marjorie, Jimmy, and two other kids said I didn't need to drop a drop for them).

Someone got an empty milk bottle, and after ceremoniously cutting into my left thumb I watched, fascinated, as my blood fell, drop by drop, down the side and onto the bottom of the clear glass container. Everyone counted together as I made my payment in full.

For the rest of the summer, I was afforded a certain status by the younger kids. They would continually ask to see the gash I had cut into my thumb.

The Fergus family moved to El Dorado Hills, California seven years later. The cherry-red swing set, complete with "Barry's Bar of Death" was left rusting and forgotten behind the fence, in the tall weeds at the edge of their property line.

Nothing is forever, except perhaps shared memories. One such shared memory, of a hot summer day, long ago, is of a small scared boy, in a red cape, walking across the sky....

*   *   *

And now Big Eddie wanted to ride our coattails to fame and fortune.

"So you and Barclay are going to Hollywood, and you thought you could cut me out of the action," he growled.

"It's one o'clock in the morning. I was sound asleep."

"You'll have plenty of time to sleep when you're dead. Anyway, after you hear why I called—you'll thank me."

"Forget it, I'm not buying."

"Relax, I'm not selling anything."

"Fergus, you're always selling."

"Hey, bad vibes man. Just listen and keep an open mind. I'm older than you guys, and know how to negotiate. It's what I do. So all I'm suggesting is you let me represent you boys with CBS. You'll end up looking a lot more professional. To sweeten your end, I'll drive, pay for the gas, meals, hotel room, and I'll bring the pot. The extra money I'll squeeze out of them will more than compensate for my 25 percent commission. So, do we have a deal, amigo?"

"Well, *amigo*, I'll need to talk to David before anything is decided. And I've been reading *Variety* lately and 10 percent is standard, and that's when the agent finds work for the client...not the other way around."

"Details. OK, you talk to Barclay and I'll settle for 15 percent."

Before we hung up, he played his strongest card.

"Let's not forget my mother changed your diapers. I'm the oldest friend you have."

David thought Fergus's proposition made sense. "Bare, he's our ride, our meal ticket and he's got a stash? He's in."

*   *   *

Paula was ecstatic about our opportunity although she told me she was worried about Pluto moving into my third house of careers, or was it my fifth house? Anyway, she volunteered to work with David and me if we could get to Berkeley.

"You and David need to come down here at once. This is bigger than the Challenge Test, and you should work just as hard. You have no time to waste. Barry, this could change your life. This is CBS, for God's sake. You really need to take this seriously. You need to rehearse every day. Let me help you. When can you come?" Paula wanted to know.

Why we didn't go rehearse with Paula isn't important. Not going was.

✳   ✳   ✳

Like any good manager, Big Eddie also thought it wouldn't hurt to practice the routine. As we got closer to LA, he kept asking to hear it... just once? Later, as he put down his MasterCard for our one room at Best Price Inn, he pleaded to hear just one line.

"Relax, Eddie," I said, "It's kinda like magic. It works...or it doesn't work."

"Doesn't work? Well, how often don't it work?" Eddie wanted to know.

When he left the room for another six-pack, David and I stared at each other. Time had run out.

"Bare, we should have gone to Berkeley. Paula really could have helped us." David stated the obvious. "So now what?"

"All we really have is the material from the talent show," I said.

"Yeah," David was saying, "as long as we got Barry and David's 'No Talent Review' we're cool."

Our convoluted theory held that by demonstrating that neither David nor I had so much as one scintilla of talent we would be appreciated as two lovable, hilarious young comics. If ignorance is bliss, it was never more so than that night, as we confidently bullet-pointed our routine:

1. Introduction: Insult/Bribe (Barry and David)
2. (Open) Nixon/Agnew (Barry and David)
3. Mexican Comedian (Barry)
4. Song: Skin Ain't No Sin (Barry and David)
5. Hold Breath/Stand On One Leg (David)
6. Breaking Plates (Barry and David)
7. Tap Dancing on LSD (David)
8. The Psychotic Psychic (Barry)
9. The Flasher (David)
10. (Close) Demand more money...walk out...return...agree to discuss contract over lunch—on them. (Barry and David)

If nothing else, we had David's exquisite blue velvet suit going for us. Under his jacket, he would wear a collarless white silk shirt. On his feet were polished black leather loafers. It was a beautifully fitted, put together outfit. He looked good in it, and he knew it.

I, on the other hand, was a Fashion Don't. The collars of my all-organic, "river washed" shirt extended out past my shoulders. Embroidered on the front were parrots, monkeys, and babes in bikinis. On the back was the national flag of Uruguay. My pants were vintage. The clerk at Salvation Army told me they were new—in 1940. Bringing my ensemble all together were my pink socks and white vinyl shoes. It was an ill-fitting, hideous outfit. I didn't look good in it, but I didn't know it.

As we waited in a conference room at CBS, David and I studied our outline. Eddie snatched it out of our hands. With a look of fear in his eyes he said, "LSD, and what's this flasher thing? No one wants to see you guys exposing yourself."

"We sure don't. We're casting for a family show," said one of the three men who had slipped into the back of the room, and now stood staring at us.

"Gentlemen, thanks for seeing us, I'm Eddie Fergus, Barry and David's manager and agent. Let me introduce you to the two funniest guys in America."

"Well, at least in this room," I said.

Fergus burst out in what can only be described as forced laughter. The three suits were not smiling.

The person who had said he was not interested in seeing us expose ourselves made the introductions.

"This is Saul Pearlman, new talent development. This is Marty Sterling, one of the producers for *The Newcomers*, our pilot program now in development, and I'm J.J. Johnson, Executive Producer of that program. Shall we get started?"

David and I jumped to shake hands with the three big shots. We both placed a five-dollar bill in our palm so that when we shook each of the producer's hands we transferred the bill from our hand to theirs.

"Don't consider this small token of appreciation as a bribe, but rest assured there is a lot more where that came from. Maybe you guys could use it to buy some decent ties," I said.

As if on cue Fergus started laughing, and shaking his head, "Didn't I tell you these boys were funny?"

David added, "Ten bucks can still get you a good haircut. Go ahead...splurge."

"They never stop, these guys," Fergus said between more strained laughter.

"Well, let's go out to the main stage and turn them loose," said J.J. as he collected the bills from his associates and handed them over to Eddie, adding, "Just so there's no possible confusion down the road."

The idea behind the bribe and insults was to set us apart from the hundreds of other "newcomers" they would be auditioning. It would have helped to get a few laughs, though.

The CBS brass and Eddie sat in folding chairs on the stage, not more than ten feet away from us. I could feel my heartbeat thumping. I also felt a cold droplet of sweat slide down my left leg, having originated somewhere near my groin.

Then I heard J.J. say, "Boys, whenever you're ready."

I turned my back on them, and when I turned around I had hunched my shoulders, dropped my head forward, and made my eyes as beady looking as possible. I spoke in my best exaggerated Nixon voice.

Me: "Spiro come in here. We need to talk." (I patted my leg, as I sat on a chair at center stage.)

David ambled over and sat on my leg looking as goofy as possible.

David: (spoken in a high pitched voice) "Gee, Dickey, I hope this doesn't take long. I'm about to make that speech condemning the morals of today's college students."

Me: "This should only take a moment. As you know Spiro, I play hardball. Whatever happens, whatever THEY find out must never, I mean never, touch the Presidency."

David: "You mean like the time I banged that cute young page in the Senate chambers, or the time I blew the slush fund in Vegas. Or the time..."

This was not going well. No one was laughing, not even Fergus. When we had performed this bit for stoned-out drunk college students, we had rocked the place. I decided to cut this segment short, skipping the dialogue about Pat Nixon's lesbian lover.

Me: (Standing up, David leaves) "And now let's go south of the border. Say hello to Chico as he works for laughs...Tijuana style."

Me: (spoken with a bad Mexican accent) "Thank you Lola wasn't she wonderful. She even looks good with her clothes...on. Ha, ha, ha...

Hey, no more farting...you might spoil the punch line...Ha, ha, ha... You don't look so good amigo...I told you no more chili con carne! Ha, ha, ha... But you know my friends I got me a woman, she ugly though. She so ugly when she comes in da casa...all da roaches dey throw demselves on da traps. Ha, ha, ha..."

Did I just hear a pin drop? And I was now starting to sweat down both legs. Fergus looked constipated and seemed to be fighting back a twitch in his left eye. It might be best to bring David back in his great looking suit.

Me: "Amigos, my radio station is T-A-C-O. One song on dat station goes like dis..." (David returns).

We both strip to our waist, and let out with a long sustained Hummmm...and then begin singing while slapping our bodies to the rhythm of the song; "At the Hop."

"Skin ain't no sin, no, no, no...
Skin ain't no sin, (slap, slap, slap,)
Just cuz you be kin, I still be singing
Skin ain't no sin, no, no, no...
Skin ain't no sin, (slap, slap, slap)
You can touch it, you can lick it,
You can rub it, you can stick it,
But skin ain't no sin, no, no, no
Skin ain't no sin..." (slap, slap, slap)

Looking at the faces of our hosts, I rejected the idea of asking them to join in the chorus.

Me: "My partner will now attempt to hold his breath for five minutes while standing on one leg. Drum roll, please."

The little tape recorder I brought blared out a continuous drum roll. David, now at center stage, made an exaggerated display of sucking in his breath, and then very slowly—looking a bit unsteady—he lifted one foot up.

Fergus was trying his best to disappear. He had one hand completely covering his face, and was looking out through a small separation in his fingers. The other three suits looked like they were frozen—eyes opened, staring coldly.

Me: (In a booming voice) "Behold the Eighth Wonder of the World!"

I ran off stage and returned with 12 dinner plates.

Me: "And now sit back and enjoy our: 'Tribute to Gravity.' "

David took five plates and ran to the opposite side of the stage. On the count of three, we started hurling them high in the air across the stage to each other.

As the plates landed, they exploded with remarkable volume. We spun in circles, trying not to get hit as they came crashing down around us.

"OK, fine," J.J. was saying as he walked toward David, "That is, shall we say, different. You can stop with the plates now. We all get the idea...Ouch! Shit!"

A sharp edged fragment had gone flying across the floor, and had somehow managed to tear a small hole in J.J.'s pant leg.

"First time I've seen a comedy act and come away bleeding," J.J. said, as he bent down and touched his cut. The other two producers were now up and showing concern for their wounded comrade. Fergus looked like he'd been hypnotized by a cheap practitioner of the trade. His twitch was now in both eyes.

David was out of plates and I had only one left, so trying something different I threw it towards David as if it were a Frisbee. The plate went sailing out past the edge of the stage smashing thunderously on the sidewall.

Me: "Ladies and Gentlemen let's hear it for the juggling artistry of Barry and David!" We walked back to the middle of the stage, and in unison bowed low, and deliberately.

This resulted in bringing Fergus out of his coma and he offered his now familiar, irritatingly phony crackle.

David: "And now who says LSD isn't funny..."

Before David had a chance to finish the introduction to his LSD routine—J.J. cut him off.

"I think we're done for today. As I said your act is, well, different."

"You mean like good different?" Fergus croaked.

"Let's just leave it at different. Thanks for coming down. Marty will show you out."

J.J. was gone before I had the chance to demand a bigger trailer and my personal masseuse. Marty was saying something about the third door on the left and that he thought David's suit was very smart looking.

* * *

Driving back north along Highway 1, the angelic sound of the Beatles' "Let It Be" filled the car. David and Eddie were both asleep.

I felt I was at a critical crossroad in my life. I didn't want to end up wandering lost in the nether world of pot smoking lethargy, wondering what the lyrics to the Beatles songs meant when you played them backwards.

Rounding a bend in the road a full moon was directly in front of me, its reflected light almost too bright for the eyes. Alone with my thoughts, I felt stupid. David and I had blown our CBS audition. It would take more than charm and a friend with a velvet suit to succeed.

My future was once again clouded. I had to find a job. The moonlight had temporarily found refuge behind a rolling California hillside. Unconsciously, I accelerated. I didn't know where I was going, but I was in a hurry to get there. I turned up the radio. The satisfying drug that was Beatles music washed over me.

"Let it be, let it be, let it be, yeah, let it be,

Wistful words of wisdom, Let it be..."

the new

universi

VOL. XLII NO. 54

TUESD

Bennis

By Tony Cipriano

President Bennis will anne
tuition or room and board i
at the spring all-University
meeting today.

Bennis will caution, howe
the final decision depends
proval of increased state su
UC by the Ohio General As

Bennis speculated Sunda
the General Assembly an
Rhodes both approve a
package providing the necess
sidy increase, "without quest
tion will be reduced for up
sion students (junior and
beginning fall quarter.

He added that fees for fr
and sophomores may not be
by approval of the state highe
tion budget proposal. Benn
however, that the Admini
and the Ohio Board of Rege
determine the final tuition p

Bennis also "doubted" that
iversity will increase tuition
the state fail to approve t
ditional subsidy UC has requ

A compromise state
package, expected to go to th
Senate Finance committee thi
would give UC $20.5 million
ditional subsidies over the ne
years. In return, the bill stip
UC must become a full state
tion by July 1, 1976.

This $20.5 million increase a
approved by the Ohio House,
million more than what Uni
officials had requested in add
subsidy from the state.

Great Expectations

"My expectations are high f
ting the money," Bennis decla

Bennis added that since he to
fice in 1972, tuition has been
only once—1.2 percent last ye

John Simmons/the newsrecord

Lunar lunacy

Moon Man gives his sales pitch to UC students gathered on the bridge. On campus three days, Moon Man collected over $180 with his unique scheme—selling acres on the moon.

Moon Man: lunar con or sale of laughter?

By Mary Haas

Self-proclaimed "Moon Man" Barry McArdle jettisoned onto campus last Thursday, selling acres on the moon.

The price was right: for $1 you

get," he said. "Once I was tossed in a holding cell with 15 men while I was dressed like this and they sure didn't want to talk about the moon.

"It's a rough way to make a living,

CHAPTER 4

HELP WANTED

With stardom on hold for the immediate future, I returned home. The house seemed smaller after my two years away at college. This perception, I felt, was due to the natural order of things. I was now 21 years old. It was time to make my own way in the world. As the only boy, the only son in the family, I felt additional pressure to succeed. Although I didn't believe either of my parents planned on having seven children, they were just one more practicing Catholic couple proving that the "rhythm method" just didn't work.

From oldest to youngest, with a 12-year span in ages, the McArdle children were christened: Patricia Kerry, Karen Dourene, Barry Anthony, Elizabeth Ann, Shelley Marie, Sheila Maureen, and Thea Mary. I believe that growing up surrounded by all that female energy played a critical roll in shaping my personality. If nothing else I learned that sensitivity—being in touch with your feelings—should not be considered a weakness. Growing up as the only boy with 6 sisters had other advantages as well. It's not that I staked out an observation post, but with 6 girls living in the same house, I was simply the beneficiary of the law of probability and through the years observed them in various stages of undress. As we got older, these random encounters decreased, although the visual enjoyment most assuredly increased.

I grew up knowing my sisters loved me and I them, but that didn't stop them from banding together for protection....

They called themselves the "Hardy Hearts—Boom Boom Club." It was started by Elizabeth, and included Shelley, Sheila and Thea. The main activity and responsibility of each Hardy Heart was to defend any other Hardy Heart whenever called to do so. Their battle cry was most often employed whenever I tried to muscle into any of their stuff.

When this happened the whole house would be filled with the banshee wailing sounds of my younger sisters chanting "Hardy Hearts— Boom Boom!! Hardy Hearts—Boom Boom!!" I secretly enjoyed letting them gang up and pound on me with their small fists until I would fall agonizingly into a heap and beg for mercy. Mercy was always granted, and I would slink, a beaten dog, back to my room with shouts of the Hardy Heart's in victorious celebration echoing down the hall.

There was, however, a dark side to the Hardy Hearts coalition. My sister Liz, as founder of the group would, on occasion, find it necessary to flex her omnipotent authority and banish one of the members from the club.

The most horrifying part of one's banishment was the official expulsion ceremony the poor untouchable had to endure. Worse yet, this excommunication was usually delayed a few days, ostensibly to give the offender one last chance to prove their worthiness. I did notice the unfortunate marked Hardy Heart arrived on the battlefield a bit faster than the rest, and fought with renewed zeal—unfortunately to no avail.

When the appointed day and hour arrived, Liz had the condemned stand opposite the somber-faced membership. Standing at attention they would all place their right hands over their hearts. Then by some unseen signal, the Hardy Hearts would in unison start walking backwards down our long hallway, chanting in a funeral-like dirge, "Hardy Hearts—Boom Boom...Hardy Hearts—Boom Boom..." over and over again, all the while tapping their fists over their hearts on the ominous refrain of..."Boom Boom!"

The reinstatement ceremony was a family event. Everyone, including my mother and father, would attend once Liz made the long- awaited announcement that the Hardy Hearts would again be reunited in full strength. This restorative ritual was a repeat of the expulsion service—only performed in reverse. The three members in good standing would convene at the far end of the hallway and then march in unison, one step at a time, closer to the outcast who waited at the other end of the corridor. Naturally, they chanted their now familiar refrain of "Hardy Hearts—Boom Boom!!" but this time with an upbeat rhythm and cadence. When they arrived in front of the former pariah, they would encircle her, everyone kissing everyone, happy to be whole once again.

Growing up is never easy, but as long as the Hardy Hearts were united, our family could once again look to the future with confidence.

Confidence was something I could use now, I thought, as I came out of my reminiscence. I had been thinking quite a bit about money lately, no doubt because I didn't have any. When you're in school, you're not expected to have money, or hold down a job. Having graduated, however, everybody's first question is always, "Now what are you going to do?" How come, "I don't know what I want to do," is never an acceptable answer?

When you need a job, and your father doesn't own the company, what are your options? I did what most desperate, unconnected job seekers with skimpy resumes do. I started reading the Help Wanted ads.

Not surprisingly, the jobs requiring little or no experience also paid little or no money. Then I saw it: "Unlimited Income Possibility." Cash paid daily. Work Outdoors. No experience necessary. Call Benny.

"Yeah, you can bring your friend," Benny said. "If you guys work good I pay good. We pick everybody up at 16th and Broadway. Bus leaves at 5 AM sharp. If you don't have a shovel we'll get ya one."

"What exactly will we be doing, and how much do we get paid?" I asked.

"You just be fillin' up bags. Guys' be makin' good money. Harder you work, more you make. It ain't nothin' to pull down $100 cash money a day. You want to make money? Be there tomorrow."

I Sold *the* Moon!

Cigarette tips glowed orange in the gloom of the bus stop. Benny's work force looked like a prison chain gang. They were all dressed in long sleeve shirts, jeans, boots, and hats, with gloves hanging out of their back pockets, and all had a shovel and a lunch box in their possession.

Keeping in mind that Benny had emphasized the fact that it would be outdoor work, we thought we were dressed appropriately: Tee shirts, Bermuda shorts and tennis shoes.

By the time we arrived, an hour and a half later, it was already getting hot. I stepped off the bus and took in the landscape. It looked like we were standing on the moon, or more accurately on the edge of a huge crater on the moon. All the men were putting on sunglasses as they disappeared down into the crater.

"Best to get as many of them bags filled up before it gets too hot," the bus driver said.

I recognized that voice. "Are you Benny?" I asked.

"I sure hope so, cause that's what everybody been calling me," he answered, and then added, "Let me get you boys a couple shovels."

Benny explained the setup. "Fill as many of them burlap sacks as you can, and bring 'em on up here, they gotta weigh in at 70 pounds or more for you to get paid. I give you one of these slugs for every bag that makes the weight, end of the day I trade you 25 cents for every slug you turn in. Harder you work, more you make."

By the time David and I made our way down to the bottom of the crater, we were both sweating and our eyes were starting to burn. We were in a brilliantly white phosphorus hole in the ground. I had never given much thought to calcium carbonate before, now I was surrounded by it. Its primary use, I found out, is for making quicklime and chalk. Now I understood why everybody brought sunglasses. The crystalline silvery white walls of the pit were impossible to look at without squinting, and the sun was just starting along its arc to mid-heaven.

In no time at all David and I were both covered with the white dust generated by everyone shoveling this carbonate stuff into their sacks. Some of the workers had 10 bags or more filled and tied off with their own identifying color twine. We decided to work together—one of us holds the sack open, the other one shovels in the lime. Twenty minutes into the effort, I understood why everyone was wearing long sleeve shirts and long pants.

"This shit itches," David so accurately announced. 10 minutes later, we discovered it also burned. And it was starting to get hot...a lot hotter. By 11 AM, it was well over 100 degrees in the pit, and my eyes were starting to swell. The sweat from my face and head would find its way into the corners of my eyes, carrying with it dust particles that burned, itched and generally made me feel like a swarm of mosquitoes were holding an eating contest on my eyeballs.

David and I had not brought anything to eat and were thankful to find that Benny had sack lunches for sale. They went for $5.00 and consisted of two pieces of bread, a piece of cheese, a small bag of potato chips, a candy bar and a piece of gum. A cold can of Coke would be an additional $1.50. All payment was transacted with Benny's slugs. We had to have that Coke. In the end, lunch cost us 52 bags out of our total morning's labor of 90 filled gunnysacks.

After lunch, we slowed down. It was now 115 degrees in the hellhole, and climbing. I was starting to lose my sense of humor. The whole scene looked liked something out of *The Building of the Great Pyramids* or some "B" prison movie where all the convicts are required to work until they die. Carrying these deadweight sacks up and out of the white furnace of Hades was not something I had gone to school to learn how to do. Was this "The Real World?"

By the time Benny blew the whistle, indicating it was time to bring any remaining sacks to the scales, David and I were two burnt, itching, scratching, sweating, hand-blistered, exhausted, eyes-swollen-shut, lime-covered members of the American workforce. We turned in twelve more bags for a couple of Cokes and then counted what we had left...58 bags. It was then that Benny told us he would have to deduct $5.00 for each of the shovels we had "rented." That left us with 18 bags. Well not quite, four of these did not make the 70-pound minimum and Benny rejected them. He did not take kindly to my suggestion of pouring lime from one of the underweight bags into the other three until they were brought up to the acceptable minimum. Our remaining 14 acceptable bags turned into 14 slugs, which brought us a total of $3.50. Split between us we each came home with $1.75.

As we got off the bus Benny said, "First day's always the toughest. You'll make more tomorrow. Remember every day's a payday, the harder you work the more you make."

Driving home, David, who I think was suffering from sunstroke said, "If we were to bring our own shovels, lunch, and drinks, we could finish the day with a lot more cash."

I barely had the strength to say, "Are you out of your fucking mind?"

After an extended pause, David answered, "Yeah, I do believe I am."

CHAPTER 5

UNREAL ESTATE

DAVID AND I DECIDED TO PASS ON FURTHER EMPLOYMENT WITH Benny and his quest to dig to the center of the earth. It was starting to appear like the world was broken into three groups: students, the employed, and the third group I now found myself in, the losers, more commonly referred to as the unemployed. I turned my attention once more to the Want Ads.

Shoe Salesman: Earn high commissions, no experience needed.

Encyclopedia Britannica: Highly motivated, self-starters earn big money.

Unique Opportunity: Be part of the fast expanding world of frozen food direct marketing. Must have reliable transportation.

Great, four years of college and I'm qualified to schlep frozen Brussels sprouts around town in the trunk of my car—that is, if I had a car.

"Let it be..." I thought of the song and the night I drove back from L.A. under the full moon. Closing my eyes, I could almost feel the moonlight surround me. Suddenly my body was covered with chicken-skin. What was it about the moon that was sending my autonomic nervous system into overdrive? No sooner had I asked this question than the answer was understood.

I Sold *the* Moon!

It had been two years since Neil Armstrong had taken his one small step for man—his one giant leap for mankind. During that time, I had done some research and discovered that my government had made no sovereignty claims on the moon. Further, I could find no evidence of any individual or nation making any claim of lunar ownership. The United Nations did have legislation designed to regulate the future of off-world claims—but did the UN have authority over individuals? It was all very *nebulous*.

Since graduating from college, I'd spent most of my time scouring the classifieds looking for a job. And now, alone at my family's kitchen table and out of work, the idea that I could lay claim to the moon with the express intent to sell it suddenly exploded with incredible intensity and clarity. I could be the first person in history to lay claim to the lunar surface!

I didn't need someone else to give me a job. I could create my own. I'd never liked working for someone else anyway, and now I wouldn't have to. With great satisfaction, I crumbled the classifieds. Let someone else sell shoes, encyclopedias or frozen food. I would sell the moon!

A rush of freedom, a feeling bordering on invincibility started to surface now that I had committed myself to following through on my new career path. I would not be discouraged by logic or common sense. I was on a mission: I would claim the moon. I would sell the moon. Wait. How does one sell the moon? The first thing would be to register my claim. No, that wouldn't work because my whole premise for assuming the right to sell the moon lay in my belief—and confirmed by my research—that nobody had the authority to grant me that claim. If I stood by the notion that there was nowhere I could go to secure authorization, then how could any agency be empowered to stop me? I would simply be the first person to take advantage of this celestial loophole.

With my legal concerns worked out (at least in my own mind), I turned my attention to marketing. Would I consider selling moon property through newspaper advertising or phone solicitation? That just didn't sound right. Yes, I wanted to make money—I had to make money—but I would want to see the people who bought. I would need to sell face to face. But was I kidding myself? Who would buy a piece of the moon when no proof of ownership could be given? This is no time to think negative, I told myself. Anyway, how would I ever know how people would react if I never tried it?

How much to charge? More to the point, how much would my speculators be willing to pay? It stood to reason that the more I charged, the more compelling my argument for buying it would have to be. I anticipated being on the defensive in explaining my right to sell it in the first place. I didn't want the additional challenge of defending my price to slow down the land rush I was looking to create.

Two prices came to mind–$5.00 or $1.00? Raising my price was always an option, but having to go down in price might send the wrong signal, as far as property value was concerned. The price would start at $1.00. This would allow *everybody* to afford one. And selling in volume sounded good for business.

How much property would $1.00 buy? Considering I would be paying nothing, I could afford to be charitable. Pricing it by the acre had a nice ring to it. An acre was not too big, yet substantial. Who could find fault with the generous offering of moon property for sale at "One Dollar One Acre?" Like any other development with parcels for sale, I would need ownership certificates.

For the next two hours, I worked on designing the first Moon Acre. Through the years, it would change colors, the artwork would be improved, and I would eventually print on the back side as well, but the Moon Acres I sold would stay at one dollar until 2007 when the price was raised to $5.00 (hey, 30 years of inflation eventually caught up with lunar real estate). And the certificates would always be printed on quality 8 ½" x 11" card stock—suitable for framing.

I knew I wanted the finished certificate to look as authentic as possible. The Moon Acre had to have at least the appearance of legitimacy. With that in mind, I worked to have my prototype look as much like currency as possible. I remembered having seen an old stock certificate and I used my memory of that genuine document in sketching out my design.

After playing around with a bunch of different names, I settled on The Lunar Development Corporation. I thought the word BAD (For Barry And David) on the front of the Moon Acre provided a degree of honesty in representation. I added the initials B.A.D. to the lower left corner and drew in three orbiting electrons. It looked cool and futuristic.

I Sold *the* Moon!

The original Moon Acre would eventually read:

The Lunar Development Company of the United States of America does hereby relinquish all rights and privileges of one (1) acre of lunar surface in section B of area 321-A of the Hartland Crater (Hartland is David's middle name, and besides liking the sound of it, it was a perfect name for a moon crater) and does on this day in the year of our Lord 1971 deed over all rights and privileges of forementioned property to:

Directly under this paragraph was provided the "Legal Owner" line. In time I would add a series of faint parallel lines printed very close together. With this safeguard in place, it would be obvious if an original signature were ever tampered with. Should anyone attempt to remove or alter it in any way, the protective layer of lightly inked parallel lines would smudge. What else could you buy for one dollar that had this level of security built in? This refinement turned out to be a big selling point for the obsessed.

I knew it was late, but I was still surprised when I discovered it was after 3 o'clock in the morning. Lying in the dark, under my prized possession—the quilt my Grandmother Leonardo had made—I looked forward to the morning, and my first day as owner of the Lunar Development Corporation.

CHAPTER 6

MOON SHADOW

I GOT UP EARLIER THAN NORMAL, WITH ONE GOAL IN MIND. I NEEDED to find a print shop that would bring my new enterprise to life. I left the house without divulging my plan. Taking my rough design, I checked out three or four printing establishments before making my choice.

The Copy Tree was located near downtown Sacramento. The moment I walked in and heard the welcoming door chimes and saw the woman behind the counter I felt I was in the right place. I introduced myself and discovered her name was Teresa. She looked to be about 18 years old, and she was beautiful. After explaining why I'd come, she excused herself and then returned with what turned out to be her father and his two apprentices. How would they react to my request?

They loved it. Everyone was speaking Spanish and laughing every time someone said what I interpreted to mean "one dollar one moon acre." They all had suggestions on how to improve the original design.

Deciding on what type of paper to print on was more involved than I had anticipated. I wanted something that felt expensive when you touched it. Not surprisingly, paper that felt expensive—was. My first choice would have been parchment, but it was way too expensive.

Juan, the owner, suggested a compromise. He showed me a sample of something called "Parchtone." It looked and felt a lot like real parchment, but for a fraction of the cost.

When it came time to pick out the color for the border, I suggested a light shade of blue. I had read somewhere that blue was far and away most peoples' favorite color. I saw nothing wrong in pandering to the masses.

With design, paper stock, and color decided, I needed only to specify the number of Moon Acres I wanted. Juan explained that the larger the print run, the less it would cost per each individual certificate. I decided on a first run of 500. The cost for that plus a one-time charge of $187.00 would total about $250.00. I could double my investment on this first printing alone. All I needed to do now was sell the 500 certificates.

I sealed my positive working relationship with Juan by giving him two $100 bills, and letting him know I would pay the balance when I picked up my order.

Juan then proudly took me on a tour of the shop. With the sound of the big printing presses clanging in the background, and the smell of ink and paper in the air, I started to feel like the legitimate executive I fantasized myself to be.

Teresa filled out the order form and gave me my copy. I took my time scrutinizing. Under quantity, she had written 500, and under description, she had put "Lunar Acres." That was close enough. I lingered with Teresa as long as I could, without completely blowing my cover as a young professional on the rise. We said our good-byes, and I opened my father's old leather briefcase, not letting her notice that the invoice was slid into an otherwise empty satchel.

Although I had spent my graduation money on a gamble, my anxiety was tempered by the satisfaction I felt for having created something of my own.

That night at dinner, my mother announced that a Teresa from the Copy Tree had called to say that my Lunar Acres would be ready in five days. She then asked, "What are Lunar Acres?"

It got very quiet, very quickly. All six of my sisters were looking at me—along with my father who had halted a forkful of mashed potatoes half way to his mouth. Dourene, who detested all vegetables, except corn, took this opportunity to slide her green beans onto Elizabeth's plate.

"Well, I was going to tell everybody once I picked up the certificates. The deal is...I've claimed the moon, and I'll be selling it for a dollar an acre."

"I want an acre!" said Thea, my youngest sister. Sheila wanted to know if she would have to pay for hers. Lizzy thought it was a great idea but wanted to know who would buy them besides Thea—who she pointed out, did not even have a dollar. Shelley said something about God owning the moon and stars, but wanted some to give to friends. Patricia, my oldest sister, was intrigued, although was concerned about the legal ramifications. Dourene was too busy off-loading the rest of her green beans to comment.

When the initial questions were answered and the conversation died down, everyone looked toward Dad and waited for him to say something.

＊ ＊ ＊

The best thing my father ever did was to marry my mother. What confluence of events, of decisions made, and decisions avoided, brought my father to a dance being held in the basement of the cathedral in Sacramento, California on a Saturday night, in 1944? My mother, too, through tens of thousands of decisions, events, roads taken, and roads avoided, beyond all logic, against all probability, somehow in body and soul stood standing with her nursing school girl friend near the punch table, trying not to look too hopeful or eager on that same Saturday night, in that same cathedral basement.

Benny Goodman was playing on the phonograph; the room was alive with dancing soldier boys and girls on the doorstep of womanhood. One soldier boy caught my mother's eye. He was a bit older than the others, a bit thinner and a whole lot better dancer. He was coming through the crowd straight towards her. Was he coming for punch? Was he coming to ask her friend to dance? She had to look away. She felt a warm confident hand touch hers.

"Care for a twirl?" he asked. She did. The dance lasted 41 years.

＊ ＊ ＊

"Mary, is there any more hot gravy? My potatoes could use some warming up."

He paused as my mom went to the stove and turned up the heat on the gravy.

Back at the table, my mother filled the growing silence by reminding my father of something she had been saying, on occasion, ever since I could remember.

"Now, Edmund, don't go getting all upset during dinner. You're putting bad juices into your system. It's not good for your digestion."

"Well, what would be good would be some hot gravy, and an answer to a simple question. Why would you sell the moon for one dollar when I would think you could make more if you charged, say, five dollars an acre?"

Whew, not bad. My dad was not demeaning the idea, he was just curious about my pricing structure. This was starting to go my way.

For the next two hours, and on and off over the next few days, all anybody wanted to talk about was how best to sell acres on the moon and speculate on the probable success or failure of my newfound enterprise.

Each night I fell asleep with the same thought. How exactly am I going to sell the Moon?

With three days left before I could pick up my certificates, I went to see Paula. I was excited to tell her about my new venture and to get her advice on how best to proceed. That conversation, I knew, would be delayed until we worked through the cycle of regret, hurt and anger over another act of infidelity on my part. (The sexual revolution had been in full swing during my two years at Chico, and I'd found it impossible not to participate).

Paula had made it clear that lovemaking was out of the question and that we were now going to be "friends." My expectations were simply to start the healing process with the hope of being forgiven one more time.

Getting to Berkeley from Sacramento when you didn't have a car was a fairly simple thing to do in 1971—you hitchhiked. I was a firm practitioner of making eye contact, smiling, looking clean and happy when you went looking for a ride. My theory was the longer you looked liked you had been waiting for a ride the longer you would wait.

No matter how long or difficult my journey may have been, once arriving at Paula's apartment, it was all worth it. She never failed to orchestrate some incredible dining experience, and tonight's meal would be no exception. There was one thing, however, that would not be on the menu.

"Barry, we're not making love tonight, so don't make it any more difficult on us than it already is," Paula suddenly said.

"Well, just so I know, do I have to sleep on the couch?"

"We can sleep together. We can even hold each other but I'm wearing pajamas, and they're staying on. You can't get naked. If you agree, and I mean it Barry, you can sleep in my bed, otherwise, yeah, you're on the couch. So what's it going to be: torture with me or torture alone?"

She let out a soft giggle at this closing line of truthfulness.

It was really no decision at all. One must never underestimate the value of proximity.

"You talked me into it. I'll bunk in with you."

"Do I have your Catholics' Honor you agree with the conditions?"

Somewhere along the way, she had learned that this was the highest, most solemn oath I could take. Once I gave my "Catholics' Honor" she knew, and so did I, that I would live up to whatever was sworn to. I'd been brought up to believe that breaking such a pledge would condemn me to eternal hell fire. However, the person you swore to had the power to relieve you of your oath. And tonight this provision would never be far from my mind.

"Yes, you do," I said.

"Say it."

"You have my Catholics' Honor. Of course, I promise nothing related to what I will be thinking, wishing and remembering."

"Remember all you want. You just can't make any new memories," she laughed.

Dinner was a five-star affair.

"Paula, if you're trying to seduce me with this meal, consider your mission accomplished."

"Very funny, but something tells me I could have skipped the Betty Crocker routine and still had a chance at seduction."

"You really are psycho, I mean psychic," I answered as I held her gaze.

Staring at each other, although only across the distance of the table, felt like we were continents apart. Paula could not hide the sadness behind the smile on her lips.

She broke our gaze by asking me to save some room for the main course, and the surprise dessert that would follow.

Although the evening was not to end the way I would have scripted it, I realized I had no one to blame but myself.

Paula was pouring wine into a hot skillet that, based on the pungent aroma, most likely had fresh garlic already browning. She told me it would be a few minutes and asked me to turn over the album.

I walked through the floor-length strands of orange and red glass beads that framed the archway separating the kitchen from the living room. The small living room looked a lot like most college students' first attempt at interior decorating, only a little messier. The cheap couch didn't match the cheap chairs or the even cheaper coffee table and lamps. Indian tie-dyed bedspreads were used as curtains and wall coverings. Posters of Isadora Duncan, Greta Garbo and Fredrick Douglass were held in place with thumbtacks. Books, candles, incense, magazines and theatre Playbills were strewn on top of every surface and piled up in the corners.

I turned over the Miles Davis album and then went into Paula's bedroom. A huge vanilla-scented candle, which I had given her a few months before, was filling the room with a sensual aroma. Another bedspread of deep purple, red and black with a mandala design covered her double bed. Moving to her nightstand, I opened the top drawer and removed what I had no business looking for. The pink circular disc of thin plastic that held her birth control pills showed that she was current. This was good news...I guess. It could mean one of two things. Either she was thinking we would get back together sooner rather than later or she wanted to be protected if she found someone else.

Putting the dispenser back, I felt a tinge of guilt—reminiscent of how I felt whenever I had read a page or two from one of my sister's diaries. Suddenly I had a sick feeling in my stomach. There was, of course, one other possibility. She could be currently seeing someone else. No, that's just paranoia talking. If that were true, she would have told me.

"We're ready Barry," I heard Paula calling from the kitchen.

The main course was no less spectacular than everything that had preceded it. Giant sea scallops had been dusted with flour and dill, then pan-fried to perfection. Creamy, garlic mashed potatoes, asparagus with slivered almonds, and grilled onions completed the dinner plate. "Paula, this meal is truly incredible. You're just the best."

Holding my gaze she let out a heavy breath, "If I'm really the best Barry, why aren't I good enough?"

I didn't have an answer that would satisfy her or make sense to me. We were stuck. There was no going forward and it was even worse when we looked back. "I don't know, sweetheart. I wish I did, but I don't."

Her eyes were filling up with tears, and as the first drop slid slowly down her cheek, she stood and left the room. A minute later, I heard the bath water running.

I spent the next two hours cleaning the kitchen. The dessert of fresh peach cobbler with vanilla ice cream would wait until morning.

I could hear her moving around in her room, and thought I heard her get into bed.

When I eventually slid in beside her, I could tell she was still awake. She was on her side, wearing a long nightgown. I took a chance and snuggled up next to her.

"Thank you," I whispered in her ear.

After a pause I heard, "You're welcome."

I laid my arm over her waist and brought my face as close as I dared to the back of her neck. She smelled newly washed – desirable.

"Good night, Toys," I said, using an endearing nickname I often called her.

"Good night, Bare," she softly, sadly replied.

I left Berkeley on a damp, leaden morning. The weather and I were in synch, even if Paula and I weren't. We had managed to get through the rest of the week without any more tears, although we both had to work hard at pretending we were OK, and even harder at pretending we believed each other.

More than a little nervous, I arrived at the Copy Tree. This case of the jitters was brought on by the anticipation of holding in my hand the physical manifestation of my overactive imagination, as well as the prospect of seeing Teresa again.

I opened the door and the now familiar chime sounded. Teresa emerged from the recesses of the shop. She was prettier than I remembered. The mother-of-pearl headband she wore in her jet-black hair complimented her lovely white gauze dress.

"Thanks for calling," I said.

"I got the feeling you were in a hurry to get them. They finished the run last night."

"How do they look?"

"Really cool. My dad was showing them around, he usually doesn't do that."

"No, I don't usually do that," her father said smiling as he came through the curtain that separated the front office from the work area.

He was carrying two brown paper-wrapped packages, which he laid on the counter. On one side of each bundle someone had written in black Kato marker, "250 MOON DEEDS."

"Here are your 500 certificates and in this envelope are an additional 40 or so that we had left over," Juan said, as he handed me the manila envelope.

I reached in and dramatically slid into view the certificate that would be part of my life—for the rest of my life.

It was perfect. It felt expensive and looked like a legitimate stock certificate. The color was a soft blue that allowed the fibers of the Parchtone paper stock to show through. It had the look and feel of currency.

"Well?" asked Juan.

With difficulty, I tore my gaze away from the Moon Acre to find both Juan and Teresa watching me.

"It's fantastic, better than I imagined. Thank you," I replied sincerely.

The boys from the back came out to share in the congratulations and the discussion that followed regarding refinements for the next order—if there was a next order.

I paid my balance in cash, shook hands with everybody, and stalled long enough to find myself alone with Teresa.

"I want to be the first person to buy one," she said, as she handed me a dollar.

"But you can have one of the extras your dad said he ran off for himself."

"Yeah, I know, but your idea is so cool I think you should be supported. I really want to buy one."

Exchanging that first Moon Acre for a dollar bill gave me a warm tingling feeling. Not only was it was proof positive that moon acres were sellable—they were sellable to beautiful young women.

"Thank you, Teresa, I'll never forget who bought the first Moon Acre."

We stared, smiling at each other.

The door opened behind me and two businessmen entered the shop. Their arrival brought Teresa and me back to our surroundings, and the now noticeable glare of the overhead fluorescent lights.

I put my two precious bundles under my arm and slid the manila folder into my briefcase. This time I was not afraid to open it in full view of everyone as I had made sure to pack it with envelopes, paper, pens and other various artifacts I identified as the necessary trappings of a legitimate, successful business man.

Snapping the case closed, I reached out and took her hand in mine. We looked straight into each other's eyes for maybe 10 seconds, during which my hand felt as if it was holding a glowing ember wrapped in velvet. Jolted, I imagined jumper cables attached to my groin and felt the current run down the line at full capacity. This could get embarrassing. I reluctantly broke the connection and thought I saw sparks fly across the widening gap between the tips of our fingers as our hands separated.

The briefcase was finally being put into service as I used it to hide my excitement—brought on by the simple, innocent act of holding hands.

I Sold *the* Moon!

Driving my mom's car home, I was gripped by the realization that I was not sure what to do next. I had been telling everybody that I had a plan. Well, what is it? I asked myself once again.

As a child, I had been successful selling any number of commodities door-to-door. It was just a matter of percentages. The more doors you knocked on, the more you would sell. My confidence started to come back as I remembered how easy it was selling packets of flower seeds, Little League baseball decals, mistletoe, and church raffle tickets. I even sold Girl Scout cookies—helping my sister Elizabeth be the first scout in Redlands to sell over 1000 boxes of those chocolate-covered cardboard confections. I had a proven track record. I was a natural born salesman. What difference did it make—decals, mistletoe, or cookies—the point was I could sell anything! Right? Yeah, right.

ONE DOLLAR ONE ACRE

MY FIRST DAY AS A MOON SALESMAN BROKE GRAY AND COLD, AS WAS to be expected on a late November morning in Sacramento. I wanted to present the image of a professional, plus reduce any anxiety the person opening his or her door on a complete stranger might feel, so I decided to wear a jacket and tie.

I counted out 100 certificates and placed them neatly into my briefcase. I thought if I could sell these before lunch, I would come back to the house and refresh before going back out with a new stash of 100—ready to satisfy what I believed would be my equally appreciative afternoon clientele.

My new career would start somewhere other than my own immediate neighborhood. This was perhaps a subconscious desire to avoid people I knew—at least until I perfected my presentation.

After walking through yet another new subdivision, I could no longer justify my reluctance to approach a house on the probability that the person answering the door might know me.

I pulled out the dollar that Teresa had given me, and that I now carried for the reassurance it provided. I had never been even mildly apprehensive about knocking on doors when I was a child. Why did I now feel like my legs were made of lead and my confidence of helium?

I Sold *the* Moon!

If I couldn't convince myself that what I was doing had value, how in the hell could I convince anyone else?

I was starting to feel conspicuous standing alone on the sidewalk, in a strange neighborhood, at 9:30 in the morning. Come on, Barry, I told myself, pull yourself together. You don't really have a choice. Do you want to go back to looking through the Want Ads?

My legs were moving. The door loomed large and foreboding. I walked down the walkway and up the three steps to the porch. My hand reached out. I hesitated. My finger, independent of my desire, pushed the white plastic button.

A moment later, the sound of my pounding heart was drowned out by the loud barking of a dog aggressively clawing and snarling on the other side of the door.

I had used barking dogs to my advantage when I was a boy selling door-to-door. I would feign fear (not all of it a put on), whenever confronted by an aggressive dog. Appearing to be frightened would usually elicit an apology from the owner and more often than not, a sale would follow.

The door opened the few inches allowed by the brass chain and I could see a gray haired woman peeking nervously through the slight opening. Her obnoxious dog was now trying to squeeze as much of his body through the door opening as he could.

"What do you want?" she croaked.

"I'm sorry to have bothered you, your dog can't get out can he?"

I started to back away, pretending to be more nervous than I actually was. She showed no concern that her dog was frightening me. Had human nature changed that much in the last ten years? No. Human nature hadn't changed. I had.

I was no longer the innocent looking child of seven or eight wearing a Little League baseball cap. The reason people had disciplined their dogs before was because their dogs had been a legitimate threat to my safety. Were they now seeing me as a threat to theirs? In that instant, I realized just how different and difficult this door-to-door selling would be.

"My dog can only get out if I let it, and you still haven't answered my question, what do you want?"

"Well, Ma'am, I've always believed the best approach is the straightforward one. You may have guessed I'm a salesman, but I don't believe you could have guessed what it is I'm selling. The truth is I would venture to bet that you have never been approached on the offer I am about to make. It will come as a bit of a shock, so I ask that you keep an open mind. I have in my briefcase..."

She cut me off.

"Is it possible that you will get to the point sometime today?"

"Yes, of course, my apologies."

I brought a Moon Acre out into what I hoped was the best viewing position—given the fact that she was still looking through the barely opened door.

"Ma'am, this document, once signed by you or the person you may choose to give it to, entitles said person to one acre of lunar surface. The value..."

"What do you mean lunar surface?"

"Well, I mean I'm offering...land on the moon. I'm selling property on the moon. The best part of all..."

SLAM!

I guess that's a no, I thought to myself.

Before I reached the sidewalk, I heard the door open. Had she changed her mind?

"If you don't leave this neighborhood at once, I will call the police."

SLAM!

That's definitely a no. Without a peddler's license, the police were not the organization I wanted alerted to my activities. Besides, I'd had some experience with the police and had found them, in general, to be lacking in the sense of humor department.

I walked another 30 minutes feeling tired, hungry and depressed. There was no way I could justify breaking for an early lunch. I hadn't sold anything, and I'd only talked to one person. Is this what Willie Loman went through in *Death of a Salesman*? Stop feeling sorry for yourself. All I need is some new motivation. Remembering that salespeople work best when they have a goal or quota they are trying to reach, I decided to give myself one. I also knew that to make the goal too high or unattainable would be counter-productive and demoralizing.

OK, I told myself, you can break for lunch but only after you have sold a total of (I paused here for serious consideration) one

Moon Acre. It's amazing how quickly one will lower expectations, especially when the prospect of lunch hangs in the balance.

The next two hours were no more fruitful than the first hour had been. One woman confided she wanted to buy one, but just couldn't.

"My husband disapproved when I bought a broom handmade by the blind. I hate to think what he'd do if I told him I bought land on the moon," she confided in me.

But I had to look on the bright side—no one else had threatened to call the police. In spite of my failure to sell a single acre, I was less depressed now than when I'd started.

My sales pitch was getting smoother and sounding more compelling with each presentation. It was only a matter of time before I made my first sale of the day. Excitement and anticipation was starting to take the place of depression and apprehension. This is a learning process, I reminded myself.

The presentation would need to continue to be refined until I discovered the right combination of persuasive language. I remembered an opening line I used to employ when I was a kid. It always seemed to get a laugh and put the person behind the door in a more relaxed frame of mind. Even as a child, I understood the value of humor as a shortcut to a sale.

"Just because I'm a door-to-door salesman doesn't make me a bad person," I said to the woman, now standing behind her screen door.

She offered me a rather weak smile.

When I realized she was waiting for me to continue I went into my evolving sales pitch.

"I don't want to waste your time, so I'll get straight to the point. What I'm selling is really all about creativity. It's an idea that I came up with and hoped there would be enough people in the country willing to support the uniqueness of the idea with a dollar bill."

"I don't know what you are talking about," she said without losing the smile on her face.

Taking out the Moon Acre, I offered it for closer inspection.

"Ma'am I'm the first person in recorded history to make a claim on the moon and then offer it for sale. I'm selling acres on the moon for one dollar an acre."

She started to laugh, and I found myself unexpectedly joining in.

"You're saying this certificate I'm holding is good for an acre on the moon, and it costs one dollar?"

"That's right, Ma'am, but I must warn you my claim has not been recognized by the United States government."

She laughed even harder.

"That hardly comes as a surprise," she giggled.

"If you know someone who might think this is funny it does make a pretty unusual gift."

This was as close to a sale as I'd come all day. I could feel it. She was laughing. She was holding the Moon Acre in her hand, and reading it.

"If I could draw your attention to the legal owner line. Should you consider giving this to someone that is where you would have him or her sign their name. Naturally, I recommend they sign in ink."

"Foolish to do otherwise," she said.

I had additional closing lines but something told me not to say anything more. My mom had always said she didn't like pushy salesmen. Although she seemed to say that after she had purchased something. I didn't want to appear desperate, so I opened my briefcase and started rearranging the contents.

"I'll take three of these. My husband is in real estate and I think he will get a kick out of this. One is for my son who is away at college and thinks his mom is a square, and one is for me. The idea that someone came to my door selling land on the moon, at a fair price I might add, is in itself worth supporting."

"Thank you very much," I said, realizing that I had just sold three Moon Acres to a complete stranger, and relieved that now I could finally have lunch.

$$* \quad * \quad *$$

The afternoon went by in a blur of "No, thank you," "Are you crazy or what?" "Is this really legal?" "Who gave you the right to do this?" And a few more doors closed in my face. I also spent a lot of time waiting, unsuccessfully, when no one was home.

The door I was currently knocking on was losing the battle of keeping the rock music, blaring inside, from escaping out into the front yard. A young man about my own age answered the door and once having an idea of what I was doing immediately asked me in to explain it to his friends. It turned out I was walking in on five college students obviously enjoying themselves with a few midday beers and the passing of the bong pipe.

They saw a contemporary in me and asked if I wanted a beer or a hit off the pipe. I wanted both, but declined, telling myself there was still a good hour of selling time left and I hoped to make the most of it.

These guys immediately understood the whole concept, and were laughing before I was able to explain much at all. They started pulling out dollars telling me what a far out idea I had.

I left the party having sold twelve acres. One of the guys bought five. "My Christmas shopping is done, man," he told me.

I was walking on air. The tiredness I'd been feeling just minutes before had miraculously vanished. Moon Acres could be sold in bunches. This was an exhilarating and energizing revelation. I had just witnessed some sort of group psychology that worked in my favor.

Although my first day had not been a total failure—I had sold a total of 21 Moon Acres—and I was improving my sales pitch customer by customer, I knew that I would need to find a better way of doing this if I hoped to be a success. The truth was if I had not encountered the stoners, my total for the day would stand at a very anemic nine certificates sold.

My problem was I needed to discover how I could be rejected or accepted at a much quicker rate. I did, however, realize my customers crossed over all age groups, gender and personality types. I especially enjoyed the young teenage boy who had been watching *Star Trek* and bought one, telling me he knew Captain James T. Kirk had sent me.

Heading home, I felt strangely hopeful and had a growing sense of resolve. I decided to spend at least three more days out in the suburbs with a bit of a different focus. My goal would not be as intently directed on selling as an end in itself. I would instead work on the technique, on the order of the presentation, and especially make note of what made people laugh.

The next three days were a lot like the first. I would make a sale, and then go to ten or fifteen houses without any success. I felt a kinship with every salesperson that had ever plied his or her products door-to-door. On occasion, I would see an Avon Lady or a vacuum cleaner salesman trudging along the sidewalk, and would exchange a brief recognition, acknowledging a fellow member of the club.

Over the four days, I sold a total of 113 moon acres, but it had taken me more than 30 hours and a lot of shoe leather to do it. And although I was getting more laughs, and fewer doors were being shut in my face, making $3.75 an hour was not going to cut it.

My last door-to-door customer turned out to be the most memorable. It was late in the afternoon, and I had 35 more dollars in my pocket than I had started with that morning. I wanted $40.00 before I called it quits.

I knew when someone was looking through a peephole at me. At this house, whoever it was either enjoyed the cheap voyeuristic thrill or was having trouble deciding whether or not to open the door. I was just about to leave when the door opened.

Wow! I was looking at a pretty 30-something woman, with curly brown hair, who was flushed-faced and sad-eyed. She was wearing a sheer pink camisole that fell short of covering her bellybutton. This "cover" somehow had the effect of making her look more naked than if she had been wearing nothing at all. Her longer but equally transparent outer gown failed to provide much additional modesty. I saw her strong shapely legs, and the palest of blue panties, even as she closed the flimsy outer garment around herself. It was hard not to notice her pink furry high heel slippers, each with a white puffball attached at the toe.

"You caught me at a bad time, you have to forgive my appearance," she said with what I detected as a slight slur. She inched behind the door, perhaps aware that I was staring.

"No, I'm the one who should apologize, but I have no way of knowing when's a good time for people, and because what I'm selling costs only a dollar it makes no sense to make an appointment. I'm sorry to have bothered you."

Willing myself to turn away, I did so reluctantly.

"Wait, now that you're here, you might as well tell me what it is you're selling."

I Sold *the* Moon!

I turned back to see that she had moved, ever so slightly, back into view.

"OK, but don't start laughing until I've had a chance to explain."

She started to laugh (as I hoped she would) before I could continue.

"I haven't laughed in days, it feels good. Thank you…and I'm going to buy at least one of whatever it is you have. Let me get my money…"

She turned to leave. I tried (and failed) not to look at her as she walked away and then she turned back.

"Would you care to join me for a drink? I could use the company."

Should I accept? She was buying an acre, I was thirsty, and she was wearing see-through clothes. I guess I could be sociable.

"Thank you. I'd like that."

"I'm drinking brandy, or I could make you something else. I have gin or vodka. I'm sorry I don't have any beer."

"Brandy would be fine."

The heater was turned up, possibly explaining her appearance. From somewhere in the house I could hear Tom Jones singing, "I'll Never Fall In Love Again."

Everything looked spotless and orderly, to the point of obsession. The furniture, artwork, and carpet were white. The kitchen was mostly white tile and white appliances. Seeing her move about in her white non-cover-up had me feeling like I was in some kind of an adult cartoon. I wondered when the anvil would fall.

She handed me my drink and I noticed she had freshened up her own. After suggesting we sit in the living room (where not much living seemed to take place) she excused herself. When she returned she was wearing a plush white terry robe. Sitting on the white couch, she blended into it and the rest of the room.

"I'm Kerry Owens."

"My name is Barry, Barry McArdle. It's nice to meet you Kerry."

"So, tell me what I'm buying."

✳ ✳ ✳

Two hours and a few drinks later, she said she wanted five acres, and all I wanted was to open her robe and lick brandy off her nipples.

Instead, I thanked her for the drinks and for the purchase. She tried to smile but failed.

"Kerry, do you mind me asking, is something bothering you? It's none of my business and I really have no right to ask, and you have no reason to answer, it's just that…"

"It's really that obvious? I guess I've been fooling myself thinking I was getting back to normal. Yes, there is something, well, two something's really. A month ago, my husband—we had been married two years—left me for another, for another…man. Nobody else knows yet. They're in Tahiti. I'm still in shock. And then a week ago…"

She stood up and went to the mantel. I could see her eyes filling with tears as she handed me the white-framed photograph.

I was looking at a young man, about my age, wearing an Army dress uniform with the American flag in the background. The family resemblance was unmistakable. I knew what was coming.

"That was my baby brother, my only brother. He is, was in Vietnam. My mother got a letter…. The funeral was three days ago."

Her tears fell freely now—one of them landing on the glass-covered photograph now on my lap.

The thought that I could have just as easily been the person in the picture flashed through my mind.

I stood up. "I'm truly sorry. I'm so, so sorry," I whispered.

She walked into my arms.

"Please just hold me," she sobbed.

I felt her body pressing into mine. I consciously suppressed all sexual thoughts. I held her gently and motionlessly.

She smelled of alcohol, sadness, and something else.

Don't, I told myself. You know the difference between right and wrong. I remained neutral.

She did not.

She lifted her head off my shoulder and without saying anything, kissed me on the lips.

Why was Paula's image suddenly in my mind? If I pushed away now, could that in some way convince both Paula and me that I was ready for commitment? But Paula and I were broken up. I was free to see other women. Why then did I still feel guilty?

Somehow, Kerry's robe had come open. I resisted the temptation to pull her closer. Kissing someone passionately for the first time is such an intimately charged experience, and I knew I couldn't trust myself to stop once we started.

Breaking off the kiss, I stood back a step, and looked directly into her eyes.

"Kerry, do you think this is a good idea?"

"I don't care," she said, shaking her head side to side and letting her robe fall to the carpet. "And I don't want to think."

She stood in the soft dusk light, her camisole damp against her body. Her skin glistened. I was past the point where logic had influence. I pulled her slowly back against me.

"I'm done thinking too," I whispered.

Sometime later, as we recovered on the carpet I noticed a small amount of brandy in the bottom of my glass. Given the opportunity to fulfill my recent fantasy...I took it.

The next morning we parted friends as well as lovers. I would see Kerry a number of times, always at her house and always with the heat turned up. She eventually sold the house and moved to Pennsylvania. We exchanged a few letters, a Christmas card or two and then faded into the mist of our individual memories of each other.

CHAPTER 8

No Transportation
Provided

My door-to-door approach to selling was over. I considered it the end of the beginning of my apprenticeship. I came to understand that the poorer the neighborhood, the more the person behind the door was ready to laugh. I learned that there was no single type of person that bought Moon Acres, other than those with a sense of humor. I just needed a way to talk to more of these connoisseurs of the absurd at the same time.

My sisters thought I was rich as I counted out over $100 of moon money on the kitchen table. My father reminded me I had made more in my first job, at the local Dairy Queen.

"And we got free cones and stuff when you had that job," Dourene reminded everyone.

"Yeah, but would you rather have a free Dilly Bar or land on the moon?" I countered.

"You've proven you can sell those things," my dad was saying, "now you need to discover how to sell them faster."

It felt nice when I realized my dad and I were on the same wavelength.

* * *

I Sold *the* Moon!

It was over dinner that night that my mother suggested I call Marilyn Fergus and ask her if I could sell my deeds at the upcoming Folsom Street Fair. Marilyn worked in Folsom, 11 miles from our house, selling a line of porcelain dolls called Madame Alexander.

Marilyn was agreeable and let me know her son Jimmy was going to be helping her during the two-day event. Jimmy Fergus and I had continued our friendship, partly because he understood why I often had disagreements with his older brother, Big Eddie.

I got to the fair early looking for a place to set up. Vendor booths tightly lined both sides of the main street. I eventually found a spot near a parking lot that nobody else seemed to have any interest in.

The lot was filling up. Hundreds of people had gone by me without so much as a passing glance. I had taken a Moon Acre out and was holding it aloft trying to generate some interest. On occasion, I would announce, "Moon acres for sale…moon acres for sale…land on the moon one dollar…one dollar an acre…get your moon acres here." I found this "barking" to have a positive effect and it ultimately resulted in a few sales. But something was telling me it could be better.

After three hours I had sold 12 acres, only slightly better than what I had been making going around the neighborhoods on foot. This was less tiring, but a long way from what I needed.

"What the hell are you doing way out here? I've been looking for you all morning."

"Hey, Jimmy, nice to see a familiar face. How goes the doll business?"

"Mom's doing great. These fairs always attract the collectors, but what about you? Is the land rush on?"

"Hardly, I've made gas money, lunch, and a few extra bucks."

"Not surprised. This location sucks. You gotta re-locate to where the action is. Follow me."

A block away, on the main street in town, you could hardly move. Wading through the throng, I didn't see how this could be any better for business. There were too many people all talking at once and everybody looked to be in a hurry to get someplace else.

I felt a tug on my sleeve.

"Not here," Jim was yelling in my ear. "There."

He was pointing to the square in the middle of the main intersection. Automobile access had been blocked off in all directions. This allowed for the thousands of people to stroll and shop at the many booths that now ringed the square.

Jimmy was standing on a slab of granite, in the middle of the crossroads.

"This is your spot. You're centralized. Everyone who comes to this fair will see you. Now go to work. And take this vendor badge. You're legal now, Mr. Moon Man."

I stepped onto a five-inch high slab of rock. It amazed me how this slight elevation gave me an intense rush of confidence and instantly made me feel more like a performer than a salesman. Wearing the vendor permit—depicting a gold miner and his mule standing next to a sluice box—gave me an additional sense of assurance.

"Well," Jimmy said, "are you going to stand there all day or are you going to try and sell something?"

As I stared out at the crowd, I recalled a day at the County Fair when I was nine years old. A carnival barker on the midway had mesmerized me. I thought he had the greatest job in the world, and when I grew up, I wanted to have a job just like him. I must have stood for two hours listening with complete rapture as he hypnotically delivered his pitch into the small microphone he wore around his neck....

"Ladies and gentlemen step right up...you've heard about him, you've read about him, now for the first time on the west coast you can actually see him.... Alive! Don't be alarmed! Every precaution has been taken to protect your safety. Once in a lifetime, you must see Kawaba the Vampire Boy. Kawaba, who in his lust for blood has been known to bite off the heads of chickens and snakes and suck the blood from their very bodies. Yes, it's Kawaba the Vampire Boy! No need to ridicule, there for the grace of God go you or I. If you live to be a hundred you will never forget the action on the inside. Alive, alive and on the inside.... Kawaba the Vampire Boy, see Kawaba, alive as you or I.... Just one thin dime, one tenth of a dollar see Kawaba, alive, alive and on the inside.... Kawaba, not pickled, not stuffed, not mummified, but alive, yes alive and all...all on the inside..."

"I'm waiting."

Jimmy had brought me back to present time. I was no longer that nine-year-old kid looking up in awe. I was the barker. I was the performer. I had gotten the job I'd always wanted. In a voice that was foreign to me, and with enough volume behind it that people fifty yards away turned their heads—I began.

"Ladies and Gentlemen, may I have your attention please? Yes, you, sir, and you, Ma'am. Please come forward. Kids, what I have to say is for you, too. Anybody within the sound of my voice that has one dollar is pre-qualified to participate in the offer I'm about to make."

To my astonishment, people were starting to gather in a semi-circle directly in front of me. I hadn't even mentioned the Moon Acre, and yet there were at least twenty people in front of me, and more coming with every sentence I spoke.

"That's right, crowd right in. Don't be alarmed, every precaution has been taken to ensure your safety."

A few people laughed at this and many were smiling. I liked this and felt energized by all the expectant faces now waiting to understand what all the shouting was about. I thought it best to have them wait just a little longer.

"You may have read about me, you may have heard about me, but today I am here in the flesh to answer any and all of your concerns, questions, or God forbid complaints, about my unique offer. I think it's safe to say I am not pickled, not stuffed, not mummified, but alive, alive and on the outside."

I noticed some people's eyes had started to glaze over.

"I know what I'm about to say will come as a shock to most of you. I also know there is no reason whatsoever that would compel you to believe what I'm about to say."

"Just what are you saying?" some guy in the front row shouted.

There were now about 100 people wondering the same thing. It was time to sell.

"Ladies and gentlemen, this man just asked me to explain what I'm I talking about."

"Good question," someone yelled from the back of the crowd, producing laughter that traveled, like a wave, through my growing audience. I realized, much to my amazement, that a theatre-like environment had been created with me at center stage. This rather large circle of spectators created an almost closed, quiet island in the middle of the cacophony of the street fair sounds and confusion. It was becoming more like theatre in the round, as the crowd was now expanding on all sides. I no longer needed to try and attract people. The size of the crowd itself was now drawing the curiosity seekers.

"What I'm talking about is doing something today that you may never, as long as you live, ever have a chance to do again. What I'm about to tell you will sound unbelievable. But the most unbelievable thing about it is it's actually happening. A few weeks ago I became the first person in recorded history—to my knowledge—ever to lay claim to the...MOON!"

I heard some nervous laughter and one woman asked her friend "What did he say?"

"Believe me, I know this sounds ridiculous, preposterous, incredible, and yet it's all true. Just because it has never happened before is no reason that it should not be happening now. If you think it's tough trying to explain what I do to all of you, you should have been there when I had to tell my parents that their only son had decided to become a moon salesman."

This line got a real honest laugh. People were enjoying this and so was I.

"Ladies and gentlemen, what I hold in my hand is an 8½" x 11" Parchtone certificate issued by the Lunar Development Corporation. This document grants the owner one acre of lunar surface for a most reasonable price of one dollar. The truth is, I have to keep my price low due to the rather high transportation costs associated with this offer."

More laughter.

"Now I know there are lots of interesting and unique things to see and buy at this fair. But I challenge any of you to find anything that even remotely comes close to the uniqueness—(remembering what Jimmy had said about the many collectors at the fair)—to the collector's value inherent in this document. And best of all, it's only one dollar. Perhaps you know somebody who will appreciate getting this in their Christmas stocking? Or you might simply have someone on your list that you don't want to spend more than a dollar on?"

More laughter.

I sensed it was time for the close.

"When you got up this morning if someone had told you that later today you would be considering buying land on the moon, you most likely would have thought them crazy. But that is exactly what I am asking you to do. Consider buying one of these Moon Acres. Take a chance on lunacy. Support your one and only…thank goodness…local Moon Man. How big a mistake can you make at one dollar an acre? OK, don't answer that."

As the crowd reacted with more laughter, I passed out five or six certificates for inspection.

"Who gave you the right to sell the moon?" someone called out.

"The gentleman over here asks a very good question; 'Who gave me the right to sell the moon?' Well, that's a fair question and I must honestly answer that nobody has given me that right, because there is no one that claims to own the moon…except for me, of course."

More laughter.

"I have never claimed that buying one of these documents is not without risk, however I do submit that the conversational value alone is well worth a dollar bill. These documents, by the way, are suitable for framing. Do you have a small crack in the wall, a chip in the paint? Cover it up with the best conversational piece in history. One dollar, one acre—Land boom on the moon!"

I strongly felt there were people who wanted to buy and yet were, for one reason or another, reluctant to come forward. I couldn't keep this group together forever, I needed someone to break the ice and soon.

"Tell me more about transportation to the property," someone joked from the back, and the audience broke out laughing.

"My friend you want a lot for a dollar. It costs you more than a buck just to drive to San Francisco and you want transportation to the moon? Just so there's no misunderstanding, I do not—at this time—provide transportation of any kind to the lunar surface. I also don't provide…air."

This line got a big laugh and I mentally made a note of it.

Looking out over the crowd I almost missed the little girl, who was about four or five years old, standing right in front of me, holding a dollar bill above her head.

"Excuse me ladies and gentlemen, but I think we have a real estate speculator in our midst. Madam, would you step up here please?"

I reached down and helped the little girl onto my elevated platform.

"Do you want to buy a Moon Acre?"

She shook her head, yes, much to the enjoyment of the crowd.

"Why do you want to buy one?"

She hunched her shoulders and started to giggle.

"Did your mommy or daddy send you up here to buy one?"

She shook her head yes, creating even more laughter.

"Where are they?"

She pointed out towards the middle of the crowd. Everybody turned to find out who this delightful child belonged to. People shifted and moved until there was a clear, unobstructed, line of sight to the now duly embarrassed parents. They sheepishly waved and joined in the general levity of the moment.

"I probably shouldn't take your dollar...but on second thought," I snatched the bill from her little hand, "I think I will. Hold on to this investment. Your mom and dad might need some help with your college fund. Would you all please give my youngest customer a big hand?"

To the sounds of applause, she went scurrying into her father's arms.

"Does anyone else have a son or daughter they want to bribe to come forward? Take a chance, this may be the only time in your entire life anybody will ever offer you the opportunity to buy land on the moon."

I noticed that the father of the little girl who had just bought the acre was surrounded by people wanting to look at the certificate.

"Please feel free to come forward and window shop. You will be under no obligation to buy. It can't hurt to take a look. Just don't read the fine print."

Some people in the back started forward.

Then from behind me, I heard those magical words.

"I'll take one."

I turned to find not one, but three people with dollars in their hands. I turned back to face the larger section of the crowd.

"Excuse me for just a moment. There are three folks here who recognize a good offer...well, at least they know an unusual offer when they see one."

I made sure to thank each buyer in a loud voice. Then I heard even better words.

I Sold *the* Moon!

"Can I have two?"

And then in rapid succession....

"One here, please."

"I need a couple."

"May I see one?"

"Can you change a twenty?"

I turned back around, and could not believe my eyes. It looked like a sea of dollar bills. The floodgates had opened. People who would ordinarily never have bought one if they had been solicited individually, allowed themselves to be caught up in the group's collective willingness to buy.

Even Jimmy bought one, telling me as he handed over his dollar, "I've never seen anything like this. You got yourself lightning in a bottle, my friend."

When the last of the original crowd had dissipated, and I had a chance to sit down, have a sarsaparilla, a plate of what they were calling Tombstone Taters, and do some bookkeeping, I found I had sold 78 Moon Acres.

I was ecstatic. I realized that this was the most money I had ever made in an hour, and I knew my presentation would only get better over time. I would continue to discover what lines brought laughter and what combinations of lines brought sales. I wolfed my food and hurried back to my improvised stage.

When I got there, two people were waiting for me.

"Are you the guy selling the moon?" one of them asked.

My heart sank. I thought I was going to be asked to leave the fair or worse yet have my money and Moon Acres confiscated.

"Yes, I'm the Moon Man."

"Great, we thought you might have left. Do you have any of those moon things left?"

Feeling immensely relieved I opened my briefcase and extracted some certificates.

"Fortunately for all of us I do. How many acres on the moon would you like?"

"I want five, and he wants three."

I counted out the eight acres, and was handed a ten-dollar bill.

"Are you thinking of giving any of these away for Christmas?" I asked the guy who was buying three.

"Yeah, I think they make trippy gifts. I always give weird stuff and this is definitely weird."

"What about one for yourself? I mean if you give all three away you might wish you had kept one," I said.

"Why not? At a buck, I think I can afford to splurge."

I passed one more acre over, and then added, "You know I always find there is somebody I forget to buy for or I get invited to a party and need a gift, you might think about getting one extra. I'll bet you'll find someone to give it to."

"Hey, are you like a super sales guy or something?"

"I don't know," I replied. "I never thought of it like that. What I was thinking though is you guys have bought 9 Moon Acres, and I appreciate it, but I just don't think you would ever regret buying one more, and like you said at a buck you can afford to splurge."

Now the guy that had bought five to begin with helped my cause by adding, "Come on man, what's the big deal? I got five, and you got more friends than I do. It's not like you're spending a hundred bucks or anything."

I started thinking I should take this guy with me.

"OK, OK I'll take one more, but that's it, and nothing you can say will get me to buy another one."

"I understand," I said as I passed over one more certificate. "Thank you guys very much. I only have one more question. Do either of you have brothers or sisters...?"

$$* \quad * \quad *$$

Back on my platform, I faced directly into the sun, imagining it to be my spotlight. This thought immediately made me feel self conscious in the sense that I was not giving my audience enough reason to look at me. If I was going to be in the spotlight, I needed to look like more of a performer. I needed a costume. I needed a Moon Man Costume!

I put my hand inside my pocket feeling the wad of bills that represented my morning's labor. That gave me energy. It was time to increase the size of this roll that created such a comforting bulge in my pocket.

Clearing my throat with a sense of conviction, I began speaking. Even as I was projecting my opening remarks, I was thinking how much more fun it was going to be once I donned my Moon Man costume.

"Ladies and gentlemen, boys and girls, please come forward. Many of you I'm sure have seen some of the hundreds of people walking around the fair today with one of these certificates."

Holding a Moon Acre high in the air, I slowly revolved 360 degrees, continuing to talk as I turned.

"You may have wondered what exactly it was they were holding with such care, or where it was they got them. My friends, what they were holding are deeds to land on the moon, and right here is where they got them. Those who invest in lunar real estate have a lot in common with the early gold prospectors. They are people who aren't afraid to take a chance. They..."

"Are you saying there's gold on the moon?" someone from the gathering crowd, interrupted me to ask.

"The question was do I claim there is gold on the moon? I assume the real question the gentleman wants answered is will there be gold on the plot he may buy?"

I heard a smattering of laughter. The wave was starting to build.

"No, I'm not guaranteeing gold on the moon. Diamonds sure, but gold, no. However, I am confident in promising all those who are willing to spend a dollar here today, that they will never regret their decision. The only decision some of you may regret is not acting on your inclination to buy one or more acres. The uniqueness of this offer alone should be enough to warrant serious consideration. The question you should be asking yourselves is not why should I buy one, but rather, what is stopping me from buying one?"

I was surprising myself with the ease I felt in verbalizing my thoughts, realizing much of what I was saying had been worked out during my long hours going door-to-door. I was also encouraged to discover the large number of people looking at me was not intimidating. On the contrary, the crowd gave me confidence and a sharper focus. The awareness that I was not just enjoying my center stage position, but loving it, was also a bit of a revelation. This was not work. This was fun.

The crowd had grown quite large by now and I felt it was time to ask for the sale, but before I could get one of my "trigger" lines out someone shouted out a question.

"What legal right do you have to sell the moon?"

This would be the single most asked question I would hear. People in all age groups, gender and from every ethnic origin would repeat it in all parts of the country. Americans, it seemed, were obsessed with the legality of what I was doing.

I would later come to understand that this question was also being asked by individuals not remotely interested in the answer, or in a purchase but who were intent on embarrassing me, and in so doing limiting my sales.

My answer, however, would invariably have the opposite effect. I could almost always get the crowd to laugh at the absurdity of expecting any legal assurances from a person dressed as a Moon Man and representing the BAD Company. And laughter, as confirmed, was the surest way of making sales.

I stood in the waning sunshine of that November California afternoon looking at over 100 people staring directly at me.

"I am not so naïve to believe that my claim on the moon will be recognized as legitimate in every court, in every state, or by every country on the planet. I think most of you would agree with me when I say I expect major resistance to my personal claim of ownership."

"You got that right," the same person shouted.

Laughter rippled through the crowd.

"Make no mistake about it. Anyone who buys one of these documents is taking a chance. After all, I work for the BAD Company. I have never denied that. However, that is what makes this document such a once-in-a-lifetime collector's artifact. Seeing is believing. Land on the moon—one dollar one acre. The conversational value alone is worth a dollar bill."

It was time to ask for the sale. I just needed to provide more cover for my self-conscious public.

"Who has a friend or relative that appreciates the unusual, the bizarre, the original, the creative side of life? As a gift, the Moon Acre is indeed one of a kind, and maybe best of all, it's only one dollar. Please feel free to step forward and take a closer look at the document."

I passed out a few certificates having learned that once the document was in hand, the chances of selling it greatly improved. I saw the first movement of green paper moving towards me through the crowd. It was important to let as many people know as soon as I could that someone was buying. No one wanted to be the first, perhaps afraid that they might also be the only one.

Pretending to hear a question, I responded. "The gentleman wants to know if I have change for a twenty? Yes, I do."

I pulled a handful of bills out of my pocket and held them above my head. Waving a fistful of money might loosen things up I thought.

What I didn't anticipate was the effect this cash in the air—like blood in the water—would have on the people milling at the edge of the crowd. The crowd was noticeably edging forward. It was as if I was holding a giant magnet and everyone was wearing an iron vest.

Three or four people in the front immediately asked to buy.

"Stake your claim. My office is now open!" I shouted out.

The sea of dollars moving in front of me was larger than before. People were laughing, asking for two and three certificates at a time. Once again, I could see a line start to form and just as quickly it disintegrated into a circle of people all jostling for position, and waving money at me.

Within ten minutes, I had sold every Moon Acre I had—all 230. I apologized to those who didn't get one, promising to return the next day with additional choice parcels.

"The good news," I said, "is that all the acreage I will be offering tomorrow is right on Moon River, and comes with an incredible view...of earth."

Before going home, I stopped at David's and convinced him to join me in the moon business. He resisted until I brought out my wad of moon cash and explained it was also a great way to meet moon maidens. "And it's not like we can't use some work on our comedy act," I concluded.

That night at dinner, my success was the main topic of discussion. I had sold 230 certificates. My father expressed more pride in the fact that I had seen my idea through than in the money it generated.

"You believed in something and followed through on it, despite the lack of encouragement. Believing in yourself even if others don't is something you can be proud of," he announced.

Everyone was happy to hear that David was going to be my

partner. They had grown accustomed to having the two of us doing things together.

I was up early the next morning, hoping to find anything that would help give me the look of a performer. With many businesses closed on Sunday, our local Thrifty drug store would have to do.

From their costume jewelry counter, I found two star-shaped rhinestone pins and a tray of Mood Rings—they were advertised as being able to change colors depending of what mood the wearer was experiencing. I bought three. Noticing the sunglasses, I was immediately attracted to an oval shaped pair with a silver mirrored coating. Just for fun, I asked the salesperson if they carried wigs. I wanted to see if they had something in silver. They didn't, but what they did have were cans of temporary hair highlighter spray. The cap was colored to match the contents. I bought four cans, all with the aluminum colored cap. My bag of cheap accessories would not provide me with the moon costume I had in mind, but with all this stuff on nobody would mistake me for a golfer. Well, OK, maybe a golfer, but it was a start.

$$* \quad * \quad *$$

After my week of door-to-door selling, coupled with all the acres I had sold to my friends and family, plus my success at the fair, I only had 112 Moon Acres left. Yesterday this would have seemed like more than enough, not so today.

With silver streaks in my hair, silver glasses on my face, light reflecting pins on my chest, and glowing rings on my fingers, people were turning their heads as I made my way through the fairgoers. My family and David, wanting to see for themselves how this worked, followed in my wake. As I got closer, I heard someone say, "I think that's the moon guy." Nearing my destination, two girls stopped me, one of whom asked, "Are you the one that was selling the moon yesterday?"

"Yes, that would be me."

"Great. They're a dollar each, right?"

"That's right, one dollar one acre," I said as I pulled out my certificates.

They both wanted three acres, and before I finished giving them their change there was a small group of people around me with dollars in their hands. I recognized three of the people from yesterday.

"Is this the property that's on Moon River like you promised?" one of the guys joked as he asked for five acres.

"That's right, as promised, this acreage fronts Moon River."

This unexpected initial rush of buyers lasted about 10 minutes and resulted in 37 acres sold—all before I'd even arrived at my location. They had found me. They had been waiting for me. I liked this job.

"Yeah, I can see why you desperately need my help," David said.

"I only get 35 cents an *hour* babysitting, and you just stand there and people give you money," my sister Lizzy lamented.

My father was shaking his head in disbelief, but had a smile on his face that I interpreted as a look of begrudging pride.

"Son," he said, "I don't think I would have believed it unless I saw it with my own eyes. You may very well have something here that you can use as a real springboard. A springboard to what, I haven't got a clue. And I think it's safe to say neither do you. But in the meantime I can't fault you for wanting to continue in this chosen line of work, even if I'm not sure what this is exactly."

My mom was wondering why people were buying before they even knew what it was they were getting into.

I was a little surprised as well. I made a mental note that returning to the same place on successive days seemed like a good thing to do, because I was benefiting from word of mouth—the cheapest and best form of advertising.

Now standing once more on "my spot," I was more nervous than I expected. Seeing my family and David all looking up expectantly brought back that old feeling I had experienced when faced with my first door-to-door customer. I had come a long way since then, I reminded myself. I knew what I was selling, and I knew I could sell it. Besides, I should be able to do at least as well today considering my attempt at costuming.

With a wad of bills in my left hand and a Moon Acre in the other—it was Show Time.

"Ladies and gentlemen, boys and girls, may I have your attention please? Some of you may have heard about the stranger that's come to these here parts. Some of you may even have heard that this here stranger is selling some kind of new fangled snake oil. Well, friends, I'm here to tell you—you heard right."

Any nervousness I had been feeling evaporated soon after I started to talk. What was more surprising was the speed in which the crowd started to gather. There must have been people in the area milling about waiting for me to begin, because as soon as I started talking, a large crowd spontaneously collected before my eyes. My family and David were forced forward in the crush of people now gathering on all sides. For the first time, I saw two or three people running from different parts of the fair to join what had become the biggest crowd I had ever addressed.

Before I could continue, someone shouted from the crowd, "When are you going to start selling the moon land?"

"The question was when will I start selling property on the moon?" I said for all to hear as I held the Moon Acre high over my head.

"Well, I think most people would agree that if they were in my business the answer to that question should be: "I will start selling these acres on the moon as soon as someone wants to buy one," and if that someone is you, sir, now would be as good a time as any."

The guy who had asked the question was starting to make his way up to the front but before he got to me there were seven or eight other people approaching me with dollars in their hands. I could see the look of confusion on a number of faces in the crowd. The ready buyers must have seen me yesterday, or had heard about it somehow. Knowing I had these sales in the bag, I decided to encourage some of the others.

"For those of you who are seeing me for the first time, it may be a little confusing as to exactly what is going on. The simple answer is I'm selling acres on the moon for the unbelievably low price of one dollar one acre. Some of these folks may well be doing a little early Christmas shopping. If you can find a better, more original stocking stuffer for one dollar, I would like to see it. Yesterday some people were worried about the legality of my enterprise. I will tell you the same thing I told them. You should be worried. This may not be the best investment you ever make."

This line got a good laugh. The confused expressions were changing to looks of amusement.

"The good news is," I continued, "your total investment is one dollar, and for your willingness to take a chance on lunacy you will become part of a very select group. A much too small select group if you ask me."

More laughter.

"While I complete these transactions let me leave the rest of you to ponder a simple question. Is the originality, the uniqueness and the inherent collector's value of this document worth a single dollar bill? Take a moment and appreciate the one-of-a-kind, the once-in-a-lifetime situation you find yourself in at this very moment. One dollar is not a lot to spend for a memory that will last a lifetime."

"Sold!" someone yelled.

What followed looked something like the day after Christmas clearance sale. The bargain hunters surrounded me as I stepped down into a group of desperate looking people, and a river of money. I sold every acre I had in ten minutes. I had been at the fair less than an hour and now had nothing to sell and was surrounded by people who wanted to buy.

My parents could not believe what they had just seen. It was a feeding frenzy with Moon Acres the only thing on the menu. My father said he had no idea my oratory skills were that good, and he wanted to know where I had learned crowd psychology, and all those sales techniques.

David thought I had missed my calling, telling me that I was perfectly suited to be a Dictator.

Lizzy said she *never* wanted to baby-sit again.

My experience at the fair had confirmed what I had come to understand. Selling the moon had to be played out in front of crowds. Not only did I enjoy the excitement, I was good at it. My father called me "a natural born showman."

It had been just a couple of weeks since my first Moon Acre had come off the press. My presentation and understanding of what I was doing had improved steadily. I now understood that what I was really selling was entertainment. I had shocked everyone, including myself, by selling 500 certificates in less than two weeks time. And today I had earned over $100.00 an hour. This idea that I could sell property on the moon all of a sudden didn't seem quite so ridiculous.

CHAPTER 9

AS SEEN ON TV

JUAN, AT THE COPY TREE, WAS SURPRISED TO HEAR FROM ME SO SOON, yet delighted that I was calling to increase my print order to 3000 Moon Acres. Before I asked, Juan told me Teresa was in Mexico seeing relatives. She'd be back in a week's time. My order could be ready in five days if needed, he assured me.

"A week will be fine." I would have waited longer I thought as I hung up.

$$* \quad * \quad *$$

Word-of-mouth had helped me at the fair and now I wanted to expand that publicity and "get some ink." I called our local paper, *The Sacramento Bee*, and was put in touch with John Burns. After some discussion, he agreed to meet the "Moon Men." A favorable article appeared a few days later, showing David, sitting in front of me, holding a framed Moon Acre, and smiling like he had just swallowed the canary.

The article explained how David and I had run a successful dating service—College Match—and an even more profitable food service business—BAD Foods—while in college. Reading about our entrepreneurial past solidified our belief that together we made things happen.

We both tacked up the article in our bedrooms. Below our picture the caption read:

Fun and Business: "Young College Grads Try Novelty Market."

The story generated a number of calls and, for the first time, mail order sales. After getting a taste of newspaper exposure, I wanted the ultimate validation—television.

A local personality, Bob Wilkins, hosted a late night TV program called *Creature Features*, and was known for having unusual guests on his show. I called the station and inquired if Bob had seen the story in the Bee. I also informed the assistant that the Moon Men would be ready to appear on a moment's notice.

I guess when you're hot; you're hot, because two days later I got the call:

Would we be available this Saturday and could we bring one of the Moon Acres? Yes, we were, and yes, we would.

Two hours later, I got another call.

"Fergus, how the hell did you find out?"

"McArdle, as your manager, I'm required to know what's going on. But I'm hurt that you didn't call me. Were you really going to cut your oldest friend out of this? I guess Barclay is calling the shots now?"

"Fergus, your stint as manager is over. Remember it went up in flames at CBS? I'm hanging up."

I didn't. I should have.

"OK, just give me two minutes. I want to explain how you can become rich, very rich," he said.

I blame it on my youth, his power of persuasion, my gullibility, and the fact that, despite everything, I liked him. When I finally hung up, it was agreed that Eddie would be joining us on the Bob Wilkins show and that David and I would participate in Fergus's newly created Events Production Company, Stairway to Heaven. That name wouldn't stick and almost overnight, it would start to be known as The BAD Company. There was one condition I insisted on: Moon Acre sales would remain separate. Big Eddie would have no claim on any revenue generated from that source.

As Fergus explained it, we would share expenses equally in the promotion of BAD Company concerts and events. He predicted we would all be rolling in the green stuff in no time at all.

"You and Barclay can still do that moon thing, and then when you want to make real money you can focus on promoting one of our events. This thing is going to be big—very, very big," Eddie assured me.

David surprised me by enthusiastically embracing Fergus's idea. He preferred the notion of being a promoter to being a space cadet, as he had been referring to himself lately.

After rummaging through several second-hand stores, David and I pieced together Moon Men costumes. I would wear a zip-up pee yellow jumpsuit with matching vinyl hood. David looked rather princely in his red and gold floor length tunic with an embroidered phoenix covering his torso. Silver gloves, mirrored glasses, capes, Mood Rings and the ever-present star pins completed the look. The costumes were not what I'd envisioned, but like the moon act, they were works in progress.

"The Moon Men" arrived at the studio with certificates and a sign that read: Buy MOON ACRES—Call (916) 961-7600.

While waiting for Bob Wilkins, Eddie Fergus made his appearance. With him were two other guys wearing matching white sweatshirts, with the words BAD Co. in black paint across the chest. With everyone else in one type of costume or another, Fergus looked especially strange in his pinstriped suit.

"As your manager, I'm here to tell you, you need to fire your costume designer," Fergus said.

Mutt and Jeff—his two companions—let out with a self-satisfied giggle.

"Fergus, you're the only one here who's been fired lately," I answered.

"We can discuss the contested dissolution of our former business relationship later, but now I think it prudent that we agree on how best to maximize our current media opportunity."

Larry and Moe nodded in support.

"Hang on, Fergus. When Barry said you had some promotion idea and wanted in on this TV gig, I said cool. But nobody said anything about Frick and Frack being included."

"David's right," I said, "I arranged for this appearance. We're here because David and I sell the moon. I don't even know these guys. Who the hell are they, anyway?"

"These are my associates. The big one is Woody, and the little one is Runt."

The two sad sacks waved self-consciously. Woody was over six feet tall and looked like a former linebacker who had been on a steady diet of cream-filled donuts and French fries, heavy on the salt. His long, dirty-blond hair hung in his eyes and he had an irritating habit of snapping his head to the side every few seconds to get it out of his line of vision. His goofy grin added to his look of nervous apprehension as if anticipating some impending disaster.

Runt looked worse. There was no mystery as to how he got his nickname. His stringy black hair and patched jeans with mushroom and pot leaf decals made him an ideal candidate for a police poster of what a Hippie looked like. Where Woody might have been smarter than he looked, I got the feeling that Runt was every bit as dimwitted as he appeared.

Fergus continued, "They're really good guys, and they've agreed to help us get the BAD Company up and going. I had to promise them they could be on TV. They won't say a word. They'll just stand behind us. It's not going to hurt anything."

Runt spoke. "Ain't nobody believed me when I said I'd be on the TV tonight. Momma and Lester and the others all gonna be watching. I ain't much of a talker, so don't worry, I won't mess nothin' up fer ya."

"Can I say something?" Woody asked. "Eddie said after we get on TV, we can buy some moon land from you boys, and me and Runt want five dollars worth each. Ain't that right Runt?"

"I brung cash money with me," Runt answered, as he proved his claim by bringing out a wad of limp bills.

"Yeah, you can buy Moon Acres, but the set might be too small for all of us to fit."

"Then we'll just have to squeeze together," Bob Wilkins announced from the back of the room.

"Hey, you're that guy on TV! Cool, man," Runt informed everyone.

Bob was chuckling, unfazed that there were five of us, three more than expected.

"That's me," Bob answered, "I'm the TV guy and these must be the Moon Men. Great idea, love it. I thought the Dead Zombies were scary, but you boys aren't far behind. Now I like to wing it on the air, so we're not going to rehearse. I'll just be asking things like: Where did you get this crazy idea? Who's buying? How much are moon condos going for? Stuff like that. Have fun with the answers and don't worry about making mistakes. In fact, mistakes are more entertaining. So nobody needs to be nervous. Now, how many microphones are we going to need?"

"Three will do it," Fergus offered. "One for each of the Moon Men and naturally I will need one for myself. These two are just... props."

"On second thought," Bob was saying, "why don't we just fix everybody up with one? No telling what they might say. OK, let's go out to the set and get everyone acquainted with the lights."

The *Creature Features* set was a Victorian drawing room decorated with posters of Frankenstein, the Werewolf and The Creature from the Black Lagoon. Bob suggested that David and I sit in the two ornate "smoking chairs" and arranged for Fergus (much to his displeasure), Woody and Runt to stand behind us.

Bob continued his orientation. "The format is straight forward. I'll talk to you before the movie starts, and then for just a minute during two breaks, and once again at the conclusion of the movie. We're on in nineteen minutes, so if anybody needs a comfort break, now would be a good time."

"What's a comfort break?" Runt wanted to know.

"If you need to take a leak, go now," David said with more than a little irritation in his voice.

"Yeah, I do, I can't hold it for a whole movie," Runt answered.

"I need to drain the old weasel myself. Which way to the head?" asked Woody.

"Follow me gentlemen, I'm going that way," Bob said, giving me a wink.

The moment the studio's big metal door closed behind them, both David and I jumped all over Fergus.

"Have you gone completely nuts? I'm not working with those Neanderthals. What were you thinking?" I screamed.

"New low, Fergus. This is bullshit, and you act like everything's cool. Well, it's not cool," David fumed.

"I should have called you yesterday. I know I fucked up, but let me explain. First off, those guys will in no way be part of your moon gig." Fergus said.

"No shit," I quickly added for emphasis.

"Let me finish. The only reason they're here is because they, well, Woody has money, lots of money, and he's agreed to help bankroll the BAD Company. Hey, it's better than using all of our money. Right? Unfortunately, Woody doesn't go anywhere without Runt. They're like best friends. Has something to do with Runt saving Woody's dog from drowning. I didn't get the whole story."

"You mean the part where Runt gives the dog mouth-to-mouth resuscitation?" David asked.

"Something like that. Look, the deal is, if we don't include Runt, we don't get Woody, and no Woody...no money. You don't have to like them. Hell, you don't even have to see them again. I'll handle everything. Trust me, by this time next month you'll be thanking me."

"You're disgusting, Fergus. As I said a new low, even for you," David groused.

"So how much does he have and how much has he given you?" I asked

"I don't really know, OK? But I know it's a lot. He hasn't given me any yet. It's really very complicated, but as I understand it, all he needs to do is get his Grandmother to sign over his inheritance before she dies, and then he can borrow cash against the old lady's property. Look, I'll handle the details. Once I've delivered on my promise of getting him on TV, he'll be obligated to me. The rest is easy. He's not interested in the business side of things. He'll be a silent partner, so to speak. Just don't say anything about his drinking. He gets real pissed off if anyone asks him why he drinks so much, so just play it cool."

David and I both started laughing in disbelief.

"What's so funny?" Bob asked, making his way back to the set.

"Yeah, did somebody fart?" Runt wanted to know.

Woody doubled over in laughter. When he recovered, he punched his friend on the arm declaring, "Jeez, Runt you're just too funny for words."

Bob Wilkins turned out to be very cool. Before the show started, he said he wanted to buy a Moon Acre, and brought out a dollar bill.

This showed a lot of class as far as I was concerned. He also said he would have no problem with us showing our sign and suggested that one of the boys standing behind us should hold it. After volunteering, Runt got the honors.

"Hey, look, I'm on TV! And you are too, Runt. Far out, dude," Woody said, as he pointed towards the floor monitor that was sending back a test picture in preparation for the start of the show.

"Boys, try not to look at the monitor once we're on the air," Bob gently suggested to the two ditwads who were now engaged in waving to themselves and contorting their faces in childlike amazement, having realized that whatever they did was instantly seen on the monitor.

A couple minutes later, we heard the floor manager say 10 seconds to air, then 5...4...3...he then held up two fingers, then one and then pointed emphatically at our host.

I noticed a little light on the top of the camera pointed towards Bob had come on, glowing a bright crimson.

"Good evening, all you night crawlers, casket dwellers, and insomniacs, and welcome to another edition of *Creature Features*. We have a good one for you this evening...*Fire Maidens From Outer Space*. This 1956 classic tells the story of a team of astronauts marooned on a moon of Jupiter, only to discover beautiful women, starved for male attention, inhabit the place. Sounds like a vacation destination to me. And speaking of moons, I have in studio with me a couple of people you may have read about in last week's *Sacramento Bee*. The two oddly dressed gentlemen sitting next to me are known as the Moon Men, and they claim to sell land on the moon for one dollar an acre. Standing behind them we have their manager, and two members of what the Moon Men are calling the BAD Company."

At the mention of the word "Manager," Big Eddie put on what he thought was his most confident self-assured smile. Unfortunately, the big boy was packed into his all wool suit and the TV lights were directing their glare and considerable heat directly on him. Sweat was already appearing in beads on his forehead and neck. A rivulet of perspiration ran down his face collecting in his damp, limp shirt collar.

Twiddle Dee and Twiddle Dumb looked like petrified pieces of wood, having taken no heed of Bob's instruction. They were both transfixed staring zombie-like directly at the studio monitor.

"Let me start by asking the obvious," Bob said. "Why should anybody buy an acre of the moon from you guys?"

"That's a good question," I said. "There probably is no one answer for everybody. Some people buy because they recognize the uniqueness, the collector's value inherent in these certificates. Others buy I'm sure as a joke or as a gift for someone they don't want to spend two dollars on."

"As to the second part of your question—why should they buy from us—that's simple. We're the only people in the world who are currently selling the moon," David added.

"Excuse me, Mr. Wilkins. Are we on TV? What I mean is, can my mom and Lester see me right now on our TV that's in our living room?" Runt wanted to know, as he continued to stare off-camera at the monitor.

"Everyone calls me Bob, and yes, we are most assuredly on the air right now. And if the TV in your living room is turned on, and tuned to channel 13, you are being seen, right now, by everyone in that room who is watching."

At this confirmation, both Runt and Woody sheepishly grinned and made small waving motions with their hands.

"Now before we start our movie I want to tell everyone I bought this Moon Acre earlier this evening (he held it up so one of the other cameras could get a close-up shot). I think it makes a heck of a conversational piece. The price is also hard to beat. It might be a good time now for your associate to hold up that sign you brought."

Runt, who held the sign backwards and hidden behind David's chair, did not pick up on the cue. I reached over and grabbed the sign, turned it around and held it steady as I had seen Bob hold the Moon Acre.

"We'll be back with the Moon Men later in the program. I want to know why the costumes and I'll try and get a comment from their Manager on what the future holds for these enterprising young men. If you want a piece of the moon, call the number you see on your screen. And now *Creature Features* is proud to present tonight's classic film, *Fire Maidens From Outer Space*."

I heard the floor manager say, "We're clear," and noticed the red light on Bob's camera was off.

The next two interview segments went well for the Moon Men. Bob asked us softball questions like: "Who really owns the moon?" and "Should investors expect a good return on their purchase?" and "Did we anticipate any possible legal problems in the future?"

The first one gave me a chance to recall watching Neil Armstrong take his historical first step, and my belief that since nobody had ever laid claim to the moon my claim could not be discarded out of hand. "And as far as the investment potential goes, Bob, it's a little like betting on the long shot at the track. On occasion, it wins. In regards to legal problems, I can only ask you: don't we look completely rock solid?"

"In fact, Bob," David jumped in, "we hope to hire one of Runt's half brothers to handle any potential legal entanglements. He's a partner with the law firm of Dewy, Cheatum and Howe."

"Lester and Chigger ain't no lawyers. 'Course they been in jail once or twice," Runt surprised everyone by announcing.

Fergus, who had yet to say anything and was looking like he might explode, decided this was his time to join the discussion.

"If I might be allowed to clarify some of the misconceptions your audience might otherwise be left with in regards to the legal position and high integrity the BAD Company will, on a go forward basis, dedicate itself to, it should be made unambiguous..."

"Sorry to interrupt," said Bob, "and it sounded like you were just getting started. I'll give you a chance to finish your thought when we return. Now let's re-join those luscious Fire Maidens and those lucky marooned astronauts."

Our last interview segment came and went without incident. Bob gave the boys in the back a chance to say something. Both Runt and Woody said "hi" to their mom, friends, and extended family members. Woody, as instructed by Fergus, had acknowledged his grandmother with a special wish for her good health and safety.

David and I both made sure we thanked Bob and made a last sales pitch for people to call in and buy Moon Acres.

Only Big Eddie got short changed out of his time.

When he finally got his moment in the spotlight, he looked like he was going to pass out from heat exhaustion and extensive gastro bloating.

"I promised we would hear from the big guy in the back. So in the short time we have left can you tell us, what does a Moon Man's Manager do?"

"Well, Bob, let me start by thanking you and the competent management team here at Channel 13 for tonight's gracious invitation and the generous hospitality you have extended. Your viewers are going to be hearing a lot about a new and exciting enterprise. I'm speaking of course about the BAD Company. My long term vision regarding the ultimate evolution and the attendant success of this venture is based in the realization that the future of global entertainment will be divided into five key spheres of influence. One..."

"Whoa, big fella, and if any of my viewers are still awake, they will just have to wait for your book to hear your analysis of the entertainment industry. I was hoping to learn more about the Moon Men but that will also have to wait as we are now out of time. Let me thank all my guests, and wish you continued success. Don't miss next week's program. It's a cult favorite, *The Brain That Wouldn't Die*. A mad surgeon keeps his girlfriend's disembodied head alive while he goes in search of a replacement body...good stuff. Until then, this is Bob Wilkins for *Creature Features* saying don't be in a hurry to turn the lights off. Good night, everybody."

After saying our good-byes and selling a few acres to the crew, we left.

"Gee, Fergus, I didn't know you were running for office. What was all that crap about your vision and the evolution of the entertainment industry? You were supposed to be hyping land on the moon and the guys who are selling it," I said.

"I was getting to that, but I wanted to establish credibility first. Shit, he cut me off every time I started to say something."

"That's because he's in the entertainment business, not in the let me establish credibility business." David joked.

"Laugh if you want to, I was just trying to present you in a more professional manner."

"Fergus," I said, "that's just the point. We don't want to be perceived as professional. I mean look at us. We're wearing cheesy, low rent space costumes. The whole thing's a joke. We want people laughing, not discussing the legal or professional nature of what we do."

"Well, I agree with one thing, those are pretty cheesy outfits," Fergus said to the approving laughter of Woody and Runt.

David and I arrived back at my house sometime after midnight. As we opened the door, Thea, Sheila, and Shelley were all screaming about people calling in to buy Moon Acres. They told us the phone had not stopped ringing since the moment the sign with our phone number was shown.

"Yes, that's right," Lizzy was saying into the phone, "as soon as we get your three dollars and fifty cents we will send you three Moon Acres the very next day. Make sure you include your address with your order. Bye."

The instant she hung-up, it started ringing.

"Moon Acres Hotline, may I take your order please?" Lizzy said, handing me a notebook, with a running list of who had called and how many Moon Acres they wanted. 82 people had called in, ordering a total of 137 certificates and still counting. With the acres we sold at the station and the $10.00 collected from Woody and Runt, the total would be over $160.00.

Even after giving my sisters a cut for answering the phone, this was not a bad way to start the new Moon Men selling duo. The working world was starting to feel exciting.

By the time everybody on this list sent in their money, I would have my new inventory and be able to deliver on my sisters' promise to send them out without delay.

The list also had one name and phone number with a circle around it, and a note in my sister's scrawl, to call a Mr. Green.

I stayed awake another hour enjoying listening to the phone ring.

—Today—

He Sells 'Acreage' On The Moon

Barry McArdle can't take prospective customers for an on-site inspection of the far-out property he sells, but the price is right.

Page A3.

● The stock market posts still another gain as its week-long rally keeps going. Page K8.

FINAL DOW AVERAGE

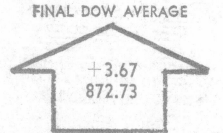

+3.67
872.73

Stock listings on Pages K8, 9.

● Women delegates snub Mrs. Rabin. Page A3.
● Tax rebates put US deeper in Red. Page K7.

FAIR

Weather details on Page E3.

CHAPTER 10

MOONLIGHTING

LARRY GREEN WAS THE ASSISTANT MANAGER IN CHARGE OF STORE promotions at White Front. I figured his last name would be of little help in advancing his career there. He had seen us on TV and called to offer the Moon Men a job standing in front of White Front's new department store between the hours of 7 PM and 11 PM during the week before Christmas. Runt, Woody, and Fergus would not be needed.

We would be paid $100 a night and, more importantly had permission to sell as many Moon Acres as we could. In fact, the whole idea of the "Moonlight Promotion" centered around the idea that you could get anything at White Front this holiday season...even land on the moon!

✳ ✳ ✳

It must have been growing up in a family with six sisters that allowed me to enjoy spending most of the morning getting ready to see Teresa.

As I entered the Copy Tree, the combination of hearing the door chimes and seeing Teresa had a trancelike quality about it. She was wearing a pale yellow dress accented with embroidered rose buds on the bodice. The short rounded sleeves were pulled down on her petite caramel shoulders. A yellow silk ribbon had been plaited in her hair.

"Hi, Barry, we saw you on TV. Are you going to forget about us now?"

"You know, Teresa," and I looked right into her eyes, "I honestly don't think I will ever forget you."

As I said this, I felt my body start to get warm. She looked away and when she turned back she was holding one of the twelve bundles I would be taking with me.

"3000 is a big jump from 500. Are you sure you can sell all these?"

"I'm not sure, but I do know I'm going to have a lot of fun trying."

She finished stacking them on the counter, and then turned her attention to the invoice.

"I have the cash and will pay in full."

"You're starting to be one of our good customers," she said, her black eyes sparkling.

As I counted out the money, my only thought was how to ask her out. What I really wanted to say was that I thought she was beautiful, and when we had held hands I noticed I had trouble breathing, that I had wanted to kiss her since the first moment I saw her, and that I thought I might be falling in love with her, and....

Our eyes met.

"Teresa, I was wondering if you, if we, I just thought..."

The phone rang. She hesitated then turned to answer it. Her father came out from the back, and thirty seconds later, the door chimes filled the room. A bride-to-be and her mother came into the shop intent on picking out wedding invitations. My chance to ask Teresa out was lost, not only for the day but forever. Leaving the shop, I had no way of knowing that I would not see Teresa again for eleven years. And when I did, she would be married and a mother of two.

I like to think she would have said yes to going out with me. And although more than thirty years have passed, when I think of her it is always in that moment—now frozen in my memory—we were gazing at each other, my heart racing, my peripheral vision obscured, my equilibrium challenged—just before the phone rang.

The White Front gig was memorable for a number of reasons. It was the first time I would be paid an appearance fee, and as it turned out it would be the last time David would don a moon suit and sell acres with me.

It was exciting seeing the ads White Front ran in our local newspaper. We were being used to attract customers: "Big Moonlight Sale...See the Moon Men...In Person," and my favorite: "As Seen on TV."

Positioned at the store's entrance, the Moon Men greeted everyone with a Merry Christmas and an offer to buy land on the moon. Within the first ten minutes of the first night, we realized people were not going to stop and listen to a long routine. Our basic sales pitch was soon edited down to a few sentences.

"Merry Christmas. You've seen us on TV and read about us in the newspaper. Now is your chance to buy land on the moon for one dollar. We have the greatest stocking stuffer of all-time and for only one dollar. Merry Christmas. Land on the moon one dollar an acre."

After a number of people bought acres as they were leaving the store, we added the line: "We will be here when you come out...think about buying at least one Moon Acre this year. Someone you know deserves to own land on the moon."

Having David selling with me was good for business, and a lot more fun than it would have been had I been forced to freeze alone in the glare of the overhead florescent lights. Although no one ever waited in line to buy, we did have some success. We averaged $225.00 a night and added to that was our nightly appearance fee of $100.00.

All of this money and more would go into the promotion and other expenses associated with the BAD Company's first rock concert, scheduled for New Year's Eve. Simultaneous with our White Front gig, we had been working to promote our first public event. The show featuring the band Redwing was to be our initial foray into the "Big Time" concert business.

We had spent weeks getting posters made and put up, printing tickets, and recording radio ads to blitz the airwaves. Since we had our phone number on the posters, flyers and in radio ads, we knew by the hundreds of calls we were getting that the word was out and the response was more than good—it was incredible. With the concert just seven days away, we were worried we might have to turn people away because of fire regulations.

Fergus assured us we would recoup all our investment for this event, and have thousands of dollars of profit to divide up…it was time to celebrate.

I had been introduced to Marty and Manny, or as we called them, the M&M boys, by a mutual acquaintance, and had developed a kind of interesting friendship. Besides being very intelligent and entertaining, they were always in possession of delightful illegal substances. Their house had an incredible sound system including speakers in every room. They were both great cooks. Well, no, Marty preferred baking and Manny did the cooking. Best of all, they never ever tried to hit on your girlfriends.

They were as obviously homosexual as I liked to think I was obviously heterosexual. Their house was meticulously furnished in 1940's decor. The artwork, the lighting, the music, the knick-knacks, and even the magazines on the coffee table were from the 1940's. Framed on the wall was their pride and joy—the 1948 *Chicago Daily Tribune* newspaper with the premature and as it turned out wrong banner headline reading: **DEWEY DEFEATS TRUMAN!!**

I especially liked playing with the four little bunny rabbits they had trained as house pets. On occasion, they liked to host their straight friends for a night of debauchery.

I had called a few days ahead and asked if I could bring Fergus, Runt, Woody, Woody's sister, and her friend. The M&M boys had met David on numerous occasions and were always happy to have him along. I told Marty we would bring all the booze and some killer pot that had just come in from Humboldt. After assuring me all my friends were invited, especially the one named Woody, Marty said he was excited to have us all try his new French currant and mango scones flavored with real lavender flower pedals.

"My scones should be the perfect compliment to Manny's truffle, champagne and lobster bisque, and just wait till you see the surprise I'm creating for our late night desert."

As we all entered their bungalow to the sweet harmonies of the Andrews Sisters and their familiar Buy War Bonds framed poster, we were handed a red capsule, and told it was very pure Psilocybin. I had always liked this drug. It was never as intense or scary as LSD and the enhanced sensitivity of touch the drug created could be quite memorable, especially if you happened to be tripping with a girlfriend.

Most of their oversized furniture was upholstered in red and gold velvet, and as I sat down, I was happy to see they still had a crystal dish full of M&M candies on their sleek polished mahogany coffee table. Pictures of Lana Turner, Betty Grable and other Hollywood starlets , of the 1940's, lined the wall.

Marty and Manny were dressed in elaborate silk smoking jackets. I noticed that Marty, dressed in red, would only sit in a gold chair and Manny, wearing the gold jacket, would only sit in the red velvet covered furniture. I guess they were both into contrast, and I do have to admit they looked very stylish, especially when they were holding one or more of their pet bunnies.

They insisted we eat almost right away before the full effect of the Psilocybin took over and we lost our appetite. Wow! The soup was fantastic and Marty was right—his mango scones were indeed the perfect compliment to his partner's lobster bisque. They both loved seeing us ask for seconds, and for Fergus—thirds. We couldn't thank them enough, especially having recently endured a meal of Runt's goulash pie covered in his own "secret sauce."

"Stop thanking us, you're making Manny blush, and pink is really not his best color. Besides, it's quite validating to see you all give in to what I know to be a natural, and dare I say, healthy impulse. Most of our friends simply won't allow themselves more than one helping of anything, you know, keeping a boyish figure and all that," Marty said.

"Except for Bobby, his boyish figure hasn't seen the light of day for years. He has seconds of everything, and I do mean *everything*," Manny offered with exaggerated inflection and conspiratorial overtones.

That drew some nervous laughter from around the table, and at least for me, a sense of a growing sexually-charged atmosphere. I knew most of this rising sexual feeling was being fueled by the drug I had taken about an hour before, but some of it, I felt, was due to the unusual situation of being in the home of two gay men.

Sure, I'd thought about what it would be like to be gay, and I never believed anybody who said they hadn't. I'd thought about it in the same way I'd thought about what it would be like to be a millionaire, a movie star, or a world famous athlete. The big difference was I thought it would be fantastic to be any of those, but to be gay never held any attraction for me. I can appreciate male beauty, but no matter how handsome a man is, the idea of intimately kissing one gives me the creeps. It would be like trying to attach two positively charged or two negatively charged magnets together. The closer they come to touching, the stronger the repellent force comes into play.

However, I also can't understand why some guys get so upset, even violent, over the fact that other men do find each other sexually attractive. Maybe it's because in some way they themselves feel some sort of forbidden attraction or interest in their same sex friends. Is this over-the-top denigration of the homosexual lifestyle their attempt to bolster their own testosterone and demonstrate to the world, and more importantly to themselves, that they are 100% hot-blooded American male? By condemning homosexuality and those that engage in it are they trying to exorcise, to "kill," any attraction or stimulation they subconsciously feel themselves?

I would think if someone is so heterosexually-charged they would thank the gay community for taking themselves out of the competition for members of the female population. And since most of the gay men I've known are not only good looking, intelligent, funny, great communicators, and very sensitive (attributes all high on most women's "What I look for in a man" list) I for one will not be complaining. It's not like we have a population shortage and the world is in dire need of more conceptions.

I hear people say, "Homosexuality is a crime against nature." I think it's a crime for society to make laws that seek to punish two consenting adults who choose to do nothing more than bring pleasure to each other. Since all of us here are in fact part of nature, indeed we are *from* nature, I find it illogical to think that because one is born with a different sexual orientation one could, by some convoluted logic, be held libel for a "crime" that their creator, that nature itself, gave birth to. Nature may very well be doing what she can to help keep the population from exploding beyond its already out of control numbers. For me the real tragedy is nature loses, for all time, the DNA from many of her best and brightest.

There are a lot of things in this world that don't make sense, but that doesn't mean because I don't understand it—it must follow that it's wrong. I can't explain my attraction to women other than to say no one taught me, and it was not a decision I consciously made nor one I could consciously un-make. It seems logical to believe that's true for homosexuals as well.

The Andrews Sisters gave way to Tommy Dorsey, followed by Liberace, and then the 1949 hit album *South Pacific*. Dessert would be ready in two hours after the Saturday Night Movie that Marty insisted we all watch, the 1944 classic with Judy Garland and Margaret O'Brien, *Meet Me In St. Louis*.

Everybody went into the living room to smoke some pot and watch the movie. Feeling as I did, watching a Judy Garland movie didn't sound that exciting. But excitement was on its way.

Woody had brought his 18-year-old sister and her girlfriend with him to the party as expected. The friend was at this moment in deep conversation with David. David was explaining how life was going to be different once he became a world famous comedian. CBS had first option on the comedy team of Barry and Dave but if they dragged their feet in negotiations over the series we have planned, well then we might be forced to consider both NBC and ABC. David let her know that CBS would most likely not relish the idea of getting into a bidding war for our services.

Woody's sister Jill was at this moment sitting across from me at the kitchen table. I had never met her before tonight, but that only added to my attraction to her. She was tall—about 5' 8" and very well proportioned. Her shoulder length blond hair, big blue eyes, and pale white skin gave her a Nordic, Viking kind of look. She had a very funny giggle that made everybody around her laugh when they heard it. Drug or no drug she was extremely sexy, in spite of over doing it. She wore too much perfume and makeup. The thick black mascara and deep red rouge and lipstick hid a natural beauty that would have been more appealing and original than the painted person she had created. Jill had no idea of how to dress other than wearing her skirt too short and her top too tight and low cut. It's not that I objected to her choice in clothing, it's just that the completed outfit looked less like stylish fashion than it did like a cry to be noticed.

On the other hand, it was working, because I was most definitely noticing her. We started to clear the table and the next thing I knew I was doing the dishes, and Jill was standing next to me hand drying the plates as I handed them, sparkling clean, over to her. Normally the idea of doing dishes while stoned on some very nice magic mushrooms, pot, and wine would be an activity that would just have to wait. But with Jill willing to share her sweet infectious laugh, long bare legs—appearing even longer coming as they did from under her short skirt—and revealing top with me, I was more than content to work for my supper.

"Do you feel all warm and glowing?" she asked.

"Yeah, even my toes feel good. I wonder why something that makes you feel so good has to be illegal?"

"Do you think it could be because nobody would want to work if they felt like this all the time? I mean they would be thinking too much about, you know, sex."

I almost dropped one of the M&M boy's 30-year-old china dinner plates.

"You're right. I was wondering if it was just me, or just because I'm here in this house, or just the drug, but it's hard for me to think about anything else, of course looking at you is not helping the situation."

She laughed, and so did I, and for the first time our eyes locked, and we both knew instantly that washing and drying dishes was a very unusual form of foreplay.

Just then, Marty came in to get another bottle of wine.

"Well, haven't we been busy little bees. Thank you so much, what a nice surprise, I can't tell you how I loath the clean up thing, especially after I've been slaving away in here all day. You kids are missing a delicious movie, but don't let me interrupt."

He started to leave with a bottle in each hand and then abruptly stopped and turned around.

"Oh here, it's not like I don't have more...but please, pretty please don't tell the others where you got this, they'll just think I'm holding out, but the truth is I promised Manny I would quit, and I will. I really will, really, just not tonight. Have fun, let it snow, let it snow, let it snow..." he sang these last few words as he left.

Jill picked up part of a page taken out of a Betty Boop comic book, folded into what looked like an origami. Unfolding it carefully, we discovered we had been given an instant party in powder form.

I had enjoyed cocaine the few times I'd tried it. I liked it so much I made a vow never to buy it. If it came my way, fine, but I intuitively knew from the first time I snorted it I could very easily become addicted, and every addict I had ever met had a lifestyle that never seemed all that appealing.

"Far out, I just love cocaine. Hmmm, do you think it will be OK to do the coke, I mean on top of the Psilocybin?" Jill wanted to know.

"Well, I'm not a pharmacist so don't take my word for it, but the Psilocybin is really a hallucinogen, the coke is a stimulant, and the wine is a depressant, leaving the pot to kind of equal everything out— yeah, I think we'll be fine."

We rushed through the remaining dishes and then went looking for a little privacy. I took her hand and led her up the stairs into the small guest bedroom with a huge king-size bed that filled up most of the room's available space. As soon as the door shut, we were in each other's arms and kissing wildly. The incredible sensation of skin on skin was no doubt enhanced by the drugs, but neither of us thought of complaining. We stood with our bodies pressed tightly together. The soft erotic pressure of her breasts rubbing against me made my legs buckle unexpectedly. The walls of the room seemed to melt away, and in their place, I saw endless circles of changing colored lights and arcing rainbows.

It was easy and natural for me to let one hand slip down her leg and up under her accommodating skirt. Just placing my hand on the outside of her panties I could feel the heat radiating through the thin cotton as they became noticeably and wonderfully damp. I started to feel her legs open slightly as she began to rotate her hips creating more pressure and rhythm on my hand that was now cupped snugly between her legs. Hearing the sound of her pubic hair rubbing against her panties had me feeling like I was about to lose consciousness. We both were having trouble standing, and as I looked down toward the dizzying sound the floor seemed to disintegrate into a vast star field of constellations and planets. Jill was leaning heavily on me for support and I felt as if I were falling through the shimmering tail of a speeding comet.

I had taken enough drugs to know I was experiencing a rush, a condition brought on when the effects of the drug were the strongest and most intense. Realizing this I knew the key was not to panic. The disorientation and hallucinations would pass. Wouldn't they? They always had, I reminded myself.

"God that feels good," Jill moaned. "I want to be naked. Don't you? But can I trust you? I mean I have a boyfriend and we promised not to have sex with anyone else, but being naked is not having sex, and besides since we have all this coke I want to try something I read about, if that's all right with you."

As she was saying this, she had put one of her hands down my pants and had used her other one to pull aside her panties. Suddenly having unencumbered access to that beautiful, magical, indescribable place of pleasure, mystery, and bliss and at the same time feeling her hand find its way around my penis, I might have promised her anything if it meant getting naked with her.

We had been swaying back and forth when suddenly we stumbled falling onto the huge bed. The awkwardness of the fall had us laughing, providing both of us a chance to recover a bit from our high state of arousal.

Lying side by side, I was able to indulge myself in her big dreamy blue eyes.

"You look beautiful and very womanly. Your cheeks are glowing a dark shade of red," I whispered as I kissed both sides of her warm, lovely face. "And yes, of course, I want to be naked with you, and yes you can trust me...I think. The odds may be around 50-50 so I hope you're the gambling type."

We both started laughing again. It felt so good to be open and up front about something as sensitive and intimate as sharing your body with someone—even if that sharing was to fall short of complete surrender. I secretly felt that I could do my part and respect her wishes, especially if she helped me by staying in control herself.

"I think I can raise those odds quite a bit. Remember I told you I wanted to try something I read about? Well, it sounds like fun and if you're up for it (we both had a good laugh at her unintended pun), I'm more than ready to try it."

"Right now I'd agree to almost anything. What did you have in mind?"

"Well, it's kind of embarrassing, but here goes. Instead of snorting all the coke, I think it would be fun if you let me cover your, a, if I put it on your um..."

"Penis?"

"Yeah, on your penis. And then I'll...you know...kiss it and stuff. The cocaine is supposed to make it numb at first and then when feeling starts to come back it's supposed to be better than anything, well at least that's what I read. And then it's my turn. You put some on me and return the favor. We can be naked together, have fun, and not worry about whether things are going to get out of control, and I break my promise not to have sex, well, intercourse with anyone else. My cheeks must really be red now. Well, what do you think?"

"Where do I sign, and where do I get a subscription to that magazine," I joked as I started to unbutton her blouse.

I had always loved these few minutes of undressing a woman for the first time. I was taking my time and more than once I had to gently stop Jill from becoming too helpful.

Her blouse was so tight I had to concentrate as I slipped each of the pearl-coated buttons through their respective holes. It was an added pleasure to see that she was wearing a bra. I first let slip her shoulder straps, and then kissed her all along the top of her breast line, and then nibbled through the satin fabric bringing her hidden nipples back to life. Hearing her moan was as exciting as thinking about what lay ahead. Reaching around her back, I felt for the bra clasp. This was always a danger zone. I usually tried to cover for any pending display of inexperience or just plain bumbling, on my part, by saying something to the effect of "I hope you're not timing me," or "does this come with instructions?" I knew these were lame attempts at easing my own lack of confidence before I ruined the mood completely by fumbling through the Rubik's Cube of locking devices.

But tonight would be different. I felt I had been in this situation enough to justify playing the part of James Bond. I would say nothing. I would just reach back and with one hand bring the two elastic end pieces together. That would relieve the tension on the clasps and allow me to delicately unfasten the usual three little hooks and eyes. Kissing her full on the mouth, I made my first attempt to free her swelling breasts from their satiny white restraints. No luck. I kissed her harder, and brought more of the back strap together. Then slowly, moving my fingers along the elastic band felt for the clasps...nothing. This was not working. Mayday! Mayday! OK, time for Plan B. Putting my other hand back there, I felt along the entire length of the back band and to my growing panic could not identify anything that might help unlock the secret of the great pyramids.

I was hearing a little giggle escape from her partially covered mouth.

"It's in the front. I tried to help but you wouldn't let me. It's a new design."

"I can take it from here," I laughed. And for the first time I was presented with a bra that hooked together in the front. It made perfect sense, of course, to have the clasp there, but it might as well have been in the bunny hutch because I never would have thought to look there.

This was now a new and wonderful experience because after some further difficulty with the interlocking clasp, not your standard hook and eye, I realized I had the option of lifting off one side at a time or peeling both covers off at once. Now that I had mastered the technique of the front sealing brassiere I enjoyed uncovering and then recovering her full, luscious breasts over and over. I might have continued playing this erotic game of hide-n-seek the rest of the night, but on the fifth or sixth uncovering, Jill grabbed the bra and threw it across the room.

For some reason this aggressive action was very much a turn on and my planned slow and deliberate removal of the rest of her clothes was now carried out in a more frenzied, chaotic fashion. I turned into a four-year-old who had just been given the OK to open his first beautifully wrapped Christmas package, and didn't want any more help from mom.

When we were both naked, I opened up Miss Betty Boop a bit more slowly. I wanted to try one line just to see how good it was. After rolling a dollar bill into straw, I asked Jill if I could put the coke between her breasts. That just seemed like a far better place than the nightstand, and considering where I would eventually be putting it I didn't think she would mind and she didn't. Licking up the white dust that was left behind was further confirmation that skipping the nightstand had been the right decision. She followed up with a line of her own off my torso. She also took her time with the residue. She surprised and delighted me by spending as much time licking and nibbling on my chest as I had spent on hers.

"Are you ready?" she finally asked.

"I don't think I've ever been more ready for anything in my life...but are you sure you don't want me to, well, I mean shouldn't it be ladies first?"

"If it was I would be in no condition to return the favor," she said as she slid her body half off the end of the bed. She started by wetting her finger, dipping it into the cocaine and then applying the powder to her lips, tongue, the vibrating head of my penis, and to the creamy white valley of her breasts. Arranging her breasts around my compliant and suddenly captured appendage she started to move herself rhythmically up and down while randomly kissing, licking, and sucking the agreeable prisoner.

The next ten minutes were a filled with a combination of pleasure so intense I almost wanted her to stop—almost. There was no question that the cocaine had a temporary deadening or anesthetic effect that ran directly opposed to the attention I was receiving. The real surprise came as the effect of the cocaine wore off and the intense feeling of stimulation returned. This delayed pleasure sensation quickly turned into my own 4th of July Fireworks Grand Finale.

"I don't think saying thank you is the proper etiquette in these situations, but I want to say it anyway, so thank you, that was beyond incredible. Shall we say same time tomorrow? Oh, and uh, for the next 20 years?"

Her laugh sounded genuine and somehow reassuring.

I continued, "I really don't recommend you turning in a book report on that article, unless of course your intent is to become teacher's pet."

We had slowly changed positions, and now I found myself kneeling on the floor at the foot of the bed. The only light in the room came from a streetlight and filtered through the drawn shade and thin-laced curtains. The yellow cast of diffused light provided a low rent, but very sexy mood to the room.

Now that my eyes were fully adjusted to the low light, the room no longer felt too dark but rather just light enough. I could see everything I needed to see without any of the flaws or blemishes I might have noticed if the room had been brighter. Looking up past Jill's glistening, blond, soft mound of femininity through her firm young breasts, I could see her eyes were closed in blissful anticipation.

I took my time applying the white powder to my sleeping beauty. Very lightly and deliberately, I rubbed the outer area of her slightly quivering genitalia. Then, repeating what Jill had done, I coated my tongue and lips as well. I slowly slid both of my hands palms up, under her warm, firm bottom, and lifted her towards me.

I Sold *the* Moon!

I always enjoy performing cunnilingus. It's extremely intimate, and equally erotic. In terms of foreplay, oral sex is always the best appetizer, although tonight, we both knew it was being served as the main course. I was getting excited all over again listening to her moaning while I luxuriated on the wonderful taste combination of cocaine and female excitement. Looking up, I was further stimulated by watching her bite her lower lip as her face contorted in spasms of both pleasure and pain.

She was now moving her lower body in a more controlled, determined rhythm, and I knew the effects of the cocaine were starting to wear off. I didn't want to do anything that would break the fuse and leave her on the launch pad, and yet I also wanted to do whatever I could to maximize her flight. Using both my hands, lips and tongue to full advantage she entered that mysterious, fantastic final countdown phase. All systems were go. Ten, nine, eight, seven six, five, four, three...

Suddenly I heard the door behind me burst open and a bright, glaring shaft of light fell across the bed. Before I had time to turn around, I felt the back of my head being yanked up and back. My toes were barely on the floor and it hurt like hell. This was not good. As I was being pulled out of the room, I got a last glimpse of Jill as she was pulling the bedspread frantically around her. Then she started screaming.

"Woody, you bastard! What the fuck are you doing? Leave us alone. I hate you! I hate you! Put him down, you asshole, put him down."

I was out in the hallway now and I could see everybody running up the stairs to see what was going on. I could also tell that Woody was very mad and worse, very drunk.

"I should throw your ass over this fucking railing. That's my sister in there you fuck head. I'm throwing your ass over," Woody was yelling in slurred wine-smelling speech about two inches from my face.

"Wait! Let me move my Kittinger coffee table first! That's an original irreplaceable heirloom," Manny shouted as he ran back down and pushed the table out of harm's way.

I am not a small person but Woody was huge, pissed off, and out of his skull with alcohol and God knows what else. I was more than a little nervous about being thrown over the railing, especially now that the table would not be there to break my fall. I also didn't enjoy being nude, held by my hair, for the entertainment of the assembled party guests. It was my turn to say something.

"Easy man. Take it easy. We didn't *do* it. Your sister is an adult, and we were not doing anything you haven't done...I hope. Put me down man, let's talk this out. Let me get some clothes on."

Woody let me down from my tip-toes, but still held a tight grip on my hair.

"I should just smash your face in," he slurred.

I felt I was making progress. My sentence had been reduced from being hurled over the banister to just getting my face bludgeoned.

Fergus was lumbering his way up the stairs, and as he approached us I saw a noticeable softening in Woody's deranged features. Jill had also come out of the bedroom and thankfully shared her bedspread wrap with me.

"Hey Woody," Fergus was saying, "we all need a drink. I know I could use one. You just got carried away because you were worried about your sister. She's fine. Let's all just shake hands and fire up a big bomber, and pour everyone a tall cold one. Come on now, let's just chill out, shake hands and let's go downstairs."

Jill reached up and peeled Woody's fingers out of my hair. He had a big goofy, ah shucks I guess I blew it kind of look on his face. He snapped his head to get his hair out of his eyes and then he put out his hand for me to shake.

I was more than relieved to shake hands, but I also knew in that moment that things were going to have to change radically. I was ready to forgive and forget, but I was not willing to continue to be in business with a borderline psychotic and Runt, his lap dog friend.

Even Marty's cognac-soaked flaming mint ice cream balls with hot caramel sauce and toasted coconut could not brighten the mood. Not surprisingly, the party broke up soon after that. I said my embarrassed good-byes to Jill. I never saw her again.

Life is strange that way. Tonight had been the first time I'd ever seen her, and we end up licking cocaine off each other's most private parts, and then we never lay eyes or anything else on each other ever again. Stranger yet may be the fact that although our time together was only a few hours, the memory is forever.

I Sold *the* Moon!

Two days later, for the first time in our lives, both David and I were speechless. Fergus was at a loss to explain how it had happened. We were all staring in disbelief at the signed contracts with two different dates. Redwing, the band, had another gig on the night Fergus had secured the auditorium and the venue had a boat show booked on the date he had contracted the band and light show. David and I had done our part handling the publicity, Woody had gotten his grandmother's money, and Fergus had made a simple but costly mistake. The tickets and posters had been printed. The radio ads had been running for two weeks. The band, the security, the liquid light show and auditorium had all been paid for. We would lose everything we had invested.

Within a week of the disaster, three different vendors wanted to sue us for breach of contract. All my Moon Man money had been lost in the venture and Runt's half-brothers Lester and Chigger were looking for us. They wanted Granny's money paid back pronto.

David went to hide out with his brother in San Francisco. Paula was in Europe with my sister Liz, and I was in my parents' house, with no car, no income, and in a state of desperation. Where had all the Moon Man momentum gone? It was too convenient to blame Fergus. After all, I was an adult. I should have known better. I hadn't.

What I did know was that I needed to get as far away from Fergus, Woody, Runt and the imploding BAD Company as fast as possible.

CHAPTER 11

RUNNING ON EMPTY

IN A CLEAN WHITE SHIRT, BACKPACK AT MY FEET, STANDING BY THE highway, I stuck out my thumb. I had $93.00 in my pocket and a sign that read EAST on one side and VIRGINIA on the other. The only thing I knew about Virginia I'd learned from the bumper stickers that read, "Virginia Is For Lovers," with "Lovers" being represented by a picture of a big red heart. I also knew that my sister Dourene and her new boyfriend Mike Dolan currently lived there.

I experienced a clarity regarding my position in the universe every time I hitchhiked. The sheer number of cars passing by was clear evidence that it was not that difficult to have one. I had to ask myself, what was I doing wrong?

Hitchhiking is unpredictable. It took me almost three days and more than 25 different rides to end up, as The Eagles song says: "Standing on a corner in Winslow, Arizona..." only 650 miles from where I'd started. And then less than 24 hours later—needing only one more ride—I would travel the remaining 1900 miles to Arlington, Virginia and be dropped off at my sister's front door.

Outside Winslow, I wasn't sure if I was seeing things or did a gleaming white and gold Cadillac just cut across three lanes of traffic and come to an abrupt stop in a cloud of dust not more than thirty yards ahead of me? Surely, this car was not stopping for me? The passenger door opened, and in the next instant, trash of all kinds: fast food bags, soda cans, plastic bottles and more were being thrown out of the car. Then came the contents from the ashtray, as it was banged against the bottom of the doorframe. This was not a simple case of littering, this person was using the side of the road as a personal dumpsite. Ripping across three lanes of busy highway just to do some tidying up seemed about as improbable as having this car pull over for me. I stood like a statue waiting for the door to close and this mirage to evaporate. Then the trunk sprang open and the horn blared. I grabbed my pack and ran to the car.

"Hello, and thanks for stopping. I wasn't sure you pulled over for me. Where're you headed?" I breathlessly asked, as I went through my practiced survey of the driver and the car's interior.

The inside was very clean (understandable now that any trash that had been inside was currently blowing into the desert), jazz was playing on the tape deck, and strangely, the back seat was covered with one and five dollar bills and layers of change. The driver was about 35 years old, huge, but handsome. He was outfitted in a bright yellow long-sleeved silk shirt, butter-colored dress pants, brown suede sandals (no socks), flashy gold rings and gold watch. His numerous thick gold neck chains included one which dangled a gold dollar sign inlaid with what appeared to be diamonds. He wore wraparound sunglasses and a friendly smile. The fact that he was black was very unusual in that I had found it a rarity to get picked up by African Americans. I reminded myself that every mass murderer, kidnapper and serial killer that I had ever heard about was white.

"Your sign says east and I'm headed east. You be standing there all day or you want to put your gear in the trunk and let me get back on the road? I got lots of ground to cover, my man."

As he said this last line, he took off his sunglasses. This gesture told me he might have been thinking I was nervous, and he was doing what he could to relieve that. It was very cool.

I hustled to put my pack in the trunk and had to move what looked like an alligator suitcase and matching smaller case. Closing the trunk, I couldn't help noticing that it too was covered with change and low denomination bills.

We sped off, and within a few seconds were traveling in the fast lane at just under 100 miles an hour. He said his name was Chili Royal, but that everybody called him Cash and I should do the same.

Turning up the music, he said, "We got a long drive, but I got plenty of sounds. You gonna get introduced to the Cash Man's Hall of Fame players: Charlie Mingus, Ray Brown, Oscar Peterson, Wes Montgomery, and what jazz education would be complete without my main man the Duke?"

The next twenty-four hours were indeed an education, and not just to the world of jazz. Cash refused to let me pay for anything. He bought me breakfast, lunch, and dinner, paying for everything by peeling large denomination bills from his huge roll. Anytime he got change of any kind—less than a ten-dollar bill—he threw it in the back seat like it was an old burger wrapper. He laughed when I offered to "kick in" for gas, saying, "You be the one doing the hitchhiking, my man."

Cash was headed to Maryland to place a big bet in the sixth race at Pimlico and to make a delivery. He didn't say what he was delivering and I didn't ask. He not only had fantastic pot—saying something about jazz being appreciated more fully when one is in the same state of mind as the musicians—he also was quick to share his never ending supply of cocaine. He kept the coke in what looked like a miniature glass baby bottle with the "nipple" designed to turn 360 degrees. This allowed for the coke to fill the "blaster" compartment and then when turned back to its upright position allow for instant snorting without ever having to open the bottle.

I would have felt paranoid with all these drugs in the car if Cash hadn't shown me his secret hiding place. He was very proud of his security system: Automatic windows on lock, fan set to level 2, humidifier at 73 degrees, and only then could you slide the back panel of the glove compartment open. Since I was sitting in the passenger seat, it was my job to retrieve and replace the pre-rolled joints and "daddy's baby bottle," as he called the coke dispenser. He must have known I would see the two huge rolls of cash money wedged behind the pot and three bottles of coke.

"Cash, I can't help noticing you carry lots of money. Shit, your backseat has more loot sliding around than most guys carry in their wallets. Are you ever nervous about that?"

"Well, my man, I ain't too worried. Some fool try and mess with the Cash Man's money, he be messin' with this."

From under the seat, Cash pulled out a big, scary-looking gun. I had never been this close to a real gun in my life. I instantly went from feeling comfortable and safe to sheer panic. I could actually hear my heart start to pound, my breathing stopped, and my body turned rigid.

"Never had to use it and don't want to," Cash was saying as he thankfully returned the gun back under the seat. "In my business it's important the boys know I have one. It's not for causing trouble, but for seeing that trouble don't get started."

This was not the time to argue with him over what I considered to be his suspect logic. I was too busy trying to get my breathing back on automatic. In the next few minutes, as Duke Ellington's syncopated music filtered back into my consciousness, I realized my moist body was giving off an overripe odor. The cold sweat of fear smelled like hamburger meat gone bad.

An hour or so later, Cash asked me if I would mind driving, telling me he hadn't slept for two days. I was more than happy, if not a bit nervous, to get behind the wheel of this powerful new machine. I had just pulled back on the freeway when I heard Cash breathing deeply and rhythmically in the reclined passenger seat.

This was the first time in my life I'd listened to jazz music for 10 hours straight, and I felt I was learning to appreciate the altered state of being that this music—which at times seemed to have no beginning and no end—transported me to. It was two or three in the morning and I was flying along at 85 miles an hour through the Smoky Mountain region of Kentucky. In spite of my reluctance, I felt compelled to reach under the seat and touch the polished steel of the gun barrel. I wondered if the gun was loaded, and why Cash would leave it here while he slept just a few feet away? I also started thinking how much I hated guns, and what they represented. I hadn't always felt this way, but then that was a long time ago....

As a child, I lived in my holster and gun set. I would practice for hours, and truly believed no one was faster on the draw than I was. "Davy Crockett" and the "Lone Ranger" were my favorite TV programs. The masked man

never shot to kill, only to protect the innocent. That's the type of cowboy I would be. I would give my sisters all the time they needed to draw against me, but in the end, their pitifully slow reaction was never a challenge to my claim as the "Fastest Gun Alive." Sometimes they would indulge me and fall to the floor as my red roll of paper caps would fire in quick succession, filling the air with the intoxicating aroma of gunpowder.

There was one particular gun set I desired more than anything I've ever wanted before or since. I was eight going on nine when I first saw them. Walking home from second grade, I was allowed to stop in a small grocery store and spend a nickel on anything I wanted—usually a "Three Musketeers" bar or sometimes a chocolate covered nougat bar called "Look."

I'll never forget the first day I saw them—two gold-handled six shooters with holsters to match. They were dazzling. The unique feature about this set was that the outside of the two holsters and the handles of the guns were made of some kind of gold metal, complete with a western design showing a cowboy riding the range. Even the bullets on the holster belt were gold, although I would have been happy with silver bullets, the kind that the Lone Ranger used. This set also had the long leather straps extending down from the bottom of the holsters so I could tie them tight against my legs. I knew only tinhorns let their holsters flop around, not allowing for easy and, most importantly, fast removal of your pistol. And everybody knew life and death in the Old West was dependent on who got their gun out first.

I had to have those guns. I also knew there was no way I was going to get them. They cost $39.95. This would be asking for something almost three times more expensive than any gift I had ever received. My entire yearly tuition at Sacred Heart School was only $18.00 and that included the books, plus an occasional free lunch on "Hotdog Thursday."

Christmas arrived with little anticipation. When you're eight years old and you know you're not going to get the only thing that matters, some of the magic is gone. That still didn't stop me from inspecting the packages under the tree that had my name on them. Failing to find a gift that might be the right size only confirmed what I already knew.

It was hard to look happy with my new socks, new shirts, and a game called Peg-O's. After the last present was opened, my sisters were busy trying on their new clothes and wondering how to get their "just like real" dolls to stop wetting themselves. In the midst of that commotion, my father said, "Barry, there's one more gift I have for your mother. Would you get it for me? It's under my bed."

I ran to get it, happy that my mom was getting something special. I handed over the present and sat down with the rest of my sisters, comforted by the soft colored lights on the tree as they reflected off the tinsel that we never seemed to hang with any sense of proportion or individuality.

"What a beautiful present," my mom said, "but this one is really for you, Barry." She handed it back to me. Could it be? It seemed like the right weight. I nervously removed the ribbon and carefully folded back the paper. There they were. Not on the shelf looking so out of place in that small grocery store, but in my own house, on my own lap. They were really mine. Tears welled up in my eyes, giving the room a golden cast as I continued to gaze in wonderment at the most magnificent gun set ever created. This was the happiest day of my life. My position as the fastest gun alive was secured. Dreams do come true...

"Hey, man, are you tired or what?"

Cash was suddenly awake bringing me back to the present.

"No, no, I'm fine. Why?"

"Well, if you ain't tired, then move. We got miles to go."

I checked the speedometer. I was going 85. Cash watched me push the needle up to 110, and then drifted back to sleep.

Soon after breakfast, Cash dropped me off.

"I'll be getting me some moon land now," he said handing over a $100 bill.

When I told him I didn't have the change, and suggested he give me one of the small bills on the back seat, he scowled, "I don't want no change," then softer, "consider it a tip for driving last night. Gotta run, my man. You be cool."

I waved as he drove away, the sounds of Herbie Hancock fading in the unfamiliar surroundings. Being given this money had to be a sign. I would continue to sell Moon Acres. I just needed a little break. David and I would team up again. Paula would come to her senses and realize she never stopped loving me. I just needed some time...and at 22 years of age, I still believed, time was on my side.

CHAPTER 12

REEEEEALLY BIG SHOW

My new East Coast surroundings reminded me of the pictures in my fifth grade Early American History book. Arlington, Virginia, was a world away from Carmichael, California. One thing wasn't different; I still needed a job.

About five blocks from Mike and Dourene's apartment, on Glebe Road, was a new restaurant called The Barnacle Goose. I stopped in one day hoping I could find some work. Walking in, I was confronted by a young girl with large brown eyes and long, curly auburn hair. She was sitting on the floor folding oversized pink cloth napkins into pyramid shapes.

"We open at 5. Please come back then. Our steamed lobster is the best in the world. If you want a drink, we can sell you one. My dad says you make your money with the bar."

"Is your dad the owner of this restaurant?"

"I wouldn't be working like a slave if he wasn't. I'm really just a kid. My name's Sofia Marie Sfarnas."

At what age do we stop using our middle name, I wondered.

"I must say Sofia Marie Sfarnas, you're pretty good at it for being just a kid."

"I'm better than my brother Steven, and he's seven."

"Can I talk to your Dad, is he here now?"

"Sure, he's in the office, back there," she hooked her thumb over her shoulder, "but he doesn't like to be bugged when he's doing his research."

"What's he researching?"

"The ponies. You know, racehorses. He makes his picks from the *Racing Form*. I need to see them in the paddock first. The jockey's important but not as much as the horse. I covered the Exacta with a 4–8 box in the third at Colonial Downs on Sunday. It paid $87.50 on a $2.00 bet."

"Who's your new friend, Sofia?"

Turning toward the lyrical voice, I saw a short woman with a friendly smile. I liked her immediately.

"I told him my name, but he didn't tell me his, maybe he forgot it," Sofia said as she continued to add to her pile of intricately folded napkins.

I laughed at the sophistication of this last remark, coming as it did from such a young child.

"I just remembered it. My name is Barry McArdle, and I'm here to apply for a job as a waiter."

"Now that you two know each other, I guess it's my turn. I'm Dolly Sfarnas, Sofia's mother," she said in that beautiful lilting voice, extending her short arm and delicate hand.

"Why don't I take you back to meet the rest of the family and then you can talk to John about what might be available."

In the kitchen, George, who looked about 14, and Johnny, a couple years younger, were loading the industrial dishwasher. They seemed to be having a blast doing it. They were telling each other jokes mimicking the voices of Jack Benny, Paul Lynde, Richard Nixon, and Jimmy Stewart.

"Rochester, where did you put the change from that nickel I gave you yesterday?" George was saying in his very good imitation of Jack Benny.

Johnny was talking like Paul Lynde. "I just hate getting old. My mind makes appointments my body can't keep."

George spoke in the voice of Tricky Dick Nixon. "All I ever really wanted was peace. A piece of Asia, a piece of Cambodia, a piece of China..."

"Speaking of China," said Johnny, imitating Jimmy Stewart, "I had dinner last night in a German-Chinese restaurant—two hours later I was hungry for power."

I wanted to stay and see the rest of the show, but Dolly guided me out of the kitchen into the salad bar area.

Seven-year-old Steven was folding napkins, too, but not with the same dexterity as his younger sister Sofia. If Sofia was precocious, Steven was, in a word, adorable. He had a soft voice and spoke with a trace of a stutter. His cherubic face was framed by long blond hair cut in a pageboy. He looked up at me with gigantic blue eyes.

"I've been on a dd-diet for a month now, and all I've lost is thirty d-days," he said.

I started laughing. This must have encouraged him because he stopped folding napkins and stood up and put his hands behind his back and then leaned forward as if he were talking into a microphone.

He began speaking in a voice that unmistakably sounded like Ed Sullivan. He was mesmerizing.

"Good evening, ladies and gen-gentlemen. We have a reeeeeally big show for you tonight. Back by popular demand is Mama Cass. When Mama sits around the house...she sits around the house. And now on our stage is my friend James Cagney. JJ-Jimmy, take it away."

Steven turned around and when he turned back to face me his face was scrunched up in a scowl, and both his hands were in the shape of guns with his index fingers pointed straight ahead and his thumbs sticking up.

"You dirty rat. I'm going to get you, just like you got my brother, see. I'm going to get you in the head with the MM-Matzo ball."

Who were these kids? There was a five-year-old Nick the Greek pushing cocktails up front while two of her older brothers were doing Jerry Lewis and Dean Martin routines in the kitchen, and now I had the best of Ed Sullivan being presented by a seven-year-old Rich Little.

"Steven," Dolly interrupted, "I'm sure Barry will have a chance to see all your impressions, but right now I want him to meet your sisters, and you need to finish folding your napkins. Sofia is almost done with hers."

"I didn't come here to be insulted," he said in a Paul Lynde voice.

"Where do you usually go?" Dolly shouted back as we walked into the main dining area.

Delores, who looked about 19, and her slightly younger sister Cindy, were setting the tables. Delores looked classically Greek, with dark, curly hair, tanned skin and deep brown eyes.

Cindy had little resemblance to her sister. Blond and blue-eyed, wth porcelain skin, she was shorter than Delores, taking after her mother in stature and complexion. She also had a body that looked illegal, confined as it was in a tight neon pink mini-skirt, and fire engine red halter-top.

They were both saying something about me working for them, but I was having trouble deciding whether to continue staring at Cindy's tiny ankles elevated in their red spiked heels, or be completely predictable and get caught fixating on the top half of her curvaceous frame. Fortunately, my need for employment took precedence and I continued staring at the not nearly so interesting carpet.

"If you work for Dee-Dee tonight, you're mine tomorrow," Cindy said in a teasing and flirtatious way.

"I'd love to work for both of you, but I haven't been hired yet."

"Mom likes you. You'll get the job," Cindy said.

"Maybe you should get back to work, girls. Barry needs to meet your father," Dolly said, leading me out of the room.

"I hope you don't mind, but I just have to ask you before I go in to meet Mr. Sfarnas..."

"Everyone calls him John," Dolly interjected.

"OK, before I meet John, is there anything you can tell me that might help my chances?"

George had been eavesdropping and now said in his President Nixon voice, "Yeah, bribe money. You know, a brown bag operation. Old Johnny Sneakers Dale loves that kind of thing."

"George, it's not polite to listen to other peoples' conversations," Dolly gently chided.

"Who is old Johnny Sneakers Dale?" I asked.

"That was John's stage name when I met him. We both were professional entertainers traveling the East Coast circuit. I was a singer. He was a standup comic who wore a formal tuxedo with tennis shoes. That's how he got the handle 'Sneakers.' He was young, very funny, and easy to fall in love with."

That explained a lot. Like father, like sons. I wondered if the girls took after their mother and had any inclination towards singing. The hit song *We've Only Just Begun* by the Carpenters started playing in my mind. I knew it was the wrong time to fantasize about Cindy singing that song to me, especially since in my flight of fancy, she was wearing nothing but her red spiked heels.

"John, darlin'," Dolly said upon opening the door, "this is Barry McArdle and he's here looking for work as a waiter."

The first thing I noticed was the utter disorganization of the room. Boxes of dinner receipts were teetering one on top of the other. Invoices mixed with horseracing magazines were scattered on the floor and desk. Newly laundered shirts, still under plastic, were hanging from cabinet knobs. Rolls of cash register paper, held in place with rubber bands, were in various-sized piles around the room. Kids' clothes, toys and books were mixed up with menus, promotional flyers, glassware and bathroom supplies. The wastepaper basket had overflowed and was now just the center of an expanding area of trash. Two framed pictures—Churchill Downs on Kentucky Derby day and a photo of a Greek taverna—were in need of straightening. A third frame holding a one dollar bill was also askew.

John Sfarnas, formally Johnny "Sneakers" Dale, put down his *Racing Form*, took off his reading glasses turned them upside down and put them back on. He looked a lot like Sofia, Delores, and George. His black hair and dark features were at odds with his boyish mannerisms and friendly face. I started to laugh when he looked up at me cross-eyed.

"Would you be kind enough to stand on your head so I can see you right side up?" he asked.

I laughed some more.

"Not responding to a direct request from the owner, the big cheese, the lord and master of all he surveys, is not recommended if you plan to get on his good side."

"That's exactly my intent. Your son George suggested the best way to do that would be to bribe you with cash."

"Thank God, there is hope for him yet. So let's see the money."

I continued to laugh.

"Sweetheart," Dolly said, "I think we should hire Barry. Remember you've promised the girls some time off."

John took his glasses off and extended his hand.

I Sold *the* Moon!

"I'm John Sfarnas, glad to meet you. I assume you've met the family and the fact that you still want to work here has me worried. But you can save yourself. What do you know about horses?"

"Only what I've learned from Sofia."

This got a little chuckle from both Dolly and John.

"Well, less important, but I feel obliged to ask, what do you know about waiting tables?"

"I worked at a restaurant in California as a bus boy and a waiter. I like people, I'm a quick learner, and I'm honest."

"OK, one last question and as long as your answer is not that you were working on a prison chain gang, or bringing cocaine up from Colombia or worst yet, working for the Republican Party, you have the job. Tell me why you're here in Virginia and not still employed in California? What I'm asking is what was your last job and why did you leave it?"

Panic. I had just said I was honest. Do I now lie and avoid telling them that my last paying job had me in a space suit selling property on the moon? Then again, would I really want to work for someone who could not appreciate the Moon Man?

"This may sound strange, but it should prove my willingness to tell the truth..."

I started at the beginning and explained how and why I came to be the first moon salesman in history, and concluded with my plans for the future.

"...And I plan on going back into the moon selling business when I've saved enough to pay off my debts, buy a car, and get a new moon suit."

After an uneasy silence, John slowly shook his head and looked up with a somber face. "Unfortunately, we have a strict hiring policy. Although Mars, Jupiter, and I believe Uranus salesmen qualify for employment, we had to draw the line somewhere, so unless Dolly can find a loophole, maybe in the fine print..."

Was he joking to let me down easy or joking to let me know I had a job? In either case, I couldn't help myself from laughing.

Dolly, who had been sitting next to me, leaned forward and pointed to one of the small printed lines in the *Racing Form*.

"She found something," John announced. "You may be in luck. It says Diamond Dancer is good in the rain... a mudder. Well, that's good enough for me. When can you start?"

"Tonight, if you need me."

"You're fired. I need someone right away."

"Hire me back and I'll start now if that's soon enough," I said, realizing that everything was a joke to the former Johnny "Sneakers" Dale.

"OK, you're hired back but be advised I'll be watching you now that you've been identified as a malcontent. A couple of things to remember, we have the best lobster and salad bar east of the Mississippi. All our steaks are USDA prime, nothing but the best. You get dinner when you work, and the law requires we pay you some kind of pittance. As you know, your money is in the tips. And above all, push the booze—that's where I make my money. The family goes to the track on Sundays and sometimes mid-week. You're invited."

When Dolly opened the office door, we discovered all six of the Sfarnas kids eavesdropping. Everyone, including John and Dolly, thought this was funny, and as I left the room cheers and applause mixed nicely with their laughter.

"One last thing," John was saying, as my new friends surrounded me, "I want to buy 10 Moon Acres as soon as possible. Let it never be said John Sfarnas doesn't know a good investment when he sees it."

Phony Deeds Hot Item
Own a Chunk of Moon

By LLOYD PLETSCH
(Enterprise-Record Staff Writer)

With one hand full [of] dollar bills and the other [full] of bogus deeds to land on [the] moon, Barry McArdle fi[res] a rapid series of jokes at [a] gathering audience.

McArdle, 28, 6819 A[p]pomattox Way, Carmicha[el] sports a silver moon suit a[nd] large plastic jewels a[nd] promises his prospecti[ve] customers nothing but [a] piece of paper. But h[e's] quick to point out it's a da[mn] nice piece of paper.

A graduate in mass co[m]munications from Chi[co] State University, McAr[dle] has been selling moon ac[res] for the last five years w[ith] considerable success.

It really works. As t[he] stack of dollars in his o[ne] hand grows, the deeds [to] moon acres disappear fr[om] the other.

To members of t[he] audience, it's obvious h[e's] having fun and maki[ng] money. It's their money, b[ut] many are eager to share [it] with him for the entertai[n]ment he provides.

He arrived on the CS[U] campus Wednesday, is pe[r]forming again today and w[ill] end his stay Friday.

"I guarantee absolute[ly] nothing," says McArdle. [He] is quick to point out he w[ill] stand behind that stateme[nt] all the way.

Those who purchase mo[on] acres actually receive [a] deed that has no value. B[ut] McArdle points out it [is] larger and cleaner than th[e] dollars he receives in retur[n].

He estimates he has so[ld] about 40,000 moon acres [in] the last five years. He g[ot] started when someon[e] suggested, during a part[y] that some things ju[st] couldn't be sold. McArd[le] accepted the challenge an[d] started going door to do[or] selling moon acres. Tha[t] technique didn't work we[ll] so he created a costume an[d] started working on campu[s]. That brought success in [a] field he says he hopes [to] follow all his life.

The moon real esta[te]

MOON ACRES — Area residents have an opportunity to snap up some moon property. Barry McArdle of Carmichael is on campus at Chico State University, complete with moon costume, selling moon acres. The deeds aren't worth anything but the humor he provides has kept sales up. (Enterprise-Record Photo

CHAPTER 13

KEEP VIRGINIA CLEAN—THROW YOUR GARBAGE IN MARYLAND

WAITING TABLES WAS A LOT DIFFERENT THAN SELLING THE MOON and yet they both taught me about human nature—about the masks people wear. I recognized my inability to see under many of those masks. For instance, tipping. It was as fascinating as it was unpredictable to guess how I would be tipped. The grumpy older woman, who didn't say much as she polished off three Rob Roys, left me 25%. The young, attractive couple that stayed till closing left 8%. Go figure.

On Friday and Saturday nights around 10 PM, John would take to the small stage in the main dining room and proclaim that the Barnacle Goose had the best lobster east of the Mississippi. He'd remind the patrons that the bar was still open, tell a joke or two and then go into his introduction.

"Ladies and gentlemen, it gives me great pleasure to introduce one of the youngest working comics in America today...the fastest rising star in his kindergarten, our own Stevie 'Funny Boy' Sfarnas."

Everybody loved little Stevie. The fact that he was so young, so cute and doing a reasonably good job impersonating famous celebrities was a tough act to follow. His signature closing joke, done in the voice of Jimmy Stewart, went like this:

"And now ladies and gg-germs, let's listen in on a phone call that Jimmy Stewart made to his valet. Hello, William, this is Jimmy. How's PP-Puffy doing? Well, Jimmy, the cat died. Now William, you could have broken the bad news to me in a much nicer way. You should have said, Jimmy, the cat was on the roof, it started to rain, the cat slipped, and unfortunately, the cat died. Now wouldn't that have been better? By the way, William, how's my mom? Well, JJ-Jimmy, she's uh...on the roof."

Johnny was next. He told the same jokes and did the same impressions as his younger brother. What made his five minutes funny was that Johnny delivered the material as if the audience was hearing it for the first time. He would then introduce George by saying, "If you like his material, I wrote it, if you don't like it, George wrote it. Please welcome...Gorgeous Georgieeee!"

George had real stage presence, and made fun of the fact that he was telling some of the same jokes for the third time. Although he clearly had better timing and much better impersonation abilities, I was still amazed that the audience laughed in all the right places. The person who laughed loudest and had the most fun was always John. He loved seeing his boys working for laughs. Even when the gags fell flat, John found something to keep him laughing. The boys, for their part, were more than happy to "bomb," as long as they heard Dad's distinctive laugh coming from his reserved booth, stage left, next to the bar and cash register.

George: "On behalf of our President I ask you to.... Free the Watergate 500."

(Laughter—Don't forget I gave you that one.)

"Remember, I don't have to do this for a living...my mother plays BINGO."

(Laughter)

"I just got back from a Hippie wedding. The bride didn't throw her bouquet...she smoked it."

(Big laughter.... When's he getting off?)

"If my father knew I was here he'd kill me...he thinks I'm in Pittsburgh stealing cars." (Laughter.... What's so funny about that?)

Now he was in the voice of John Wayne.

"I killed so many Indians in my movies.... I've started to get hate mail from Jane Fonda." (One snicker.... Oh, too bad.)

"OK, folks, let's all hold hands and try to communicate...with the living."

(Laughter.... Good comeback, I'll remember that one.)

"Definition of a loser: Someone who marries Raquel Welch...for her money."

(More laughter.... The kid's good...hell, he's a natural.)

"Thank you ladies and gentlemen, and now the star of our show... that's what he told me to say anyway. The only Moon Man in America... Strawaaaaaaaaaaa...Barry."

Because I followed George, I felt torn. I wanted him to get laughs, but not so many that I would look dull by comparison. After all, I was almost 10 years older and had auditioned at CBS. Besides my material was fresh, not jokes that were being told for the third time. My God, if he got more laughs out of that retread material, what would that say about my routine?

"Thank you George, and thank you for stealing all my good material."

(Silence)

"Let's hear it one more time for all the Sfarnas kids."

(Big applause)

"I don't do impersonations. I thought I'd try something new...like comedy."

(Silence)

"Just kidding boys, but if you guys keep getting more laughs than me I might have to turn your father over to the child labor authorities."

(Silence)

"You know, as a public service announcement, I want to say don't drop out of school...especially if you're on the third floor."

(Someone clearing his throat, some silverware being set down on a plate.)

"And as a good citizen I do need to add, never drink while you drive...you might spill some."

(Ice tinkling in a glass)

"I heard the restaurant down the street, the Chinese Wok, was held up last night. But when the gunman demanded "Give me all your money," the cashier said, "To take out?"

(Complete silence. Maybe it was time to bring back David's Flasher routine?)

"You know Chinese food...take out?"

I felt myself getting hot around the collar. It's never a good idea to insult the audience, but I was on a roll....

Tapping on the microphone.... "Test. Test. Is this thing on? Did the batteries in your hearing aids all go dead at once? Don't worry, the bus has arrived, and everybody will be going back to the home shortly. I'm sure you haven't missed your cookies and milk."

(I recognized Sofia's little laugh.)

"Just kidding. You all have a great future...as mannequins. Sir, you better show some signs of life or you might be mistaken...for a corpse."

(A small giggle from the man's wife)

"And all this time I thought the Sphinx was in Egypt. OK, well... fortunately for all of you and especially for me, I'm out of time..."

(Applause.)

"Just remember... Keep Virginia clean... Throw your garbage in Maryland."

The summer turned into a most spectacular fall. The months flew by. I was becoming a professional waiter, I was learning how difficult it is to win a Daily Double and, for better or worse, I was logging valuable hours of stage experience.

One night, I opened the door to Mike and Dourene's apartment around midnight, my pockets full of that night's tip money. The room was aglow in candlelight and the aroma of sandalwood incense. My "bed" of the six couch cushions held together by a fitted sheet, was made up, and turned down. Sitting in the middle was Paula, legs folded in a yoga position, and looking as beautiful as I'd ever seen her. I recognized the cream-colored silk nightgown she wore as one I had given her. Even in the flickering light, I could tell this was all she wore. Her hair was cut into a short shag, giving her both a sexy and sophisticated look. She had lost some weight, adding an aura of delicacy, which only increased her attractiveness.

"Paula, I can't believe you're here. You look radiant."

"Shhh...we'll talk tomorrow. Come to bed."

"I need to shower first. When did you…?"

"Shhh…hurry."

I took a short shower. The words "come to bed" and "hurry," sounded good together. It had been five months since I'd seen her and much longer since we'd made love. I couldn't be sure we would be lovers tonight, but seeing Paula, surrounded by incense and candlelight, I had to think my chances were pretty good.

Paula lived her life with an exaggerated sense of the dramatic. Returning from her extended trip to Europe unannounced was characteristic. And, if she had decided to end our current cycle of separation without the usual tears, my apologies and renewed promises of fidelity, that would also be very theatrical.

After drying off, I looked at myself in the mirror. Are you finally ready to commit to Paula? You could take advantage of this new beginning. You could do that with four simple words. "Will you marry me?" How's that for drama? Do it! I will. Go on then, what's stopping you? I don't know. That's very convenient, I told myself, turning away from the conflicted image that stared back at me.

One candle burned as I dropped my towel and carefully got into bed. We were lying on our sides facing each other. Paula put her finger to her lips. I waited. We looked at each other without talking and without touching for some time. It was sensual, intimate, and for me very arousing, although I felt I was letting Paula down on some level because I could not stop wondering if she, too, was naked. She reached out and took my hand and pulled me towards her…she was. I wanted to ask her what new perfume she was wearing, but that could wait.

Over the next half-hour, I rediscovered all of her familiar beauty marks. Our tender kisses and gentle touching would soon give way to uninhibited lovemaking, which I anticipated would be all the more intense, considering our long and distant separation.

Ideally, of course, I would want us to reach climax together, but attempting that tonight would be too much of a gamble. As it was, I needed to think about anything except how fantastic she felt. What about my laundry? Don't forget to separate the darks from the whites. How 'bout those Dodgers?

As with most lasting and satisfying relationships, ours had always been held together by more than sex. Discussions with Paula had taken me to the end of the known universe and beyond. She explained how the planets, moving in predictable orbits, had influence on the oceans within us. Just as the moon has predictable gravitational pull on the tides, so too, Paula claimed, did our moon and planets affect the billions of cells, or mini tide pools, that make up the human body. In her next sentence, she might fantasize that we were the only two people in the world, in the only room, in the only bed, the last two pair of eyes staring into each other in the hope of seeing back to the moment of creation and then forward to the end of time.

"All of us have been here from before the beginning and we all will be here at the end of the end, which is really just a new beginning," Paula had told me years ago. I was still trying to figure out what she meant, but at least it sounded like I was going to have plenty of time to do it.

We fell asleep in each other's arms. I realized this unspoken sense of togetherness was subject to change once we woke up and had to talk about it.

Over the next few days, we came to a new understanding. Paula explained how our relationship might work and I agreed. The only real change, it seemed, would be in our outlook. I would still need to be monogamous, but for the immediate future, we would take the pressure off trying to understand why, if we truly loved each other, we weren't making plans to marry.

"We love each other and that's enough for now," Paula concluded.

Paula seemed more mature, more of a woman. Maybe I needed to become more of a man. Maybe I needed to go to Europe? The moment the thought came to me I knew it was something I had to do and soon.

THE DARK SIDE

THE NEXT FEW MONTHS WERE SPENT SAVING MONEY, PRETENDING that Paula and I would live together forever, and following the national drama of a President in crisis.

On November 7, 1972 Richard Nixon beat George McGovern in the presidential popular vote, 60.7% to McGovern's 37.5%. Since then, his administration had been spending most of its time denying, protesting, and covering up their involvement in what they labeled "a third rate burglary." The rest of the world referred to the scandal, and the noose that was slowly closing around the President's neck, as Watergate.

Paula and I would fight over the front section of the *Washington Post* to get our daily fix of the growing morass the Nixon Administration was inexorably sinking into. We were also glued to the television whenever the Watergate hearings were on. At last, we thought the world would know what we had never doubted—that Nixon was a petty, vindictive, paranoid, lying, cheating scumbag.

In 1968, I'd cut my hair (to appear less radical), and I canvassed middle class neighborhoods for Bobby Kennedy. He went on to win the California primary, making him the odds-on favorite to win the Democratic nomination and most likely the Presidency. The hope was that with Bobby in the White House, the wounds still felt by the assassination of his brother John could be healed. But rather than healing, the injuries were torn open anew that year as the assassinations of both Martin Luther King Jr. and Robert Kennedy would forever scar and temper the potential of those who would dream of a better world.

Nixon, more than anyone, was the beneficiary of RFK's tragic death. Having lost the White House to one Kennedy already, running against the martyred President's brother was not a prospect he relished. Now with Bobby dead, Nixon suddenly became the frontrunner. More astonishing was the fact that he was even in the race to begin with. After his humiliating loss to Pat Brown for the Governorship of California, in 1962, he bitterly proclaimed: "You won't have Dick Nixon to kick around anymore because, gentlemen, this is my last press conference..." If only that had been true, but Nixon never was big on truth telling. Out of the ashes of political defeat and personal disgrace, and with help from the hand of fate, he narrowly eked out a victory over the loquacious Hubert Humphrey and the divided, dispirited Democrats to become the nation's 37th President.

I felt embarrassed to live in a country with Richard Nixon as my President. Why were so many people blind to the true character of this man? I saw him as nothing less than evil, hiding behind his Vietnam propaganda slogan of "Peace with Honor" while thousands of casualties, both military and civilian, continued to pile up, all in the name of peace, all in the name of honor.

But now, once more, we did have Nixon to kick around, and it felt good. It felt very good. With each new revelation, each new indictment and conviction, the snarling wolves on the White House lawn had to be sounding louder, and no amount of barricading, or denying, was going to stop them from the raw meat they knew to be decaying and cowering behind the door of the Oval Office.

I wanted to delay my trip to Europe so I could be in Washington, DC, when the ax of retribution finally fell on King Richard, however a call I received from David changed my mind. Two months earlier, David had instantly agreed to travel to the Continent with me. He called now to say his Uncle Kent, in Bristol, England had written, suggesting we arrive in time to attend a celebration that would be going on in their fair city. "The Bristol 600" would commemorate 600 years of the town's history. The Queen herself might attend, and the whole event was anticipated to be quite a splendid affair.

With this encouragement, almost $3,000 saved, and the fact that the Watergate investigation was now slowed down in the courts, I decided it was time to leave.

Once my date for departure was set, Paula decided to split as well.

"It's less painful for me to leave now than to stay and feel left behind," she explained. "Maybe when you come back you'll be ready to really commit for good. It's my favorite daydream. I suppose if it's meant to happen it will, and if not, there is nothing either of us can do to change that."

On the bed watching her pack, I felt more alone than if she were already gone. Why, if we both wanted to be together, had we both chosen to leave? That night our lovemaking was tender, disjointed, and sad.

We fell asleep holding on to each other, feeling worlds apart.

A week later, I said my goodbyes to the Sfarnas family. It was harder than I anticipated. I had rarely been treated so well and accepted so completely. I would miss performing and laughing as the Sfarnas boys kept improving their routines. I would miss Dolly's sweet, gentle disposition. And it would be hard not to miss the best lobster east of the Mississippi, and the steady money adding up in my account. Most of all, I knew I would miss relating to Johnny "Sneakers" Dale.

Tomorrow I would be in England. I called my family and said my goodbyes. Paula was already out of touch headed to Southern California to study at something called the Rosicrucian Center.

On the eve of this grand adventure, I was as excited as I'd ever been in my life. No, there was a time I had been more excited, but it was a bittersweet memory....

All year long, my fellow kindergarten students and I had been creating arts and crafts to take home. Our refrigerator was covered with my past contributions to the art world, but all that was prelude to the year-end masterpiece now in production.

I Sold *the* Moon!

There had to be at least 100 or more steps to go through to complete the project. Make a mistake anywhere along the line and you would need to start over. In short, it went like this: after adding water to some white powder, you poured the mixture into a tin pan. Then, you stuck your hand into the goop and let it dry around your fingers. Eventually, and oh so carefully, you lifted your hand up leaving a perfect mold of the artist's hand.

Once this delicate stage had been successfully completed, you were ready to paint. I chose metallic gold to cover this prized possession. On the back of the sculpture (with help) I printed: "To Mom Love Barry."

My sister Dourene had gone to the same kindergarten the year before. She had brought home her hand-mold on the last day of school, and everyone had made a big deal about it. She had gone on about how hard it was to make. I didn't believe her then, but now I knew she hadn't exaggerated. Her hand was painted purple, and now a year later it had started to fade, and even chip in places.

All my sisters and their friends were forever trying to fit their own hand into the mold. I don't think I was alone in secretly envying Dourene as having the only hand that fit perfectly.

But soon my own elegant golden hand would find a place of honor above the kitchen sink, next to the perennial avocado pit held in place over a water dish by three toothpicks.

Finally it was finished. I was overwhelmed with anticipation, pride, and sheer joy at the prospect of being able to give my mother something of real value.

After the last day of school I left with my prized treasure, now gift-wrapped and safely nestled in a bag with my other important cubbyhole possessions. I was in a state of bliss knowing how much my mom was going to cherish my gift.

Three blocks from home, I could no longer restrain my excitement, and broke into an all out sprint. What happened next is still unclear, but somehow I tripped, sending the bag and its priceless contents flying into the air.

I picked myself up and made my way through the carnage now strewn across the sidewalk. My double-decker box of crayons lay opened with less than half of its coloring sticks still inside. The glass jar that held my penny collection (exactly 100 to demonstrate how many pennies are in a dollar) had shattered, sending pieces of broken glass into the Davy Crockett coonskin hat that I had brought to school for Show and Tell. Even my oversized yellow report card showing four check marks in the boxes indicating I played well with others had come flying out of my carrying bag.

Looking further up the sidewalk I saw the white tissue-papered wrapped gift with the red ribbon bow—the ends of the ribbon still curled, having been pulled across the scissors by Mrs. Gregory. Something didn't look right.

Sitting crossed legged, I carefully unwrapped it. My golden hand had shattered on impact, and now, so too, did my childhood innocence. I had no idea that grief could be so all encompassing and life could be so cruel. I was crying uncontrollably and emitting sounds of anguish in a voice that was strange to me.

How long I sat weeping, I don't remember. I do remember having a woman I had never seen before and have never seen since, call to me from her car asking what was the matter. I showed her what I was holding and told her, through my tears, what had happened and why it had meant so much to me.

She helped me gather up my possessions, and told me she would drive me home or, if I wanted, she would take me to buy my mother another gift from a store of my choice. I counted 94 cents, having lost 6 pennies somewhere back on the sidewalk. My new guardian told me not to worry, that she wanted to buy the present for me, just to tell her where I wanted to go. One store I knew well was Woolworth Five and Dime.

I took my time and after walking the well-worn wooden floor of every aisle I selected a teacup and saucer decorated with small pink rosebuds. My driver insisted on having it put in a box and gift-wrapped.

On the way back to my house, she told me she didn't have any children, but if she did, she would be very proud if they loved her as much as I seemed to love my mom. I thanked her as best I could and invited her in to meet my mother, but she said she had to go. I was only seven at the time, but looking at her, she seemed somehow sad and almost ready to cry herself. I remember she gave me a hug goodbye, and her perfume was different from any thing I had smelled before.

For the next few weeks my family felt sorry for me and treated me like they did when I got sick or like the time I had broken my arm. Everyone was very interested in the mystery woman and wanted me to retell the story of her finding me and taking me to buy the teacup.

I Sold *the* Moon!

My oldest sister, Patricia, tried to glue the hand back together, but halfway through the reconstruction, everybody agreed it looked terrible, and I was not unhappy when she gave up trying to restore it.

The day came, near the end of the summer, when I realized the sadness of seeing my half-glued broken hand atop my dresser was worse than the inevitable conclusion I had reached. After carefully wrapping it up, I secretly buried it in the back yard next to Goldie, the goldfish. I did save out one small piece, though. It was a nondescript flat portion painted that gleaming gold on the front, and with the words, "To Mom," written in my own novice hand, on the white chalky backside. I wrapped this artifact in tissue paper and hid it in the back corner of my closet. It later found its way into the suitcase that holds my prized possessions of childhood.

I realized that thinking of my past helped me believe in my future. And even though I hadn't left for Europe yet, there was a part of me already looking forward to returning. I knew I wanted to come back to Paula, and to resurrect my other life as Moon Man.

CHAPTER 15

IN HER MAJESTY'S
SECRET SERVICE

WE ARRIVED AT HEATHROW AIRPORT, OUTSIDE OF LONDON, ON A chilly, gray morning in mid-August, 1973. David and I joined the queue to show our passports and get the visa stamp. This was the first time I had need of a passport. I suddenly felt grown up, proud and embarrassed all at the same time. I felt pride coming from the country that had gone to the moon and had turned the tide of World War II. America had, after all, saved the collective futures of the world's democracies, not the least of which was Great Britain's. This feeling of pride was tempered, however, by the shame I felt for our current involvement in Vietnam.

With my half-Irish heritage, I also anticipated disliking the English for their historically harsh treatment and repression of my ancestry. And so, it was with some resentment I handed over my passport for inspection.

"Sorry to keep you waiting, sir. Is this your first visit to the United Kingdom?" the smiling official, in his crisp blue blazer and red tie, cheerfully inquired.

"Yes, it is."

"Would this visit be for business or pleasure, sir?"

"Pleasure and educational, I hope."

"Jolly good, sir, and where might you be staying while on holiday?"

"With relatives of my friend, they live in Bristol."

"Splendid. Beautiful countryside, I daresay. I believe they have some sort of celebration going on now. Should do for a bit of local color. Do try and visit Bath while you're out that way. Simply marvelous. Lovely, really. I might recommend waiting a fortnight however, the weather being so dreadful these past few weeks."

He stamped my book.

"Right. All set then, Mr. McArdle. I do hope you have a most enjoyable stay with us. Pick up your luggage through those doors and to the left. Cheerio, sir."

I thanked him and as I left, I overheard him apologizing to the woman behind me for having kept her waiting. Was this person for real? Just this short interaction left me feeling like I wanted to be especially nice to the next person I met. What made his civility even more surprising was my own appearance. I had been awake for 24 hours, the last 12 of them on an airplane. In jeans, a wrinkled denim shirt, cowboy boots and my "Impeach Nixon Now" button, I looked liked an extra in the movie *Night of the Living Dead*. Yet, this official called me sir, Mr. McArdle, and wished me well. Is this what they meant when they talked about the English being civilized?

How could this small island nation, with people this congenial, think they had the duty, if not the divine right, to rule the world? But their devastating losses suffered during WWII changed all that. Their far-flung empire crumbled. Unfortunately, because of the geographical proximity, they continued to force their dominance on Ireland. The sun may not have completely set on Britain's global influence, but most assuredly, the sunrise was finding a lot fewer Union Jacks still waving over foreign shores.

The "Bristol 600" was being held on the Commons. Much like a county fair, there were food booths, entertainment stages, rides, carnival games and displays with memorabilia highlighting 600 years of Bristol's history. While in the information tent, I saw a notice that read: Day Laborer Wanted–Inquire Here. I did, and was told to see Peter Flaxton, who could be found in the stables at the far end of the grounds.

I think my interest was stimulated by an article I'd read on the plane that stated, "The only real way to get to know a culture and a people is to work for a time as a member of the society you find yourself in." The story went on to say, "Tourists and long time visitors alike are relegated to the observation class. However, once employed, that status changes from observer to participant—well worth the experience." With this encouragement, I found my way to the horse stables.

Peter Flaxton's crew looked as if they'd just stepped out of a Dickens novel. I felt somewhat conspicuous as my clothing was not splattered with mud and I had been to the dentist more than once in the last decade.

The position offered was that of "Fouled Straw Removal and Replacement Attendant." It meant I would be pushing a cart throughout the exposition, shoveling up muddy and soiled straw, most of which had been fouled by one or more of the barnyard animals in attendance. I would then replace this sullied groundcover with a new layer of clean, dry straw.

"Well, Yank," Peter was saying as he poured himself a cup of tea, "you look like you could do the job. I daresay the work's a bit dodgy, and you would need to start now, old boy. No training necessary, wouldn't imagine. With eight days left till the close of the fair, your pay packet would be worth, say, 34 quid 50P. Oh blimey, we'll make it 35 pounds even. We have a pair of Wellingtons and rubber bibs that should do nicely. Well, lad, hip, hip, yes or no?"

My quick calculation told me I'd be making around $12.00 a day for shoveling shit, but I reminded myself I'd be on the inside. David, not ready to stop his vacation after only two days, had already indicated he would be staying on the outside, so I would be on my own.

"Peter, you got your man."

"Jolly good, old sport, that's the spirit. You can pick up your kit out back. One of the lads will show you the procedures. It's been simply dreadful weather, so you'd best get cracking. Let me know if you need anything. Cheers."

I found my knee-high rubber boots, or Wellingtons, and was struggling with the fastening clips on my rubber pants and bib combination when one of my new co-workers found me.

"Say Governor, Pete wants me to make sure you know where the slop wagon is and where to dump your load, so to speak. This used to be my job, but you being a Yank and all, I got promoted. I learned some things, though. Now I can tell the difference between cow shit, horse shit, pig shit, sheep shit, and goat shit. 'Course, I already knew what dog shit looked like."

Maybe being on the inside was overrated.

Pulling my wagon around the fair and performing the simple task of making the public areas nice gave me an unexpected sense of satisfaction. Perhaps because I was in a foreign country, I felt no shame or hesitation in doing what I knew to be the lowest paying job at the very bottom of the exposition's employment ladder.

After four days, I realized I was actually enjoying the work. I realized, too, that I was invisible to all the attendees or at least no one seemed to notice me, and this anonymity gave me a great chance to observe without feeling intrusive. One telling observation came when I accidentally ran my cart into a man who was standing near the main walkway. Before I had a chance to apologize, the man—upon being hit—instantly said, "So sorry."

This reaction took me by such surprise I had to ask if I'd heard him right.

"Sir, *I'm* sorry. I ran into you. But if you don't mind me asking, why would you tell me you're sorry when it was obviously my fault?"

The gentleman reflected with a bemused look on his face and then answered.

"You're quite right, actually. I daresay I never really thought about it. Bit of a habit, I should think."

Being willing to apologize for something that was not your fault seemed like a very evolved way to interact. In America, receiving an apology from someone who knew they were at fault was not always a certainty, let alone hearing one from an innocent. The probability of a chance encounter escalating into violence because one person accidentally stumbled into another was mitigated almost entirely in England by this simple expression of regret.

I also discovered that when someone didn't hear or understand what I was saying, he or she would also say, "Sorry?" implying it was the listener that was having the problem not the person speaking. I liked this genteel way the British dealt with these two everyday interactions. These may have been minor observations, but something told me these unwritten codes of social interaction were meaningful enough to allow their police, or Bobbies, to get by carrying nightsticks and not guns.

$$* \quad * \quad *$$

It was Saturday night and the exposition had closed for the day. The fair's last day would be tomorrow, the employees had been called together for a meeting at the main stage pavilion. I arrived and had no trouble finding the menial laborer's group. They were sitting in the back with plenty of empty chairs around them.

"Evening, lads," I said as I took my seat.

They all responded with one form of pleasant greeting or another, with most of them calling me Yank or Governor. For days, the rumor mill had been saying that Queen Elizabeth herself would be making an appearance.

The meeting was called to order and after a few pleasantries, the President of the "Bristol 600" board of directors introduced Sir Philip Harrington, liaison to her Majesty Queen Elizabeth II of England.

A noticeable hush descended over the gathering. Sir Philip took center stage and dramatically paused before he began speaking.

"Queen Elizabeth, along with members of the royal family, will be attending this exposition tomorrow afternoon."

The crowd went wild with applause.

Sir Philip Harrington looked like a man who was comfortable on stage. He was rather short of stature and slight of build. Pale, even by local standards, he stood ramrod straight with not a hair out of place, although that worked in his favor, seeing as how he could ill afford to lose track of the few he had left. He wore an impeccably tailored three-piece suit—dark blue with gray pinstripes. His cream-colored, over-starched shirt complimented his gold silk tie and the matching handkerchief that just peeked out of his breast pocket. His rimless glasses supported his no nonsense persona. The black Wingtip shoes were newly polished and dust free, and although I have no evidence, were most likely the home to a pair of lifts that added a few inches to his otherwise 5' 4" height. His voice, on the other hand, was completely authentic, precise but with a trace of condescension.

"I won't be taking up much of your time, but there are certain protocols we all must be aware of to insure a proper and pleasant visit by her Majesty, family, and friends. Right. First and foremost, do not attempt to meet, touch or talk with the Queen unless she speaks to you first. Should that happen, it is customary for the ladies to curtsy and for the men to bow or simply nod your head. I should like a man and woman to come forward and demonstrate both the proper way to curtsy and bow."

While royal etiquette training 1A was going on, I started to drift away, thinking about our planned departure in three days for Rome and then on to Greece. I was not unhappy I had taken this job and had to admit my experience in England had been richer for it. As Sir Philip droned on, I was thinking about my favorite fish and chips vendor. Who would have thought that vinegar on french-fries would taste so good?

"...And I daresay absolutely no mud on her shoes. Who, may I ask is responsible for keeping the walkways clean, dry and free from any and all...unpleasantness?"

Everyone in the pavilion turned toward the motley group in the back and everyone in that group turned toward me. "And the last shall be first," I thought as I felt my face getting warm and registered a sudden loss of appetite. It was one thing to freshen up the paths for the local citizenry, but now Sir Philip was talking the Queen of England. The main benefit to most menial jobs is that there is no stress related to the work. As with most experiences in life, it's a trade-off. I was trading off decent wages for a job that required little or no skill and certainly no anxiety that having to please the Queen of England would create.

Peter Flaxton stood up and by the look on his face, I knew he too was starting to feel the royal heat.

"Right. Not to worry, Sir. I'll have my best man on the job. You can count on us, Sir, hip hip."

I slept uneasily that night, my anxiety made more intense by the sound of rain pounding against my bedroom window. The grassy field of the Commons was already wet and soggy. This new downpour would turn the entire fairgrounds into a muddy bog.

When I arrived at the stables, I found Peter in conversation with Sir Philip. Peter looked as if he'd slept in a horse stall. Sir Philip appeared nattily turned out in British tweed and knee-high brown leather riding boots. He was holding court and enjoying center stage.

"Been through this all before, old boy. If we had to cancel every time the weather turned a bit inclement, I daresay the Queen would never go anywhere. However, due to the severity of the storm there is a request I simply must require of you. What you and the lads will need to do is to lay down the dry straw just moments before her Majesty passes through. I have her schedule and route so the coordination should be rather simple, I'd say."

As scheduled, the Queen and her party arrived at the front entrance at 11 AM. At 11:01, I was frantically pitchforking dry straw over the muddy walkways.

The large crowd was applauding as best they could, while still holding on to their umbrellas. I got a glimpse of her as she came through the gates. Dressed in blue except for her purse and shoes, which were, oh shit...white! I had two immediate thoughts. One—why would the Queen carry a purse? And two—I bet I was the only person there who had hoped she'd be wearing brown shoes.

The crowd was starting to close off my view but before the Queen and her entourage were swallowed up completely I caught the eye of Sir Philip who gave me a discreet nod and just a hint of a smile. As the circle closed in front of me, the last things I saw were the Queen's shoes. They looked clean and dry.

Her tour was scheduled to last 48 minutes. It seemed like 10. Being in the presence of someone that carries the title of Queen was more exciting than I would have thought. I pretended I was a Knight of the Round Table and the straw was really my velvet cloak that I gallantly sacrificed in service to my fair damsel. Had I caught a reflection of myself in a mirror or in one of the mud puddles, I more likely would have thought of myself as one of the insane villagers that carried a pitchfork or burning torch up to Dr. Frankenstein's castle.

Because the movement of a crowd is unpredictable, and considering people would naturally part and make way for her to pass, I found myself on numerous occasions having a direct, unobstructed, almost intimate view of one of the most famous people in the world and undeniably the most famous person in all of England. On one occasion, I felt she might have noticed me, although I can't be certain.

I continued to lay down the flaxen straw road just ahead of Her Majesty, and for those 48 minutes, we were in some way connected. I also knew that without having taken this job the closest connection I could have hoped to make with the Queen of England would have been to buy a postcard with her image.

The tour was over and she was now pausing in front of her limousine to accept some flowers from the children who had gathered to see her off. With one final wave, she disappeared into the soft, rich leather interior of her modern day carriage. The last image I saw, as the doors closed, were what appeared to be her clean white shoes looking as if they had just come out of the box.

Peter Flaxton was so relieved everything had gone well that he ended up giving me 37 pounds—not the promised 35—and his high compliment of "Well done, lad."

Our last evening in Bristol, David's aunt and uncle took us to a party. It was held at the country estate of Dr. Brian Coals and his wife. The main topic of discussion was how much tonic is required for the perfect G&T (almost none seemed to be the consensus) and to wish the "American Lads" Godspeed. After taste-testing the endless variations of tonic, gin, and lime, David and I found ourselves in front of the group performing the best of our bad comedy routines.

They loved us. And we basked in their laughter and applause. My closing line: "And remember keep Bristol clean…throw your garbage in London," went over quite well.

What we didn't know was this would be the last time we would perform set material as the comedy team, briefly known, as Barry and David.

The McArdle's: Redlands, CA 1963 (L to R) Thea, Sheila, Shelley, Elizabeth, Dourene, Patricia, Mom, Dad and future Moon Man. (Photo by Howard Avey)

Early Moon Men, David and myself in first edition costumes. 1971 (Photo by Hal Hammond)

Moon Man Headquarters—Corner of Telegraph and Bancroft, Berkeley, 1974 (Photo by Peter Gerba)

Big Finish! Moon Man and Ms Honey Moon, University Reno Nevada , 1974 (Photo by Barbara Harrison)

Moon Acre Certificate. "World's Greatest Collector's Item."

Business is good. Long Beach State University, 1976
(Photo by Gary Ambrose)

Day at the office, Madison WI,
1976 (Photo by Michael Kienitz)

Ms. Honey Moon. University Reno
Nevada, 1974
(Photo by Barbara Harrison)

Big Crowds, return appearance Long Beach State University, 1977 (Photo by McCarrier)

Selling laughs, University of California Davis, 1977 (Photo by Monica Roberts)

Lunch time sale, University California Berkeley, 1974 (Photo by Peter Gerba)

STRANGERS IN THE NIGHT

I WATCHED THE WHITE CLIFFS OF DOVER RECEDE IN THE DISTANCE AS the Hovercraft made its way to France on the Normandy coast. I could not help but think of the tens of thousands of young men, the vast majority of which would have been my age or near it, who had made this same crossing about 30 years earlier. As they disembarked, they were met with barbed wire, machine gun fire and death. I understood that my trip today, as a free man, was made possible by their combined sacrifice. I offered up a silent prayer of remembrance and of gratitude, impossible to repay.

The first thing I noticed about France was that nobody was speaking English. My second observation was that I would not be missing the fish and chips and shepherd's pie as much as I thought I would. French food, even on our limited budget, was fantastic. We had the same looking food in America, but it didn't taste like this. It would not be Paris, the museums, the historical cathedrals, the quaint country villages or even the continuous immersion in the land of beautiful women that I would remember long after leaving. Eating French food was the best culinary experience of my life—that is, until we arrived in Italy.

I was born to eat Italian food. It all tasted so fresh, and comforting. And unlike the French, the Italians seemed happier and displayed none

of the conceit around their food that I had felt in France. My Italian language skills were as non-existent as my French, yet I had no trouble communicating in Italy.

After two weeks of camping out, seeing the sights, but mainly waiting to be hungry again, we reluctantly decided it was time to leave. We would be taking the train from Rome, to the port town of Brindisi. From there, we would take a boat to Athens.

As we boarded the train David and I got separated in the confusion of finding a seat. It would be a long, uncomfortable night if it had to be spent standing outside the bathrooms or having to squeeze against the aisle window every time someone needed to pass by.

Seeing a reserved card in the door slot of a closed compartment and deciding I had nothing to lose, I opened the door with feigned confidence while I made a show of studying my ticket. A well-dressed couple with a small child sat on one side while much to my delight, the two opposite plush seats were unoccupied. Smiling, I put my beat-up luggage in the overhead rack and then looked out the door to see if I could spot Barclay.

He was nowhere in sight but against the wall slumped in a corner and completely surrounded by a group of admiring Italian Lotharios was a breathtakingly beautiful girl. She was speaking English and fending off more than their verbal advances and looked like she had resigned herself to a completely miserable journey. On closer inspection, I thought I detected something else other than annoyance on her face. She was scared. The half-smile on her lips could not mask the fear I saw in her eyes. Suddenly, those eyes were looking right at mine. Instead of turning away I took a chance.

"Oh, there you are. I've been looking everywhere for you," I called down the hall, over the noise of the train. "I've found our compartment," as I waved for her to join me.

She hesitated only a second and then gathered her belongings and quickly walked towards me as if she knew me. With catcalls, whistles and laments from her fan club filling the hallway behind her she joined me in our tenuous sanctuary. I immediately closed the door.

"Thank you," she whispered as she flopped down in the plush window seat. Then, with a bit more energy in her voice she continued, "Do you always look to save damsels in distress?"

I picked up her bags and put them next to mine. "You did seem to be outnumbered and I guess my natural protective instincts took over. I have six sisters, so yeah, maybe I do look for damsels...in distress, I mean."

We looked at each other for the second time, both of us smiling.

Her name was Brenda MacTish. She was from Scotland and in the last week of her two month European tour. She had been traveling with friends who left her in Rome as they needed to go back to Aberdeen a few days earlier in preparation for their second year of college. Brenda and her friends were all art students and had spent most of their vacation in galleries, museums and churches. It was Brenda's first time away from home and away from her very protective parents. Who were not, as Brenda explained, "...going to be very happy when they discover that I've extended my trip by a few days and will be traveling on my own."

"I was sure I had made a bad decision when I was trapped in the corner out there with all those guys around me, but it's better now."

"That's why they call traveling an adventure. If we always knew what was going to happen it wouldn't be much of a journey. I guess the same could be said of life," I offered.

At the still tender age of 18, Brenda looked like a Botticelli model come to life. She had dark eyes, a strong nose, blooming lips and generous breasts. Her body in general was fully rounded and proportioned. She was tall, around 5'9" and well nourished. Her skin was flawless—the color of Devonshire cream. She was womanly rather than girlish. Her rich auburn hair was held in place by a copper-colored silk scarf. Whatever else she had on was not registering because as I looked at her all I could think about was what she would look like wearing nothing at all.

An hour later, the conductor arrived to check our tickets. To my complete surprise, he just smiled conspiratorially and punched them.

With our seats secured for the night, I went looking for some dinner. In the dining car I ordered a couple of cappuccinos, cheese and tomato sandwiches, apples and a bar of Toblerone chocolate...to go.

When I got back to compartment, a black curtain had been pulled across the center of the cubicle providing a modicum of privacy for the parties on both sides.

The couple across the way wanted to see if they could get their child to fall asleep, Brenda told me. I was unaware the curtain existed, but was not unhappy by this turn of events. We ate our dinner, saving some

of the coffee to have with the delicious chocolate. How was it possible America could put a man on the moon, but couldn't make chocolate like this? But what was really on my mind was wondering what it would be like to kiss Brenda.

Maybe I should get some help. The hallways were packed with people and their luggage, making me feel secretly smug as I maneuvered my way to the bar car and bought four small bottles of red wine and some mints. Stopping at the bathroom, I washed my face and hands, and brushed my teeth.

"A night cap?" I whispered as I quietly entered our half of the compartment.

"Thank you. That sounds lovely."

The first two bottles, containing about two glasses each, went down easily and I was glad to have had the foresight to buy a couple of backups. I opened them and refilled our glasses. We talked in hushed tones, discussing her school, her boyfriend, Paula, politics, our families, and our dreams.

"My boyfriend and I want to be virgins when we get married. It's not that I don't like guys, I really do. In fact, that's one of the reasons I wanted to come on this trip with my girlfriends and not my boyfriend. I knew I would have a chance to meet and talk to guys and see I was right. I would not have met you. But meeting someone is worlds apart from sleeping with them. I'm not sure why a lot of the guys I've met on this trip have a hard time accepting that. But you seem somehow different. You're the first American guy I've met—I've always wanted to. You're not like what I thought an American guy would be like."

Hearing her talk about her future plans or what she thought American guys would be like was not nearly as interesting as hearing her mention her virginity. It didn't matter that it was said in the context of explaining that she would not be having sex with me—what was exciting was the thought that when saying that word, it would be almost impossible not to be thinking about sex or the avoidance of sex. Either way, the subject of sex was now definitely and openly in the air. Hearing the word virgin had an erotically charged effect on me. It was almost as if she had said the word panties. If nothing else I knew her panties provided a symbolic protection for her virginity, so there was a connection. Virginity is a reference, no matter how oblique, to what I was imagining to be her golden-brown, silky soft, enveloping....

"Barry, you look hypnotized or something. Are you OK?"

Before I could answer, and let her know that American men were different from most of the recent guys she had been meeting—the light on the other side of the curtain was turned off. Now the illumination on our side suddenly seemed garish. Using my liquid courage and the opportunity just provided, I moved to the light switch on our side.

"I think they're trying to sleep. Do you mind?"

She shook her head no. The ensuing darkness was brightened only by light from the hallway filtering through the shade-drawn door and the occasional outside lights that would flash strobe-like through our curtain-drawn viewing window as we flew by.

When the wine was finished, we shared the last of the chocolate and then both had a couple of the mints. I searched the length of the armrest until I found what I hoped would be there. Pushing the release button, I lifted the shared armrest until flush with the seat backs. It was now or never. I found her hand. It was hot, soft, and more delicate than I'd imagined.

"If we both put our legs out toward the window we can almost fit comfortably lengthwise. We might even be able to get some sleep." Yeah, sleep. Right.

My back was now against the wall, my legs stretched across both seats. Brenda maneuvered herself between my legs with her back against my chest. My arms fell naturally around her waist. It felt good having her weight against me, and better when my lips brushed her cheek or neck when she or I readjusted for more comfort.

The train entered a tunnel and the compartment went black. I felt a subtle shift as she moved further down on my chest and brought her knees up to make room for her legs at the far end of the seats. This would make it much easier for me to bend down and kiss her. She was still holding my hand and had not protested when I let her hair down by untying her scarf. In the darkness, I found her cheek and just the corner of her mouth. I waited. She turned slowly but fully. This was wonderful. We kissed softly. I found it hard to hold back wanting to devour her mouth. I got the feeling she was not sure she should be doing this. I sensed apprehension if not fear.

"Brenda," I whispered directly into her ear. "we can stop. All you have to do is say no. I won't argue with you. (Reasoning is different from arguing, I reminded myself). Remember when you said that

meeting guys is not the same as sleeping with them? Well, kissing guys is not the same as losing your virginity. We are not going to have sex tonight. I promise you I won't try. We will leave all our clothes on. You don't need to worry. But if you want, we can still kiss. Being on this train with you is the stuff romantic novels are written about. I mean, why be young if we can't act like it? Neither you nor I will be young forever. One day, if we're lucky, we'll both be old and eventually we'll both pass away from this place. But tonight we're alive, we're here and as you know, you're so beautiful."

I waited. I believed what I had just said and although I didn't know what effect it would have on Brenda, it had put me in a state of hyper-arousal. I could not see her face clearly, but I had no trouble feeling her hand pull down on mine. This time when our lips met, there was no ambivalence in her kiss. It was wet, hungry, and ardent. Just knowing there would be no intercourse had me imagining our mouths were making love to each other. Trying to stay as quiet as possible just added to the arousal we both felt.

I had been sliding further down the wall and now my head was on the seat and Brenda, lying on her back, was fully on top of me. With a slight adjustment, her hips were now directly over mine. Without having to move, we both felt the motion and vibration of the train transfer up from the rails and into our rhythmically jostling hips. Within a few minutes, Brenda was rocking with an independent and more determined pressure.

Caught up in the thrill ride of simulated sex I wanted it to be as realistic as possible. I readjusted my fully erect penis to be snugly held in place between her thighs. Almost immediately, I felt the humid heat of her jeans-covered, virgin, vagina.

When she realized what I'd done, she tightened her legs. The movements of her hips now changed into more of a grinding motion. It might not be real sex, but both of us were thinking about real sex at the same time, and that was real enough.

By the sound of her breathing, interspersed with tiny yelps of pleasure that escaped her throat, and the quickening rhythm of her hips I knew she was nearing rapture. I now let myself catch up to her and for the first time started to move my lower body in synch with hers. When I sensed we were both seconds from tumbling head first over the falls of pleasure—with my left hand and through her blouse

and bra, I gently pinched her hidden nipples. Then waiting until the last possible instant I put my right hand firmly between her legs and palpated in rhythm to our now wildly bucking hips. Moments later she was biting my arm in an attempt to muffle the sounds of her release.

We dissolved into dreamland. On waking, I whispered in her ear.

"Wow, that was incredible. Thank you. I just have one question. Can we start over?"

We held each other falling in and out of sleep comforted by the melodic cadence of the steel wheels riding on their steel rails, moving southeast through the darkness and towards the quickly approaching dawn.

...ers Ralph Garcia (left) and Richard
...er lead Moon Man Barry McArdle off
...rside City College campus as students
...w. Apparently concerned for its safety,

Officer Fisher carries the Moon Man's sa...
el. Police cleared the incident as a "ps...
unfounded" report, the Moon Man was sp...
arrest and granted an interview.

...ghter 'a legitimate business'

Moon Man's dollar-an-acre sale o
lunar lots interrupted by police

By BEN BRADLEE

Moon Man as students booed and
...

Garcia then took some ri...
from the other officers. "Soun...

CHAPTER 17

WHAT ARE FRIENDS FOR?

DAVID AND I WATCHED THE PORT CITY OF BRINDISI RECEDING into the horizon from the Greek transport ferry *Argos*. The morning September sun was warm, and would soon be hot.

Staring out at the blue skyline, I thought of Brenda. We had said our goodbye's at the station kissing softly like old friends.

"I'll tell you all about it on the boat," I told David, who had arrived on the platform to find Brenda and me in a loving embrace.

It was a glorious day near the end of summer, and I felt suddenly connected to all the travelers that had gone before me. They had had their time. This was mine.

It's a good time to be alive, I thought. I felt guilty for not missing Paula more. But we had our whole lives to be together. Didn't we? I could give myself one last summer of no regrets. Couldn't I?

The bow of the ship was gently rising and falling as it cut its way through the calm, azure water. It was at that moment that I saw her. She sat in a deck chair, her feet on the rail, reading a book. Her hair, not so much blonde as it was white gold in color, pooled on the deck behind her. Her bronze tan offset the platinum of her hair in a way that was both fascinating and eccentric.

I Sold *the* Moon!

From my vantage point, it was hard to tell how old she was. I could just make out what appeared to be pubescent breasts providing minimal shape to an oversized colorful jersey top. Her pleated white cotton shorts, brown sandals (whose leather straps crisscrossed around her dainty ankles) and woven straw bag at her side, all looked foreign to me. On her wrists, she wore a polished nut bracelet and what looked like black wire—which I would later learn was elephant hair.

Dressed, as I was, in my cutoff jeans, cheap tee-shirt, and clunky sandals that would unfortunately never wear out, given that the soles were made from steel-belted radial tires, I suddenly felt and looked way too American. Thankfully, I was wearing my new light-sensitive sunglasses. I turned my face directly into the sun, and darkened them to full strength. It never hurt to appear mysterious. Women like that, I told myself. Additionally, my own fashion statement—the three leather bands of rawhide that symbolized my love for Paula—were in full view on my left wrist. Seeing them now reminded me of the promise I'd made to her: "These bands will have to wear off before I take them off."

I casually walked past the girl with the flowing blond hair, stopping slightly to her right, at the rail. With a bit of guilt, I slid my left hand along the bar showing off the rawhide bands to their full advantage. For maximum effect, I turned my face into the breeze allowing my hair to catch the wind. With this confident profile—chin slightly elevated—I contemplated the horizon.

Nonchalantly I turned to see what result my posing was having. Say something, you idiot, before she looks up and catches you staring at her.

She looked up. Caught. I smiled.

She appeared to be between 15 and 20 years of age. She wasn't as much beautiful as she was cute—impossibly cute. Her small round face presented a mixture of delicate features including her perfectly proportioned nose and mouth. Her lower lip was invitingly larger than her upper and when she smiled two diamond shaped dimples appeared in her peach-sized cheeks. As I continued to stare into her intelligent-looking large hazel eyes, I blurted out the first thing that came into my mind.

"Are you from Paris?"

"No, I'm from Gaggenau. I can't see your eyes."

I took off my glasses. So much for mystery.

The accent was definitely not French and since I had never heard of Gaggenau, I could only guess at her nationality. However, I was not willing to blow the image of the man with the strong profile whose hair trailed behind him in the wind by admitting my ignorance of geography. I went fishing.

"Gaggenau? Sure, isn't that somewhere near, I mean it's just south of..."

"Germany. Gaggenau is a small town in the Black Forest region of Germany."

"Ah, I was right. It's south of, well it's south of the North Pole. I think that's safe to say. So my guess is you're...don't tell me...German!"

Her small girlish laugh fit her petite body and softened what I detected as an underlying seriousness.

"I guessed you were from Germany and I'll guess you're going to Athens and that because by midnight it will be my birthday you will agree to have a drink with me."

"I told you I was from Germany, you did not guess it. This boat goes only to Athens so this is not so smart, but for your birthday, I would be OK to have a drink."

At first, I thought she might be joking with me, but over the next four hours, I discovered joking was not her strong suit. She enjoyed laughing, and did so when my humor was not too sarcastic, or culturally specific. I loved hearing her laugh and did not give up when some of my best material resulted in silence or her question, "Now you are funny?"

I realized I had never met someone so completely void of pretense. She exuded a strange combination of strength and vulnerability. This unusual personality, coming as it did in such a small attractive package, was both seductive and a bit intimidating.

Her name was Katrina Werner. She was 19 years old and was traveling alone, having just finished three years working for a company called Club Mediterranean. Her most recent assignment had been on the coast of Tanzania, in Africa. She was fluent in five languages and conversant in three others. I impressed her with my Spanish by saying, "Please pass meatballs and big butter. Tomorrow I study salt and pepper under the library."

"Barry.... Hey, Barry."

I turned to see David standing above us on the top deck.

"Stay there. We're coming up," I yelled back.

As we approached, I couldn't help but notice David staring transfixed at Katrina. After camping out for the past two weeks, David's normally thin appearance was leaning dangerously close to gaunt. Not helping his appeal was the limp cheese sandwich in his hand.

"Just in time, I was about to eat this but I'll split it. Would you like half?" David asked while never taking his eyes off Katrina.

Katrina thanked him but declined. I excused myself to get my bottle of "good" wine I'd been saving.

David followed me down the three decks into the luggage hold.

"Hey, Barry, you're not going to believe me but I think...I'm in love. I mean this is *really* weird. Like in the book, *The Godfather*. Remember when Michael sees that girl, and seeing her, he felt he got hit with a lighting bolt? Well, you're my best friend and if I can't tell you who can I tell? Where is she going? How long will she be in Athens? Does she have a boyfriend? Where is she staying? Do you think I...? "

"Hold on. Maybe if you'd had a tuna sandwich. The day -old cheese on white bread just doesn't impress like it used to."

"Barry, this is not funny. Do you see me laughing? God, I was an idiot. I didn't know what I was saying but I couldn't stop myself. I'm really serious."

"Well, I'm serious too. I've asked her to have a birthday drink with me once we get settled in Athens and she's agreed."

"You're not listening to me. I think I'm in love. Oh my God, I've said it again."

"You can say it all you want, but that doesn't change anything."

Looking straight at me David slowly answered, "You're wrong Barry, it changes everything."

We returned in a silence that was increasing in volume with every deck we ascended. The wine was shared in forced togetherness. David would look in Katrina's direction every time he thought I wouldn't notice. With the wine finished, and night settling in, I took Katrina's hand and went looking for some privacy. Remembering a movie I'd seen, I lifted the canvas covering off one of the lifeboats, and we crawled under.

We spent most of the night finding out about each other and peeking out to marvel at the brilliant stars filling the Mediterranean sky. It was equally breathtaking, in the dim light, to see the ancient hieroglyphics carved into the towering sandstone walls as the ship carefully made its way through the narrow Isthmus of Corinth.

By the time we docked, Katrina had agreed to share my hotel room for the night and join us for my birthday dinner the following evening. David would be staying at a hotel that advertised "Beds on the Roof —$1.00." With my birthday and Katrina to celebrate, I was more than willing to blow my budget. Our room, at $15.00 a night, was worth it: high ceilings, comfortable bed, and the real luxury—a private bathroom.

After my bath, I put on a clean pair of boxer underwear. She was wearing an oversized shirt covered with images of the cartoon character Snoopy. Her freshly washed hair fell in great waves down her back disappearing under the covers. She looked lovely and completely at ease. As I slid under the covers, my leg came in contact with her bare thigh. It felt like warm silk. She turned the bedside light off.

Our lovemaking was conventional and gentle and over way too fast. I forgave myself for my poor performance, blaming it on the combination of travel exhaustion, her beauty, and the exotic location. It's enough to know we have this room for another night, I told myself. And tomorrow I'll make it special. I will.... But fatigue overtook me and on this my 23rd birthday, I fell asleep in a billowy cloud of blonde hair, feeling not quite as young as I had yesterday, but still believing I had a lifetime of tomorrows.

What was that noise? There it was again. A steady pounding on the door brought me out of a deep sleep.

"Go away," I yelled.

"Bare, it's me. Open up."

It was David and he was shouting.

David started barking questions the moment I opened the door and he saw I was alone. "Where is she? What happened? I mean why did she leave? Is she coming back?"

"Hey, hold on. I just woke up. I have no idea where she went or when she's coming back."

David looked like he was going to be sick.

"But," having noticed her travel satchel, I continued, "she left her bag here and she said she was going to have dinner with us tonight and after that she's staying another night here...with me."

"Barry, listen, I couldn't sleep last night. You just have to believe me, something is happening and it's all because of her. It's very strange. I don't feel so good."

"Let me get dressed and get us some coffee before you faint on me."

"Yeah, OK. But I think I'll wait here in case she comes back. Did she say anything about me? Did she.... Did you.... What did you say about me?"

"David, relax. The only thing I said was that your flatulence was getting a bit worse, and that the drugs you take to control your bladder weren't working."

"Kalimera," Katrina said as she entered and started pulling cups and containers from a bag. "It means good morning in Greek."

She had brought back two cups of coffee, some yogurt, a big cinnamon roll, grapes, and (I knew I liked this girl) some chocolate.

"I'm sorry I didn't know David was here. I would have brought more, " she said looking at David, who suddenly had his best Cary Grant smile back on.

The coffee, pastry and chocolate were not nearly as good as they had been in Italy, but the yogurt, unlike anything I had ever tasted before, was nearly orgasmic.

"We're going to the Acropolis around noon. You're coming too, aren't you Katrina?" David almost pleaded.

"Yes, of course. That's why I came to Athens. Tomorrow I go to Santorini."

"Great! We're going to Santorini, too. We can leave tomorrow as well. Right, Bare? Wow, that's really great. Cool. Maybe we can see each other, you know, go to the beach or something one day. I've always wanted to learn German."

At least my best friend wasn't trying to steal my girl from behind my back.

The Acropolis was magical. It was hard for me to fully appreciate that I was seeing and touching marble columns that had been standing since before the birth of Christ. In America, our oldest buildings were, at most, 200 years old. The recorded history of Athens originates around 2000 BC.

The three of us now sat together atop the Acropolis, in the late afternoon sun. We looked out over the yellowish haze that enveloped the sprawling metropolis of modern day Athens. My best friend and I were enjoying making Katrina laugh with exaggerated highlights of our college days and audition at CBS. David made sure to talk about Paula and how much I loved her. It was harder, yet no less entertaining, explaining the Moon Men.

Our audience of one was left feeling that the two mercurial Americans that had burst into her life were capable of achieving whatever they wanted. The possibilities were endless. The future was ours for the taking. We were able to convince her of this, if for no other reason, than on this day, when thoughts of civilizations long past converged with dreams yet to be realized, we believed it ourselves.

university times

Vol. LXVII No. 45   California State University, Los Angeles   Wednesday, March 10, 1976

Moon Man sells CSLA students 'piece of rock'

"Not only do I guarantee nothing, but I firmly stand behind my guarantee," claimed Barry McArdle yesterday as he alternately urged students in the Free Speech Area to buy property on the moon and barraged them with one-liners.

McArdle, calling himself the Moon Man, is the embodiment of the Lunar Development Co. of the United States of America, which for the past three years has been selling lunar real estate for one dollar an acre. His three-day appearance at Cal State L.A. is being sponsored by the A.S. which will receive ten per cent of his profits here.

"I'm doing this in the name of individuality, originality, freedom of expression and survival," said McArdle. "It keeps me off of welfare, and I got tired of frying burgers. I'll keep on doing it as long as I find it educational and satisfying."

As for survival, he is apparently finding his occupation satisfying enough, since for two years it has been his sole means of support.

But it has not been all that easy. "I've been punched out, egged and water-ballooned," he explained, adding that he has found himself behind bars 12 times, always temporarily.

"People ask me what good it is, I

Frank Brown gets 'burned'

Gallery director's proba period option not rene

By KEITH HALL

"Are three rats worth my job?," cried Frank Brown, University Student Union Art Gallery Director, after notification last Monday he will be terminated April 2, 13 days before completion of his 12-month probationary period.

The rats which Brown claims cost him his job, were part of an exhibit staged Feb. 19 in the Union's gallery by artist Kim Jones. Jones torched

the rats to give his st[...] said Brown.

"However, this job [...] than three rats. And I [...] he said. "But they'll n[...] They'll shut this place [...] rats.

"I really thought [...] going to walk around [...] didn't think he was g[...] he did to those rodent[...] realize I made a mista[...] ment. But is it worth [...] asked.

"Seriously, I think I h[...] tastic job," said Brown[...] give it up in a mome[...] came along who was [...]

Con[...]

Trustees ready to abandon 'merit review' layoff policy

By JEFFREY WEIR

The gathering faculty stormclouds over "merit review" were dispelled yesterday when Academic Senate Chairperson Eloise King announced that "a large majority" of the CSUC Board of Trustees had agreed to scrap the controversial layoff procedures.

of "merit review" to persuade the Trustees that merit was not implementable.

Smoking ban adopted

Following King's revelations on the imminent demise of "merit," the Academic Senate adopted a policy that

No cheese, just $1 for a plot of land on the moon

By Marie Denunzio
Staff Writer

There really is a man in the moon and he was on campus Wednesday and Thursday selling shares of his planet. His real name is Moon Man (although his parents gave him the earth name of Barry McArdle) and he claimed the moon in 1971. He is sponsored by the Campus Speakers Board and the university will receive a share of the profits.

Since he claimed the moon he has been selling moon land deeds for $1 an acre. However Moon Man does not promise transportation or water rights on the planet.

In fact he doesn't promise much of anything except that the certificate will cover a crack in the wall and will not break, even if dropped from a two-story building.

No guarantee

"I can't guarantee you anything," said Moon Man, who was clad in silver pants, boots and a cape with a silver-glittered helmet. "Do I look like someone who could guarantee anything? But I'll say one thing — I don't guarantee anything, and I stand behind that."

Moon Man said the certificates are conversation

pieces, collector's items and they make great gif[...] the man who has everything. He said he wanted te[...] credit the rumor that the certificates can be gr[...] down and smoked in order to get high.

"I know it doesn't work because I tried it—ju[...] make sure," he said.

Acid gave idea

The 26-year-old Moon Man said he got the id[...] selling shares of the moon from "bad acid." He sa[...] had gone to Chico State University and found the[...] only people who were getting jobs were the drop-[...]

"I was out of a job and tired of frying burgers[...] was bad for my acne—so I decided to try this," N[...] Man said.

Moon Man began traveling around the country [...] Ms. Honeymoon selling moon land. They later b[...] up because of personal conflicts. Since that [...] Moon Man has traveled all over the world. He ha[...] about 20,000 shares during his career.

Already 'sold'?

A prospective customer once asked Moon Ma[...] he could be sure that he was not getting an acre[...] was not already sold. Moon Man said, "You c[...] sure I have. All moon acres are exactly alike"[...]

(continued on pa[...])

Daily Trojan

CHAPTER 18

COMES A TIME

THE RESTAURANT I SELECTED TO CELEBRATE MY BIRTHDAY SERVED meals outdoors, under an arbor of grapevines. Strings of tiny white lights were twinkling around the patio and overhead as well.

When I saw David, I knew he had dressed with care and purpose. He wore a bright red silk shirt, black jeans, and a new pair of stylish Greek sandals. If I had worn that shirt, I would have looked like an accident victim.

Katrina was in a simple white dress accented with an African trim design, her hair falling endlessly behind her. She wore a single bracelet made from elephant hair, and very little makeup. She looked glowing—without appearing to have tried.

Maybe my problem was I tried too much. I had decided to "go native" and wore a ceremonial goat herder's knee length alb. When I brought up the attached hood with its colorful tassel and small bell, I looked like a monk who should have stayed wandering in the desert for another 40 years. The pattern depicting skinned lambs being spit-roasted was less than appetizing. Not surprisingly, my hiking boots didn't help.

We feasted on Greek salads, shish-ka-bobs cooked over an open flame, moussaka, baklava and wine. I discovered that the more wine I drank, the easier it was to forgive David for staring at Katrina all night.

I Sold *the* Moon!

"A toast," David said as he stood swaying with his glass of Retsina wine.

"I raise my glass to Barry—the best friend I've ever had. To his health, to adventure, long life, and to true love." This last statement he said in a whisper as he turned his gaze on Katrina.

We all clinked our glasses together and as we did so, I wanted this exact moment in time to last forever. Simultaneously, I understood that this instant was over before the tinkling sound completely faded away.

While Katrina was in the bathroom, I turned off the lights and lit some candles. Placing them around the room created a warm and sensuous glow. I really wanted tonight to be better for both of us. Better in what way? I asked myself. I knew what it was. What it had always been. As much as I wanted to believe that I could separate the physical act of lovemaking from some greater need to share and connect emotionally and spiritually with my partner, I found I could not. I had grown up hearing that it was girls who needed "love" before they would consider sex. It was understood that boys always wanted to "get some," while girls were taught to wait until marriage. Did growing up with six sisters somehow dilute my male perception, some might say prerogative, regarding sex?

The image of David staring at Katrina came to mind. I knew I was not looking at her in that same way. There was this sense that behind his look, there was a lifetime of longing, a passion held in check that wanted and needed to be expressed.

Our lovemaking that night was better and yet not.

The next morning I was packing my suitcase as I always had, making sure to separate my dirty clothes from my clean. This was made especially easy because my suitcase was equipped with a separator that snapped in place dividing the case into two equally-sized compartments. I was wearing my steel belted sandals, leaving my hiking boots and my "going out" black loafers still to be packed. These I placed, soles up, on the top of the dirty clothes and then attached the divider.

"What are you doing?" Katrina sharply asked.

"I'm packing. Why? What does it look like I'm doing?"

"You can't put your dirty shoes in with your clothes. I have cord. Tie them to the outside of your bag."

"It's OK. All my clothes are dirty on this side. They don't come near my clean stuff."

"It doesn't matter, you can't have them in your suitcase."

Her voice sounded strained and she was no longer talking to me as much as she was giving orders

"I'm sorry, but I'll put my shoes anywhere I want. And please don't tell me what to do."

I closed the case and went into the bathroom. When I came out I was startled, and more than a little upset, to see my two pair of shoes tied to the outside of my bag.

"Shoes don't belong inside a suitcase with the clothes," Katrina said with some finality and more than a trace of satisfaction.

Now I *was* mad. I tore the shoes from their neatly tied moorings, opened the suitcase and started to stuff them back where I'd had them.

"My shoes go wherever the hell I want them to go. I don't give a shit where you think they should go."

She seemed as upset as I was and to my further disbelief, she tried to stop me from closing my case. I pushed her hands away and lost what little connection I still had on sanity.

"What the fuck are you doing? I know Germans are arrogant but this is bullshit!"

"What you do is bullshit," Katrina angrily spat back at me. She grabbed her belongings that were arranged uniformly by the door, and without looking back stomped out of the room.

"Sieg Heil, Sieg Heil," I shouted after her as I raised my right arm in the Hitler salute.

✳   ✳   ✳

Twenty minutes later, I was sitting on the floor, still wondering what the hell had happened, when David walked in.

"Where is she? We got a boat to catch. Barry, where is Katrina?"

"David, I think Katrina has left for the port. It really was never going to work out. So I guess it's back to just you and me."

"Left for the port? What are you saying? What happened? We're all going to Santorini together—remember? Why would she just leave without saying goodbye?"

"I'll explain everything. I just gotta check out, and then we're on our way. Barclay, are you OK? You look sick."

"I'll meet you at the boat," he uttered in a barely audible voice. Turning, he bolted from the room.

David and I spent the next two months very differently. I continued traveling wherever the tides and events of freedom took me. David went wherever Katrina went. When our paths crossed, I would often see him waiting outside a discotheque or restaurant on whatever small Greek island we happened to be visiting. He was hoping to get a glimpse of Katrina as she made her way past, escorted by some new bronze Adonis, and always speaking in a language other than English.

As his best friend, I didn't have the heart to tell him that Katrina's choice in men, excluding myself, seemed to be European in flavor, body beautiful in stature, and fashion exquisite in dress. The saying "Three strikes and you're out" came to mind.

"I think I'm making progress. She smiled at me yesterday, well, in my direction anyway. It's been hard digging out of the hole you put me in. I still can't believe you shouted 'Heil Hitler' at her. That was not cool." David was telling me this, for the twentieth time, as I waited to board the inter-island ferry.

"She's agreed to have coffee with me, as soon as Dax goes back to Florence. A friend of hers from Club Med has invited her to stay in some villa on Naxos, so I'll be going there. Well, not to the villa, but to the island. But who knows? I mean, how long can she hold out? Remember when I first met her and I told you I thought I was in love with her?"

"Yeah."

"It's worse now. I can't think of anything else, and I've been feeling sick."

"It's called lovesick my friend, and you got it bad."

My ferry arrived and the boarding process started.

"For what it's worth, I wish you luck. See you back in Athens."

I started up the gangplank then turned around.

"David, remember to keep your footwear out of your backpack," I yelled.

Two weeks later, I awoke to find them standing together, hand in hand, in my hotel room.

"We have lots to tell you, so get up. I'm starving and I'm buying. Let's go eat," David said as he pulled back the sheet.

They did have lots to tell me. The most significant revelation however, needed no explanation. A blind man could see they were in love. I had never seen David so happy or look better. The disheveled, gaunt, depressed stalker I had left standing on the dock in Paros two weeks earlier had been transformed into a handsome, confident, well-fed, tanned and satisfied young man.

Katrina and I had patched things up to the point of being civil to each other, but this new relationship she now had with my best friend would demand a greater effort and acceptance on both our parts. I had no illusions. David had been right; this did change everything.

On our flight back to London, David told me he would not be going to Ireland the following week as we had planned, nor would he be on the our flight back to San Francisco four weeks later. He had been invited to Germany to spend Christmas with Katrina and to meet her family. He had enthusiastically accepted.

"When I do come back to the States, I'm bringing Katrina with me. I won't come back without her," he said.

I had no reason to doubt him.

Staff photo by Jebb Harr

Moon man, Barry McArdle.

Caped crusader selling little pieces of lunacy

By DENNIS KELLY
Sun-Telegram Staff Writer

SAN BERNARDINO — "The moon man is back!" the caped crusading salesman shouted into the wind from the truck of a Toyo-

jockey and worked in radio and television. He earned his mass communications degree from Chico State College.

When he's "off" these days, McArdle said, he generally travels and "fights court cases."

30 buy plot at £1 an ac

OR SALE, one acre of land. Price £1, Location, Moon, d if occupation of the Moon ever comes about, at least 30 Irish people will be laying claim to ownership.

ey bought the land after last ight's Late Late Show on RTE from a 24-year-old Cali-

silver-speckled cape and top boots, Ba "Our legal advisers ling our case be American courts, claiming that we ha to sell the land on th The first to buy afte show was 22-year-ol

CHAPTER 19

A BAD TRIP

A FEW DAYS AFTER OUR ARRIVAL BACK IN ENGLAND, WE accompanied David's aunt and uncle, Diana and Kent, to a gala. Once again, the event was to be held at the Coals' estate, where David and I had entertained the partygoers some months earlier.

Getting ready for the party, David made a fateful decision— one he has always regretted.

Back in Bristol, our mail was waiting. One package, from Big Eddie Fergus, provided more than news from home. It also contained LSD. For whatever reason, I decided not to indulge. Had I, I might have studied the instructions regarding dosage more carefully. As we would later discover, David had overlooked one of the "and then cut in half..." Instead of taking what he thought was one dose; David took four "hits" of very potent LSD.

Thirty minutes after taking the drug, it was time to leave for the party. David wondered aloud if he should stay behind, as he wasn't feeling all that chipper.

"Not to worry, nothing a stiff gin and tonic won't fix, old boy," his uncle pronounced.

I Sold *the* Moon!

I was apprehensive, looking at David's flushed face as we rode in the back of Kent's late model Jaguar. Under my breath I asked him, "How are you feeling?"

"Why are you whispering?" David almost shouted.

"No secrets, now, boys," Diana chided from the front seat.

We drove for a few minutes in silence leaving the city of Bristol behind us.

"It's really dark in here," David suddenly announced.

Oh, shit. This could get out of hand. What to do?

"Funny how that works, old boy. When the sun goes down it gets dark. On average once a day," Kent lightheartedly bantered.

Diana laughed and I joined in, although a bit late. I wanted to tell David to shut the hell up, but unsure how he'd react, I could do nothing but sit and squirm.

"Some people are scared of the dark," David pontificated.

Just great, now he thinks he's some nitwit psychology professor. This was not going well. How much longer to the house?

"You know that because you're a product of the fine American educational system?" Kent chuckled, and pulled into the tree-lined lane that led to the Coals' manor.

Maybe it was me. Maybe David's insipid chatter was not as asinine as I thought.

When the car stopped, I lingered a moment allowing time for Kent and Diana to get out.

"David, are you going to be OK?"

"OK?" he asked

"You need to mellow out. Just stay by me and don't talk to anyone."

I opened the door, thankful no one heard David say, "Please don't let me stare at the sun."

Walking up the impressive stone staircase, under a massive cedar tree to the front entrance, I momentarily considered taking David by the hand and disappearing into the countryside. In retrospect, I wish I had.

Two sets of oversized French doors, each with large panels of beautifully etched glass depicting biblical scenes provided entrance to the manor. Moses parting the Red Sea, Daniel in the lion's den and the Crucifixion presented themselves as we ascended to the spacious

landing. Kent opened one of the doors revealing a long reception line. Many of the faces were familiar to me, if their names were not. The men were in tuxedos, the women in formal gowns.

I took a chance, turned around and asked David, "Are you alright?"

"I would be if you stop asking me that," he answered.

Cool, it was me. He's fine. I hope.

Moving through the line I was more aware of what David was saying than I was of my own conversation.

"Oh, jolly good, it's the American lads. I daresay safely back from the continent?"

It was our hostess, Mrs. Coals. She was beaming while shaking my hand.

"Right. I do so hope you will favor us with a bit more of your comedy this evening."

Turning to face David she continued, "Just yesterday I was telling Maggie, my tennis partner, how you lads had performed your comedy act for us when you first arrived."

Without missing a beat David answered, "Yes, I remember and I do hope you've forgiven us by now."

That's my man! What a perfect, very British, bit of repartee. Everyone who had been listening to this banter laughed appropriately. What was I worried about? He's smoother on acid than I am straight. Everything is going to be fine.

I entered the main parlor room. Soft amber light reflected off sterling silver platters and the coats-of-arms displayed on the mantel. The hearth was alive with a crackling fire—adding to the festive mood in the well-appointed, mahogany-paneled room. String music softly played somewhere nearby.

"Barry, old boy, what say you to a gin and tonic?" Kent was coming towards me with a drink outstretched in his hand.

"Marvelous, I'd love one, actually." I heard myself answer, falling into what I'd perceived to be the English style of speaking. Which seemed to be achieved by simply using more words than necessary—I daresay.

I see the drink. I see the lime wedge, its pulp slightly frayed. I see a single drop of condensation start its slide down the side of the glass. I reach out. I feel the coolness surrounding the ice-filled tumbler. Smiling, I start to close my hand around the glass. I don't complete this simple action.

In that same moment, there was a heart-stopping explosion of shattering glass. All activity and conversation instantly stopped.

My first and only thought was...David!

For two seconds the only sound I could hear was the hissing and popping of the fire. The uneasy stillness was quickly broken by a second equally loud and terrifying blast of breaking glass. With this second deafening noise came the sound of screaming as women came running into the room where most of us still stood frozen in our places. I turned after hearing a third thunderclap, in time to see shards of splintering glass go flying down the hallway, shattering further as they landed on the beautifully polished marble floor.

As I returned to the now deserted foyer, I could not avoid crushing pieces of glass as I walked. The inspiring French doors were shattered. The damp night air was rushing through the jagged openings where moments ago, and for decades prior, one-of-a-kind glass panels had kept the English weather safely at bay.

Someone wearing a yellow sweater was darting between the cars parked in the circular driveway.

"David! David! Did you see who did it?" I yelled out through the breached doorframe.

"He bloody well did it!" a man wearing a red silk lined cape, standing at the top of the stairs screamed. He pointed directly at the shadowy figure who now stood swaying in the darkness, staring back at us.

I knew people were starting to congregate behind me because I could hear the cracking of the glass under their feet. Without turning around, and without having to open the door, I stepped through the newly created opening and uneasily went to talk to my friend.

"David, are you alright?"

"Get away from me. You're one of them!" he screeched and ran down the drive disappearing into the English fog and moonless night.

I had no choice but to follow him. Having taken LSD before, I knew it provided an additional source of energy and strength—that is until you crashed. He was pulling further ahead, when unexpectedly he turned and started running toward me. It took more willpower than I care to admit to keep me standing in my place.

David stopped two feet from me. He looked different—scary different. Besides the perspiration covering his scarlet face, his hair looked wildly snarled, and his eyes were ablaze and unfocused. Blood had seeped through his sweater at his right elbow, drying reddish brown in color.

"Why did you take me there? I thought I could trust you," David said in a faraway sad voice.

"David, it's going to be OK. You know you can trust me."

He started to say something but couldn't get it out. It looked like he was in conflict with himself. When he finally spoke he sounded better, and his eyes were clearer and more focused.

"Barry, what did I do back there? The doors...I remember now. This is bad, I mean, really bad. Why would I do that?"

"It's the acid. And, yeah, it's bad, but it could have been worse...I guess."

As I was talking, I watched fascinated as David's face completed a metamorphosis. He was once again the person with blazing eyes and fiery skin. His few moments of clarity were dissipating. He turned away and started to run.

Oh, shit! I could see a man working on his car ahead of us. Maybe David would run past. I sped up in the hope of diverting him before he...hell, I had no idea what he might do.

I caught up, completely out of breath.

"What's that you say, lad? Ring the police? Blimey, why on earth should I do that? Best not to muck about with the Bobbies, I should think."

"Yes, call police now. Not sure what I'll do. Need to turn myself in," David demanded.

This was exactly the kind of conversation I wanted to avoid.

"Sorry to bother you, sir," I interjected, as I arrived. "This is our first day in England and I think your beer here is much stronger than in the States."

"Oh, so that's it? Well, no harm done. I've been known to bend the elbow a time or two, wink, wink, nod, nod."

David had turned away and was now on the porch of the man's house.

"Need to call police," David announced as he opened the front door and disappeared inside.

I dashed to the door calling back over my shoulder, "Not to worry sir, I'll get him out."

"Bloody hell! I bloody will ring the force if he's not out before I bloody hell get to the phone."

He continued to yell as I rushed to get my friend. David entered a tiny den occupied by three small children, their mother and a TV. They were eating dinner on trays while watching *Monty Python's Flying Circus*. All the laughing stopped when they saw the wild-eyed stranger in the yellow sweater walk in. It got even quieter as I came up behind him and grabbed his wrist.

"Good evening M'am. I am so sorry to have bothered you. My friend and I are just leaving. Aren't we?" He didn't budge.

"Need phone. Call police."

Great, now along with looking like a zombie, he was starting to sound like one.

"Mummy, who are they?" The oldest of the children asked, as one of the younger ones scurried onto her mother's lap.

"Whoever they are they're bloody well leaving now." The man from the carport bellowed as he grabbed David by the collar, and with my encouragement took him out of the house.

"Bloody Yanks," I heard him say as we turned the corner with David having thankfully started to run again. To my dismay, I saw two young women carrying grocery bags coming towards us on the sidewalk. I felt we had just gotten out of the proverbial frying pan and now....

"What are you trying to hide?" David demanded.

"Sorry?" Questioned the woman directly in front of him.

"My friend's a little drunk, please forgive our intrusion. We're leaving now," I said.

"The devil is in there," David continued.

"Oh no, Sir, I just have me produce and some sweets for the wee ones."

Unconvinced, David reached into the bag and removed a bottle of milk.

"I was right, Satan's poison," David triumphantly proclaimed as he held the bottle high over his head.

"No, Sir, that's just me milk," she said in a fragile sounding voice.

"Liar! It's the devil's brew," David screeched as he poured the milk on the sidewalk. Frightened, both women ran into the street and away from the maniac who was now stomping in the white puddles of liquid venom.

We wandered aimlessly for the next few hours. Around midnight, much to my apprehension, we entered a graveyard. It was dark and the fog had gotten thicker. David suddenly stopped and turned around.

"I know why I freaked out."

His voice sounded normal.

"They were all vampires. I was there to be initiated. When I saw the ghoul in the red lined cape, I snapped. I knew they were going to kill me, but I wouldn't let them do it without a fight. I used my elbow as a battering ram. The worst thing was, I thought you were one of them. I've never felt more paranoid and alone."

Four hours later, we sat exhausted on a park bench, with the Bristol Cathedral looming gray and gothic behind us. The drug had finally worked its way out of his system. The fog was lifting and although it was still gloomy, light was less than an hour away. David must have felt it, too.

"I really need to see the sun come up. I won't feel completely safe until I do. What I told you about seeing vampires was true. It seemed as real as me talking to you now. I guess my worst fears were brought to life tonight. I'm not sure I believe in heaven. But after this, I believe in hell. I'm really embarrassed. Kent and Diana have been so good to us, and now I totally fucked up. What are we going to tell them? What should we tell them?"

"The only thing we can tell them, David."

"The truth?"

"Yeah, the truth. We owe them that much and it's the only explanation that makes any sense."

"You're right, of course, but I'll leave out the part where I saw blood running out of their friends' eye sockets."

Then, to my surprise, David got down on his knees, put his hands together and asked God to forgive him. He continued praying silently for a few minutes and when he stood up, I could see that he'd been crying. He sat down and together in private contemplation we waited for the sun to bring us light, warmth, and redemption.

Had no licence to sell acres of the moon!

A 24-year-old American who said he was a "student of life" was charged in the Dublin District Court today with selling "lunar certificates" in Henry St., Dublin, without a street trader's licence, between 4 and 6 p.m. yesterday.

He is Barry McArdle, who said he was staying with friends at St. Margaret's Road, Malahide, Co. Dublin. He told Justice Good that selling lunar certificates was only a joke and a gimmick.

McArdle said he had sold the certificates in American cities, and it was crazy to sell them and more crazy to buy them." He had appeared on the "Late Late Show" on Saturday night in his moon costume, but did not want to wear it in court as it might be a distraction.

"I wear my costume when selling the certificates, give a show and make a fool of myself, but I make people laugh and that's an honest way to make a living," he said. He said the whole thing was a joke and he told people not to take him seriously. He agreed that the moon suit was ridiculous. The certificates, he said, entitled those who bought them to an acre of lunar surface but he could not provide the transportation to the moon and agree he had no legal rights to sell any part of

years ago as a joke and to get money at Christmas. He said people bought crazy things at Christmas time like lunar certificates to give them to their friends. He said he had sold no certificates in London and when the Justice remarked "I suppose you thought the English were not as gullible as the Irish," McArdle replied. "No, but I did not have my costume or enough certificates".

He had sold everything from encyclopaedias to peanuts. When he sold an acre of lunar surface he gave a specially prepared certificate to the buyer and this entitled him to an acre of the lunar surface. McArdle said that people in Dublin had recognised him from the T.V. show, but he had sold very little. He admitted he had no licence but he was told by people who were selling balloons in Henry Street that he did not need one. He agreed with the Justice that the whole thing was ridiculous.

BIG CROWD

Garda Sylvester Nolan, Store St., said he watched McArdle for some time in Henry St., where a big crowd had gathered around him. He later followed him to O'Connell St. and asked him if he had a street trader's licence. He said

assurance he would not sell certificates in Dublin as he was returning to America on December 3.

Imposing the fine, Justice Good said it was an extraordinary story told by an extraordinary young man. He appeared to be intelligent and educated, but he told him there were more useful

Barry McArdle

Pitchman Barry McArdler offered a crowd at Polk Gulch the stuff that dreams are made of — a piece of the moon — and a young buyer (right) took a whirl

Photo by Terry

Little Bit of Everything at Polk Gulch Fa

CHAPTER 20

JESUS, MARY AND JOSEPH

W E MADE OUR EMBARRASSED APOLOGIES TO KENT AND DIANA. DAVID insisted on paying for the damages, although plain glass would now take the place of the exquisite etched panels. A week later, we left. He was going east to Germany and Katrina. I would go west to Ireland and then home to Paula.

Paula's last letter told of a "hobbit cottage" she had rented in Berkeley, and that she was ready to start our lives together again—if I was finally ready.

I am ready, I told myself as I rode the bus across Dublin, and I resolved to remain celibate until I was with her. This commitment of unassailable loyalty remained unshakable until 45 minutes later, when Breanna Ryan opened her front door. The Ryan's were my father's first cousins and on hearing of my trip had insisted I come for a wee bit of a visit.

"The Saints be praised! If my eyes weren't playing tricks on me, I'd swear it's himself standing on our doorstep. I'm Breanna Ryan. Welcome."

She was enthralling. I was immediately and helplessly attracted to her. Her intelligent looking face, blessed with a flawless complexion, was framed by short copper hair that reflected reddish sparks when it caught the light. Without a trace of makeup, her lips were a sensual coral pink.

She smiled at me through soulful blue eyes. Her heavy Donegal sweater failed to conceal her womanly figure. She exuded an air of confidence, which seemed to add an inch or two to what I guessed to be her 5' 6" stature. I knew her age to be twenty-one.

More than her beauty, I felt myself drawn to her on some unexplainable level. My ancestors and hers had, down through the ages, lived out their lives on this bit of Celtic rock in the North Atlantic Sea. Our bloodlines and genetic history were connected.

"Will you be coming in then, or do I stand here all day with the door opened to the world?"

As I maneuvered my large suitcase through the small doorframe, we brushed chests. I was also treated to the smell of wool from her sweater and the femininity from her neck and hair.

"Da, Gabrielle, Barry McArdle has come to visit," Breanna called down the short hallway of the modest but well-kept house.

Bob Ryan was first to come into the small foyer. He was a slight, fragile-looking man, with thin, graying hair. The lines around his clear blue eyes looked like they had been helped along more from a lifetime of smiling than from his 60-plus years of living. He looked quite dapper, being nattily attired in a bright green wool vest and red tie. I would come to discover that Bob wore a tie every day, even when he had no plans of leaving the house. He greeted me with a warm, beaming smile and firm handshake.

"Ah, is it Barry McArdle, then? Let me take a good look at you. You're a strapping big lad if I may say so. Ah, but you do favor your mother's side of the family a wee bit more. But not all is lost. You do carry the McArdle resemblance, no denying that. Ah, here's Gabrielle, our little actress. Say hello to Barry McArdle, he's come to us all the way from America."

Gabrielle looked older than her 10 years and, like her sister Breanna, walked with a self-confidence not often seen with American girls her age.

"Nice to meet you, Barry McArdle. Have you ever been to Hollywood, then?"

"I'm sure Barry McArdle has been many places and I want to hear all about them as well," said Breanna, "but not here in the draft. I'll put the kettle on. Gabrielle, show Barry to his room, and Da, if you would add some turf to the fire that would be grand."

For the next three hours, we sat in the cozy parlor, and talked about my heritage and the tragic history of Ireland itself.

Gabrielle informed me I should feel special as the tea set we were using was generally reserved for Christmas, New Year's Day, to celebrate First Communions, or if there was a priest come to visit.

That night over dinner, the subject of selling land on the moon came up.

"Go on now. Do you think we're completely daft? Jesus, Mary, and Joseph who in their right mind would buy one?" Breanna asked in disbelief.

"It's hard to describe without seeing the Moon Man. It's more the comedy that people pay for."

"Well then, you'll just have to do your Moon Man show for us so we can judge for ourselves," Breanna said with an air of finality.

"Oh, I can't wait to tell my friends that the Moon Man from America will be putting on a wee bit of a show. This will be something grand," Gabrielle announced with great excitement.

Not to be left out, Bob had his own questions. "So then Barry McArdle, when will the big day be, and where might you be thinking of having this Moon Man of yours perform?"

"I would love to do my show, but without my Moon Acres and costume it really is impossible. You'll just have to come to America and see me there," I said, thinking that would end the discussion.

Wrong. Before dinner was over, Breanna had me call home and ask that certificates be rushed to Dublin. This done, she sketched out three different costume designs, telling me to pick the one I liked best.

"I'll wager you a pint at O'Malley's that I'll have your costume made before the certificates arrive," Breanna challenged.

Looking into her confident, almost fierce eyes, I had no doubt I would lose the wager. I answered, "Make it two pints and you have a bet."

Later that evening, with everyone gone to bed, Breanna and I settled in front of the hearth with yet another cup of my new drug of choice—Irish tea. We sat facing each other in the darkened room, illuminated only by the fire's ambient glow. Since I'd arrived, our conversations had been effortless. Now, suddenly, we found

ourselves in an uneasy silence, due perhaps to the realization that we were attracted to each other.

The costume design we settled on was simple yet elegant. I would wear calf-high rubber boots sprayed metallic silver, trimmed with 2" blue felt ribbon. My pants, a matte gray material, looked appropriately otherworldly. The bottom of these moon-pants would be tucked into my silver boots and held up at the waist with a wide belt covered with shimmering material. A long-sleeved turtleneck sewn from brilliant silver fabric became my tunic. On the front of the shirt, running diagonally from my left shoulder down my torso, was a matching piece of blue felt ribbon. A rhinestone crescent moon and two star pins were attached to the ribbon sash.

The same blue- and gold-flecked fabric used to cover my belt was fashioned for use as my flowing cape. Besides the silver gloves and mirrored sunglasses, there was one other element of my costume that enhanced my appearance. Completing my new moon suit would be a bullet-shaped skullcap. Made from the same silver cloth as my moon shirt, it was accented with two pieces of blue felt that came together in the shape of a "**V**." At the point of the "V," Breanna attached a brilliant 20-point rhinestone star.

"Thank you, Breanna. It's fantastic," I said, seeing my reflection in the full-length mirror.

"Just looking at you, I've half a mind to buy one of those deeds myself, but seeing as how they have yet to arrive, I believe you'll be owing me a couple of pints."

While waiting for my package to arrive, I did some reconnaissance. In the very heart of downtown, on Henry Street, there was a furniture store that was closed for renovation. It had a curved entry area that would allow room for a crowd to gather. And on Saturdays—the day I would be appearing—Henry Street was closed to automobiles. I also discovered I would need a license.

"It's not actually land on the moon I'm selling. The documents are just novelty items—a conversational gift," I explained.

The desk Sergeant continued to stare at me. I tried to clarify.

"The deeds are called Moon Acres, but it's really entertainment I'm selling, a souvenir if you will. They told me at City Hall I could get my license here."

"Lad, selling land on the moon—real or not—sounds like it's a bit out of my jurisdiction. We best wait till the Captain gets back from holiday. He'll know how to proceed."

I pressed on.

"If you won't issue me a license can I at least apply for one?" I asked.

"No harm in that. I'll be needing two pounds then, but until the Captain signs off, it will be doing you no good at all."

I left the station with a receipt showing I had applied for a Dublin Street Trader's license.

✳ ✳ ✳

Breanna was waiting for me when I arrived back at the house.

"You won't believe what I have to tell you. I still can't believe it myself."

There were half a dozen people I'd never seen before, along with Bob, Gabrielle, and for the first time out of her sick room, Breanna's mother, Patricia Ryan.

"Be on with it Breanna. Tell the man the news," Patricia said, breaking into a wide, self-satisfied smile.

"First you should know that my mother's been making calls for the past week to the *Late Late Show*. She told them that if they wanted the Moon Man from America on their program they had better be on with it. Well, not more than two hours ago, the man himself, Mr. Gay Byrne, called. At first I thought it was just Patty O'Shay giving me the Mickey, but when he asked about the Moon Man, and told me he wanted you for tomorrow night's show, well Jesus, Mary, and Joseph, I about fainted on the spot."

I had heard of the *Late Late Show* and its host Gay Byrne. Being in Dublin it was impossible not to. His picture was on busses, taxis and billboards. I had seen television and heard radio commercials promoting the show. It was far and away the number-one-rated television program throughout Ireland. Gay Byrne was to Ireland what Johnny Carson was to America. He went out of his way to be controversial in a society that

175

had grown weary of being conventional. Being on *The Late Late Show* was no Sacramento *Creature Features*. This was the epicenter of prime time Irish television and Moon Man was going to be a guest star. Jesus, Mary, and Joseph!

Breanna continued. "He wanted to know if you were the Moon Man from California. I assured him you were. He then asked if you had your moon suit and certificates with you. I assured him you had everything and that you would call the minute you came in. Here's the number. You are to ask for Claire Hennessy, she's Mr. Byrne's assistant. You get paid something, I don't know how much. Oh, and you get four tickets to the show. Ma says she wants to go, and she plans on wearing her Christmas coat. This is really grand."

I sat down, but was immediately encouraged back to my feet, maneuvered into the kitchen, and handed the phone. Everyone closed in while I made the call.

"*The Late Late Show*, how may I help you?"

"May I speak with Claire Hennessy, please?"

"One moment, please."

"This is Claire, how may I help you?"

"Hello Claire, this is Barry McArdle and I was told to..."

"Is this the Moon Man from America, then?"

"Yes, it is."

"Splendid. Mr. Byrne talked with a, just a minute now, yes here it is, a Breanna Ryan who we understand is the daughter of a Mrs. Patricia Ryan, and that you are currently in residence in her home on St. Margaret's Road in Malahide. Is that right?"

"Yes, that's right."

"What's right?" Breanna wanted to know.

Claire continued. "We also understand that you have agreed to appear on our program tomorrow night in your full Moon Man costume. Is that right?"

"Yes, that's right."

"What's right?" Breanna, Bob, and Patricia all whispered to me at the same time.

"Splendid. We'll need you here by 7 PM. The show starts at 10:00. Right now, we have you penciled in as our third guest. Mr. Byrne will meet with you prior to air and go over the format. As a first time guest, you will receive the standard 48 pounds. We also reserve four audience seats

in your name. It's a good idea to have your guests arrive a little early just to be safe. I think that covers it, unless, of course, you have any questions?"

"Just one if I might? Will I be doing some of my act? I mean will I be able to sell Moon Acres to the audience?"

"That's really a question for Mr. Byrne. Splendid then, I'll see you tomorrow at 7:00. Bye now."

Over tea, I was introduced to the neighbors who wanted their picture taken with the Moon Man. Once in costume, my natural instincts took over and five of the curious became proud, although confused, owners of lunar real estate.

'MOON SALE' MAN BUMPS BACK TO EARTH.

MOONMAN Barry McArdle was brought down to earth with a bump yesterday.

For his "space mission" in Dublin — selling res of the Moon — landed him in court before Justice Hermann Good.

By MALCOLM NICHOLL

Littlejohns 'date set'

APPEALS by the Littlejohn brothers, Kenneth and Keith, against rison sentences for a 67,000 bank robbery in ublin, are likely to be eard in January.

Mrs. Christine Littlejhn, wife of Kenneth, aid yesterday that this ate had been given to er by her husband's licitor in Ireland.

Kenneth was sentenced 20 years and Keith to 5 at their trial in ublin last July.

And Barry, who wears a silver sparkle space suit when "working," got a rocket.

His behaviour was extraordinary, said the judge. He had no licence to sell, and the offence would cost him a £2 fine.

Barry, a 24 - year - old American, describing himself as "a student of life," admitted that Earthmen were far from starry-eyed about his venture.

In fact, there were few takers for his "lunar licences," he told Dublin District Court.

Then, perhaps in mitigation, he added: "I wear my Moon costume when selling the certificates, give a show and make a fool of myself.

"But I make people laugh, and that's an honest way to make a living.

"You have to be a little crazy to sell them, and more crazy to buy them."

Crowd

The certificates entitled the buyer to an acre of lunar surface, but Barry agreed he could not provide transportation — and had no legal rights to sell any part of the Moon.

It was all a joke, said Barry, who is staying in St. Margaret's Ro hide, Co. Dublin.

But the fun en a big crowd round him in Henry Street.

Civic Guard Nolan nabbed B not having trader's licence.

Justice Good sa a most extra story, told by an dinary young m appeared to be i and educated.

"But there a useful ways of living," he told th salesman.

Later, Barry sa sold about 50 Moon land in Ir

In two years at £1 an acre, made about £3,0

COONEY PLANS A NEW DEAL

WIDE-RANGING law reforms are expected o be unveiled tomorrow y Irish Justice Minister Ir. Patrick Cooney.

He will be introducing is Department's estinate in the Dail.

Reforms are expected the controversial adoption laws, which now bar couples of mixed marriages from adopting children.

In family law, special attention will be focussed on a wife's right's in the family home and property. There may also be better deals for deserted wives and for young offenders, with a reorganisation of the children's court.

Mr Cooney is expected to outline prison reforms, especially in the light of recent riots and demonstrations.

WATERWAY GETS GO-A

The first step yesterday tow £2,400,000 imp scheme for Sou shire canals and

Environment Geoffrey Rippon mission for th Waterways Boar duce a Parliame for the scheme.

CHAPTER 21

THE LATE LATE SHOW

THE FOLLOWING EVENING BOB DROVE PATRICIA, BREANNA, GABRIELLE, and me to the Montrose Studio. They picked up their tickets, wished me luck and then went in search of dinner.

Claire—maybe in her early 30's, looked competent. She was short, trim, and conservatively dressed. She walked quickly towards me with one hand extended and the other holding a well-worn clipboard.

Her handshake was firm. "So nice to meet you. Let's get you settled in our Green Room. We have a little paperwork to fill out, and then I'll show you the buffet. Mr. Byrne will be seeing you shortly, after which you should have plenty of time to get into costume, visit makeup, and enjoy a second cup of tea. Have you ever been on live television before?"

"Yes I have," I answered with more confidence than I felt.

"Good. Then I won't worry about you freezing up. You'd be surprised by how some people have trouble remembering their own name the first time they experience it."

Once in the Green Room, I met the other three scheduled guests. One was an Englishman who was running for a seat in the British Parliament. His controversial platform supporting a united Ireland would be enthusiastically received by the studio audience.

The president of W.A.R.S.—Women Against the Round System—would follow him. Her organization preached that the pressure to "buy the next round" had created a generation of Irish alcoholics and had to stop.

After these two heavyweights, I would be brought on for comic relief. Following me—and the guest most of the viewers would be tuning in to see—was Father Callahan. This Dominican priest would dare to suggest that not all types of birth control were necessarily mortal sins. For a vast number of viewers, this deliverance from the eternal fires of hell was reason enough to watch.

Claire returned to escort me into Mr. Byrne's spacious, comfortable office. A short well-built man with sandy-blond hair, and large, happy green eyes got out of his chair to shake my hand.

"Ah, the American Moon Man. Delighted you could make it. Tell me what brings you to Ireland?"

"Excuse me Gay, I'll be back in twenty with Father Callahan," Claire said as she left the room.

"First and foremost I'm Irish, well, half Irish," I answered. "And I've always wanted to see where my father's parents were born."

"And where is that exactly?"

"County Armagh."

"That's up north near Crossmaglen. It's a real hotbed of IRA activities, situated as it is on the border. But we're not here to discuss the troubles."

He took a sip of what looked like tea, "Half Irish?"

"My mother is full blooded Portuguese."

"Oh, you're lucky. Hard working people, the Portuguese. If you were all Irish you might be selling Pluto, or trying to get there. It's the Irish half that has you thinking you can do what you do. And, of course, growing up in America allows one the freedom to believe in dreams. Well that's enough philosophy. Let's talk about our segment. Claire mentioned your idea of selling moon certificates..."

We were both laughing when we heard a soft knock on the door and Claire entered with Father Callahan. I shook hands with Mr. Byrne again, wishing I could have stayed and talked longer.

"Remember, Barry, have fun. If you're having a good time, so will the audience," Mr. Byrne advised as I left.

The show seemed to be going well. More than once I caught a glimpse of the Ryans, when the director cut away for an audience reaction shot. Seeing people I knew on a nationally televised broadcast, in Ireland, while I nervously watched backstage in a moon costume, waiting to go on that same program, had me thinking how unpredictable and wonderful life can be.

It was a matter of minutes. My body was moist but my mouth was bone dry. Was I panicking? I heard the introductory words, "Direct from America..."

The President of W.A.R.S. walked past me. She whispered cheerfully, "Good luck." It was as if I was looking through the wrong end of a telescope. How far was my mark? Oh shit, I can't remember my own name.

"Claire, is there any..."

She handed me a glass of water before I could finish my sentence.

"...And so in keeping with the Late Late Show's tradition of presenting the most unusual personalities we can find, here is the one, the only...Moooooooon Man!"

"Have fun," I heard Claire say as she pushed me forward past the edge of the curtain and into the blinding bank of lights, blaring music, and the encouraging sound of applause.

My cape fluttered behind me and I could see the light refract off my silver tunic and rhinestone pendants. Seeing my cape catch the air as I looked through my mirrored glasses suddenly had me transported back in time to the day I attempted to walk across the "Bar of Death." I felt some comfort knowing Big Eddie Fergus was not in the audience.

Have fun, I reminded myself as I stopped on the barely visible chalk mark on the floor. My legs felt like Jell-O. I smiled, and remembered to wave in the direction of Mr. Byrne. I was only a few feet away from the front row of people and staring into the big glass eye of one of the cameras. The little red light on top of the camera was glowing brightly. After the clapping had passed its high point and before the music faded completely, I launched into my recently rehearsed monologue.

I Sold *the* Moon!

"Thank you, ladies and gentlemen. Thank you very much. My name is Barry McArdle but across America I'm known as the Moon Man." (A bit of an exaggeration, but, hey, this was show business.) "As my family name indicates, I'm Irish."

At the announcement of my heritage, there erupted spontaneous applause, enveloping me like a soft warm blanket.

"I also am the first person in recorded history to lay claim to the lunar surface and then sell that property by the acre. Ladies and gentlemen, I know what I'm saying must sound ridiculous and I'm not surprised when people call me...well, they call me a lunatic."

I heard a fair amount of easy laughter. This was a good sign. "All over America people ask me the same question, 'What gives you the right to sell the moon?' And my answer is always the same. The only right I have to sell the moon comes from the fact that I was the first to claim it. But please understand, those of you who decide to purchase an acre of the moon from me tonight must do so with the knowledge that you are taking somewhat of a chance, somewhat of a gamble. My legal claim to the moon has not been, shall we say, completely authenticated. I ask you, do I look like someone you could have legal confidence in?"

The audience was laughing again.

"Mr. Byrne told me I would have no more than three minutes in which to persuade you to buy one of my lunar certificates. As you might imagine, it usually requires more like three or four months of brainwashing, I mean discussion, before someone sees the light."

More laughter. I was having fun and so were they.

Dramatically, I pulled out a moon certificate, and holding it with both my hands, I extended my arms fully, talking as I slowly rotated the Moon Acre for all to see.

"My question, simply put, is how many times in your entire life have you been offered a chance to buy land on the moon? The very fact that this may be the first time, and quite possibly the last, acquiring an acre should, at the very least, be considered. And remember if you don't want one for yourself, you might just know the perfect person to give it to."

The audience had grown quiet. They were thinking. I was too. This may have been a situation where I should have broken my self-imposed rule to never plant a shill. But I knew that if just one person

would break the ice, others would follow. I desperately wanted that first person to be anyone other than Mr. Byrne. Knowing my time was running out, I skipped ahead to the end of my prepared remarks.

"Ladies and gentlemen, in the days, weeks, and years to come when in conversation it is discovered that you were here on this night, that you were among the first people in all of Europe to see the Moon Man and that you were offered a chance to buy this one-of-a-kind collectible, what will you tell your family and friends? At the cost of only one pound an acre I think you might agree that the story you tell of this evening would be made all the more interesting, all the more believable, if at the end you produce one of these moon certificates—with your signature on this line, as the legal owner."

I paused for dramatic effect, and then bellowed. "Moon Acres are now on sale—one pound one acre. Who would like to be the first person to own land on the moon?"

What happened next was as unexpected as it was wonderful. No sooner had I finished asking my last question when, to my amazement and delight, I heard five or six people from all different parts of the audience shout out their intent to buy.

"That would be me."

"I'll be buying one."

"I'll take one, God knows I can't afford property down here."

"My kids are watching. They'd lock me out if I didn't get one."

"One here, please."

A circle of people were gathering in front of the stage, all with pound notes waving in their hands. One of the first to buy was my radiant-looking costume designer—Breanna. I smiled broadly as I accepted her money and was instantly aroused when she squeezed my hand as she accepted her certificate.

Not one to be left out, Mr. Byrne left his chair and joined me. When he ceremoniously handed over his pound note, the audience broke into applause. His purchase had a positive effect because once again, the circle of buyers was growing rather than shrinking. The land rush was on, and I was having no trouble whatsoever having fun.

When I finally sat down, the floor manager was holding up a "4 minutes" time card.

"Let me start by asking you where this idea to sell the moon came from?"

"Well, Mr. Byrne, the seed was really planted when I was about seventeen years old and saw Neil Armstrong walk on the moon. That got me thinking about the whole issue of who owns the moon and would it ever be sold."

"And in your opinion, who does own the moon?"

"You mean besides you and all the other folks who bought Moon Acres here tonight?"

The audience started clapping and cheering, some waved their certificates in the air.

I continued. "The truth is the legal ownership of the moon and for that matter the planets, in my opinion, is open for discussion. If any government or nation were to claim sovereignty, there would be more than a little disagreement from other countries—and rightly so. But just because no nation or individual has every done so does that automatically invalidate my claim?"

A chorus of "No," "Never," was heard from the audience.

"So if I understand, nobody has recognized your claim, and further, you are under no illusion that your claim will ever be certified."

"That's right, but I would add that if my claim could be, as you say, certified, that would imply that the group or nation doing the certification had such authority begin with, and that, as we have discussed, is not the case."

"I'm starting to see how we could continue this discussion forever and end up where we started. Let me change direction. What kind of person do you think is most inclined to buy one of your Moon Acres?"

"Besides intelligent talk show hosts, it would be accurate to say that all types of people, in all age brackets, from all different backgrounds have purchased my certificates. But if I had to guess what personality traits would be most common in my customers, a couple obvious ones jump to mind. First and foremost, they have a highly developed sense of humor. They have the ability to think in the abstract and can appreciate the intangible value inherent in the document. I also think they have a strong streak of individuality, and when they recognize that in someone else they are inclined to support and encourage that effort. Then again, many of the buyers may just be looking for a good investment or a parcel of land on which to build their retirement home."

This got a laugh from Mr. Byrne and the audience as well.

"Now I understand you are staying with relatives in Malahide. How are they handling having a Moon Man in the house?"

"My cousins have been terrific. In fact, they are in the audience tonight."

I pointed out to where the four of them sat, now suddenly looking very self-conscious.

"Would the Ryans please stand up?" Mr. Byrne asked.

With the audience breaking into applause, my four hosts stood and shyly waved to the crowd before quickly settling back into their seats.

"Mr. Moon Man, I wish we had more time because what you're doing is fascinating and just a lot of fun. The world can always use more laughter. Thank you for coming on tonight and I wish you much success. Ladies and gentlemen...the Moon Man."

"Mr. Byrne if I might just have 30 seconds more I would like to make a closing statement."

A look of mild concern crossed his face, but he knew, as I did, it would be more awkward not to let me have my moment.

"We are running behind, but if you're brief—please proceed."

Two recent news stories were fresh in everyone's mind and were the inspiration for the remarks I was about to make. The first had taken place a few weeks earlier on October 20th. Richard Nixon had ordered the firing of Archibald Cox, the Watergate Special Prosecutor. The obvious reason being that Mr. Cox was actually doing the job he had been appointed to do. Rather that carry out this unethical order from the President, Elliot Richardson, the Attorney General of the United States resigned. When the Deputy Attorney General, William Ruckelshaus also refused to comply, he was summarily fired. Nixon then turned to Robert Bork, the then acting Attorney General, who did fire Mr. Cox. This series of events had come to be known as "The Saturday Night Massacre."

The second event had happened less than a week earlier. Three high-ranking IRA prisoners, or patriots, as they were called in the Irish Republic, had escaped from the Maze, a maximum-security prison located 10 miles outside of Belfast. It was not just the escape that captured the attention of the country, but the manner in which the escape was executed. The IRA had copied to perfection

a *Mission Impossible* TV episode that had aired a month prior. The escape combined courage, surprise, luck, and most of all daring. In broad daylight, a helicopter, with the proper British insignia, landed in the prison's main exercise yard. Two "British Officers" got out and at gunpoint "ordered" the three IRA prisoners into the chopper. What really appealed to the Irish sense of humor was the photograph that kept appearing in the papers and on the nightly news. It showed two English prison guards standing at attention and saluting just as the helicopter was lifting off.

I took a few steps toward the audience. It had gotten very quiet.

"Reading the papers lately I've noticed that America and Ireland, have some differences. One difference is evident when it comes to housing political prisoners."

I heard an unmistakable low murmur run through the audience.

"I'm happy to see that in Ireland not all your political prisoners are able to be kept behind bars."

There was an immediate eruption of cheers and applause. I waited to let the noise die down and then continued.

"In America we have a different system. In America, it seems, we keep our political prisoners...in office."

In a country where many keep a framed picture of President John Kennedy next to one of the Pope and Christ on the cross, this incrimination of Nixon, coming as it did from an American, an Irish American, touched a nerve. The entire audience was on their feet cheering wildly, and applauding.

I floated off the stage, out of the lights, and out of the tens of thousands of TV sets tuned into the program. It would be years later when I first heard the expression "peak experience." I didn't know it then, but as I walked off that stage, to the sound of that ovation, I was having one of my life's peak experiences.

CHAPTER 22

MOON MAN FACES DUBLIN SNAG

FULLY SUBMERGED IN THE RYANS LARGE CERAMIC TUB, I MELTED INTO the hot sudsy water with the echo of applause still ringing in my ears. The rush of being on live television was a powerful aphrodisiac.

It was a joyous ride back from the studio. Gabrielle and I had a grand time counting aloud every pound note. I had sold 139 moon acres, and when added to my appearance stipend of 48 pounds, my 15 minutes "on the air" had netted me 187 pounds. Doing a rough conversion that would be somewhere in the neighborhood of $430.00. Wow! Maybe I should just move to Ireland? After all, I am half-Irish. I love the beer, the potatoes and the tea...and the women...I came up for air.

Later, Breanna and I settled in close to the peat-burning hearth.

"Before you leave, you really should see more of the country. Is there anywhere particular you wanted to go?" Breanna asked in a soft voice.

"Yes, I'd really love to go to the West Coast, maybe Galway Bay?"

"It's truly beautiful there, no denying that."

Without taking her eyes off the fire, she continued.

"I could take a Monday or Friday off and we could rent a car. A three-day weekend would be enough time to see a good bit of the area. That is if you don't mind the company?"

"Mind? That would be fantastic. I'm ready whenever you say. And after tonight I'm happy to pay for the car and the room, I mean rooms."

A few small embers were still dimly glowing in the hearth.

"It's been a grand evening. One to remember, that's for sure. But now it's a wee bit past my bedtime, so I best be saying my good night to you," Breanna said as she rose from her chair.

As she passed in front of me, I could not help but notice her robe had parted. Underneath, she wore a floor length linen nightgown. Seeing the outline of her body through the gossamer gown had a heart-jolting effect on me. Without thinking, I reached out and grabbed her hand. Standing to face her, I closed the distance between us.

With the fire almost out there was a chill in the room, but not where I was standing. I took her other hand in mine as well. Would she take that half step separating us if I encouraged her gently forward? I looked directly into her eyes.

"Breanna, thank you for all you've done. I wish I'd come here sooner. I wish I had more time here. I just hope you know I appreciate everything."

Her hands had gone from warm to hot, or were they mine? It was taking all my willpower not to lower my eyes and fully admire the translucency of Irish linen. I wanted to kiss her. I wanted....

Someone had just opened the refrigerator and was moving about in the kitchen.

"It's Da, he has trouble sleeping."

Noticing her robe, she dropped my hands, and pulled it tightly around her.

"Goodnight now, Barry McArdle," she whispered, turned and was gone.

The hearth was dark. I could feel the full chill of the room now, and the tea had long since gone cold.

I felt a bit like Clark Kent, even though I had changed in a department store bathroom and not a phone booth. As I took one last look in the mirror, I had to admit this new moon suit was sparklingly dramatic. The moment I walked out of the bathroom and into the crowd of bustling Dublin shoppers I felt alive, transformed, and energized.

Knowing where I was headed gave me confidence. I crossed the street to my "office" under the awning of the closed furniture store. Much to my surprise, I had been followed by a sizable group of people who now stood staring at me as I stepped up onto the star-covered crate I had brought with me. People were starting to converge from all sides, others simply stopped where they were as they saw the growing crowd or noticed the alien-looking creature at the center of all the attention. Before saying a word, a crowd had gathered. My long cape filled the space behind me as it fluttered on intermittent gusts of wind. In my announcer's voice, I began.

"Ladies and gentlemen it is a great pleasure to be here today…"

"Kevin, look. As sure as I'm standing here, it's that moon guy from the *Late Late Show*," someone across the street shouted to his companion, as they both now came running towards me.

"I know I must look strange, but please don't hold that against me. What does look really strange to me is in Belfast there are uniformed, gun-toting British soldiers on Irish soil."

The crowd suddenly erupted into boisterous cheering and shouting, making them sound less like a crowd and more like a mob. I felt strongly about what I had said but had not expected such a visceral, intense reaction. I'm a showman, not a politician I reminded myself.

"My name is Barry McArdle, my Grandparents were born in County Armagh, and now I live in California. In the United States I'm known as…the Moon Man."

The crowd had doubled in size in less than two minutes. People were being forced to stand in the street.

"Some of you may have seen me on the *Late Late Show* last week."

Immediately, there was general applause and one person yelled out, "I'll be buying myself a piece of the moon."

"Well, Sir, you've come to the right place. I only hope you're not the only one."

It was encouraging to hear a few people laugh.

"For those of you who did not see the program, you must be wondering what exactly is going on and what did the gentleman mean when he said he wanted a piece of the moon? The story is really simple although hard to believe. A little over a year ago I made

my claim on the moon and I've been selling it ever since. But please understand and be forewarned. The American government has not, I repeat has not, certified my claim."

The audience had been listening intently and now broke out in genuine laughter.

"Because of my shaky legal status I can not guarantee water rights. I can not guarantee mineral rights, I can not even guarantee…air."

I heard more laughter from the crowd.

"And I may as well get it into the open now, I do not provide transportation—that is something you will need to arrange on your own."

I heard more laughter. Even though I hadn't been performing my Moon Man routine much—save my recent appearance on Irish television —my timing was good and I was having no trouble deciding what I wanted to say next. Maybe selling the moon was like riding a bike.

My one concern was that the crowd was getting too big. Before it got out of hand, it might be a good idea to sell as many acres as I could now —even knowing I was most likely going to lose some business by not providing enough "softening up" of the audience. But I had forgotten about the power of television.

Someone shouted from the audience. "You don't provide much of anything then, do you?"

"This gentleman," I pointed at the person who had called out, "suggests that I don't provide much of anything. And he most certainly is right if he is referring to the legality or the amenities of what I offer. However, in my own defense, I believe in offering these documents (I slowly and dramatically pulled a Moon Acre from my silver lined satchel), I provide originality, creativity and, on occasion, humor.

I raised the volume of my voice. "And so I ask you. Who is willing to take a chance on lunacy? Is what I'm doing ridiculous? Of course it is. And yet therein lies the value. In years to come, as you admire this moon certificate framed and on your wall, do any of you really believe that you would regret having made the decision to buy one today? The conversational value alone is worth one pound."

I could feel a restlessness start to spread through the crowd. I knew there were buyers out there. All I had to do was give them a little more cover and I could ask for the sale. Casting my net wider still, I continued.

"Remember, Christmas is almost here. If you can find a more original gift at the price of one pound, or at any price for that matter, I suggest you buy it. If not for yourself, then consider giving a Moon Acre to that hard to shop for person on your list. And I think it's safe to say that the person you give it to...won't already have one. One pound, one acre! Land on the moon! Who wants to beat the rush? Who wants to own land on the moon?"

"I know just the person, a bit daft," said a man standing directly in front of me.

I knew this was a critical juncture in the process. Just like the Veg-a-Matic pitchman at the State Fair, once his presentation was over, his job switched from selling to trying to accommodate all those people who had made up their mind to buy before they had a chance to change their mind again. My experience had also taught me that having a lot of people buy helped "pull through" other people who were still undecided. In short, sales created sales.

As I had done before, I thanked every person who was stepping forward in a voice directed to the back of the crowd. The pound notes in my hand were starting to add up and, remembering my street fair experience, I held them high over my head so people in the back would know that others were buying. The objective was to keep the excitement and activity alive as long as possible. With that in mind, I would yell out answers to imaginary questions.

"Yes, I will be happy to autograph the moon certificate. The question is can you read the document before you buy? Yes, of course, but skip the fine print. What's that? Yes, I have change for a 20-pound note. Is Moon River really filled with Guinness? Yes, that's absolutely true—another reason to own a piece of the moon."

Twenty minutes later, sales had slowed to a trickle. It was time for another presentation. How many acres had I sold? My best guess was more than fifty and somewhere south of eighty. But that was in pounds I reminded myself.

Holding a Moon Acre high over my head, I started again.

"What or who gives me the right to sell the moon? A good question, and one I get asked a lot. Well, my friends..."

I felt it before I saw it. Someone had thrown a tomato and it had hit me on the shoulder splattering against my new silver tunic—the red juice now running down my chest and arm. Scanning the crowd,

I Sold *the* Moon!

I saw the second tomato just as it was thrown, and reacted in time to have it fly by, missing me completely. The culprits turned out to be two street urchins. The boys could not have been more than 10 years old, and now, out of ammo, they ran across the street and disappeared around a corner. I wiped myself off as best I could, and turned back to face my audience.

"Ladies and gentlemen, it's not true that the kids who threw the tomatoes have been to the property I'm selling and found it to be all bog land. I repeat that is simply not true. It's not all bog land, just... mostly bog land."

The audience was once more smiling and laughing. I was relieved to find my voice sounded steady and confident, although I felt neither. It was the first time Moon Man had suffered any abuse other than verbal. I felt vulnerable. If I could be hit with an overripe piece of fruit by a couple of pre-adolescent boys, what else could happen? I had never thought of myself as a target before. A rush of sadness washed over me—from now on, part of my awareness would need to be concerned with my safety. The feeling of innocence while performing in front of a crowd was lost forever.

Although still shaken, I muddled through a shortened, uninspired presentation, and not surprisingly made only a few more sales. Before beginning my third moon show for the day and while there were still a group of people milling around asking questions and studying the certificate, I saw a policeman walking straight towards me.

"I'd be needing a word with you, sir," he said in a pleasant voice.

"Yes, of course, Officer, how can I help you?"

"I've been observing you for some time now and I can't say you're doing much harm. But you are engaged in a form of commerce that would require a street vendor's permit. Now if you can produce that license I'll be on my way and sorry to have bothered you."

Producing my receipt only stalled the inevitable. Garda Sylvester Nolan, on the way to the station, explained that having applied for a license was not the same as having the license. After two hours of paperwork, I was free to go.

"Sorry for the delay in processing, but as it's the weekend it's to be expected," Officer Nolan said in his kind voice.

I thought I would be paying a fine and that would be the end of it—not so. My court case was set for the following Tuesday, in three

days time. I would need to appear in person, as I was now officially charged with two violations. The first: Selling the moon without a license. And the second: Blocking a thoroughfare. The good news was they didn't take any of my money, but they did confiscate five Moon Acres as "evidence."

✳ ✶ ✳

It was embarrassing telling my story to the Ryans that night at dinner. Everything had been going so well nobody wanted my visit to end on a bad note. And getting myself arrested seemed like a pretty good way to do just that. I tried to reassure them that it wasn't all that bad—and it really wasn't. I had made almost $200.00 in less than two hours, and after a proper cleaning, the red stain left from the tomato was nearly invisible.

Maybe I should have been concerned about my pending court case, but I wasn't. I didn't feel like a criminal. In fact, the more I thought about it the more I realized I was actually looking forward to my day in court.

"National television one day and prison the next. As sure as I'm sitting here, it's never dull having a Moon Man come to visit," Bob Ryan proclaimed shaking his head as he loosened his tie.

The next morning, half asleep, I could hear commotion and muffled conversation outside my bedroom door.

"I'm going to wake him up. He'll be wanting to see this." Breanna's voice sounded excited.

"Let the man sleep. He'll be seeing it soon enough, now." I could hear Bob's reply.

Then Gabrielle added her opinion. "Da, don't be daft. Barry would want us to show him this now. I'm going to knock."

Before her threat was completed, I threw open the door.

"What would I want you to show me?" I said with a laugh.

Breanna, holding *The Sunday Press* (November 25, 1973) newspaper, turned it around. There in the center of the front page, under the headline: "**MOONSELLER**" was a very large picture of the Moon Man. I was caught smiling and holding up a certificate. The entire article with picture was 11 inches long and four inches wide. It seemed to take up the entire front page. Under my picture in smaller font the caption read:

"30 buy plots at one pound an acre." The article included mention of my appearance on the *Late Late Show*, an interview with one of the happy buyers, and a few quotations from my street performance. I especially liked the following:

"Our legal advisers are battling our case before the American courts. We are claiming that we have a right to sell land on the moon."

The reporter had obviously left before my arrest, because there was no mention of that development, and I had sold many more that 30 acres. After breakfast, I went out and bought 25 copies of the paper, sending the front page to Paula, David, now in Germany, the Sfarnas' and my family. It was hard to believe that I had been in Ireland less than three weeks and had appeared on their number-one-rated television show, had my picture on the front page of the Sunday paper, and now was going to court to plead my case. Either there was nothing of an unusual nature going on and the Irish were starved for entertainment, or my moon shtick was something fairly unique and warranted all this attention. Naturally, I chose to believe the latter.

That Tuesday, as I arrived at the courthouse, I was surprised to see a number of onlookers in the gallery section. More surprising was that most of them were in possession of very expensive looking cameras. I had decided against wearing my moon costume into court, opting instead for my nice dress pants, pressed white shirt, and conservative tie—on loan from the Bob Ryan collection.

My case was held in the Dublin District Court with Justice Herman Good presiding. After a number of petty theft and disorderly conduct cases were adjudicated, my name and case was called. As I made my way to the front of room, I noticed those with the nice cameras were taking out pad and paper. It was then it registered with me that the press was in attendance. After being sworn in, I was directed to the witness chair. The judge was to my left, and a few feet above me.

"Mr. McArdle, you are from America, is that right?"

"Yes, your honor."

"And you're staying with relatives in Malahide?"

"Yes, your honor."

"Would you explain to the court how you came to be selling what you refer to as 'Moon Acres' on Henry Street Saturday last?"

"Your honor, it really all started because I didn't want to go on welfare, or as you call it here, the dole. I wanted a job where I could make people laugh and make some money doing it. The whole idea of selling the moon really started out as a joke. I don't claim to have clear ownership of the moon, but I do contend there is some confusion as to who does. I also make a point in my presentation to remind the audience that I don't guarantee transportation to the property."

The courtroom broke out in muffled laughter.

"Quiet, please," Justice Good, rather gently, told the spectators. "Continue, Mr. McArdle."

I could tell or at least thought I could tell that the Judge was enjoying himself. The expression he had been wearing all morning, a mixture of seriousness and boredom, had morphed into one of animated bemusement. Far from being hostile towards me, he seemed genuinely interested in my story. It was hard to tell his age. My best guess put him at about 65, and I had to believe this was the first time anybody had been brought before him for selling the moon—with or without a license.

"I admit you have to be a little crazy to sell moon property and a little crazy to buy it. I'm really a student of life. And I think most of the people that buy one are supporting the creativity and uniqueness of what I do. I wear a moon costume but I think it's an honest way to make a living."

"Why are you not wearing your moon costume now?"

"I thought it might be a distraction, your honor."

"Did you come direct from America to Ireland with the express intention of conducting your business?"

"No, your honor. I've been traveling in England, France, and Greece. I arrived here from England. This is my last..."

"And did you sell your moon certificates in England?"

"No, your honor. I..."

"I suppose you thought the English were not as gullible as the Irish?"

A soft ripple of laughter moved through the courtroom.

"No, it wasn't that. I didn't have my moon suit with me and I only had a few certificates."

"What do you have to say in regards to the charges brought against you today? The first of which is that your activities resulted

in blocking a thoroughfare. According to Garda Sylvester Nolan's report, Henry Street was blocked by pedestrians standing in the road as they listened to your, to your…" he studied the report, "…'moon show.' Is that true?"

"Yes, your honor, that is true. The crowd got rather large and extended out into the street."

"That offense does carry a fine. But for the moment let's proceed to the second charge. You…"

"Your honor, if I might, I would like to make the court aware that I chose Henry Street to perform for the very reason that the street is closed to automobiles on Saturdays. The road, in essence, became an extension of the sidewalk. I don't see how I was blocking something that was, at the time, not really a thoroughfare at all."

The courtroom became very quiet as the judge sat staring at me. I got the impression he was having trouble suppressing a smile. With a small nod of his head, he began speaking.

"You are entirely correct, not only in your assertion that the road would have been closed to traffic at the time of the citation, but as to your conclusion as well. I am dismissing this charge."

"Thank you, your honor."

"Now as to the second offense—selling the moon without a license—do you have anything to say on your behalf?"

"It's true I did not have a license. I did, however, apply for one over a week ago and paid an application fee. I have that receipt with me."

The court bailiff handed the receipt to the judge, who studied the document.

"Ladies and gentlemen, here is a lad who tried to do the right thing. He made the effort to get his permit and for that I commend you, but why did you fail to get the license itself?"

"Your honor, the Sergeant at the desk said that issuing me a license to sell the moon was…out of his jurisdiction and that…"

The court erupted in laughter. Even the judge allowed himself a small chuckle.

"Order, please," the justice said, rapping his gavel three times in quick succession.

"And that…what Mr. McArdle?"

"And that I would need to wait until Captain O'Riley got back from vacation to approve my application."

"Yes, I believe the Captain is on a two week holiday. Fishing in Scotland, if I'm not mistaken. But you chose to ignore the Sergeant's instructions and took to the streets, selling your certificates, without a proper license? Is that true?"

"Yes, your honor that's true."

"You have a remarkable story and I believe you are a remarkable young man, who appears to be intelligent and educated. I must tell you, however, there are more useful ways to make a living. I am going to fine you three pounds for street trading without a license, but I will waive that fine if you promise the court one thing."

"Yes, your honor?"

"You need to promise that you will go back to England and sell as many of your moon certificates as you possibly can."

Everyone was laughing as the judge pounded his gavel once and announced that court stood in recess until 2 PM.

Outside on the courthouse steps, members of the Dublin press awaited me. I answered questions for about an hour and "gave away" 14 Moon Acres. The people I "gave" them to, in turn "loaned" me a pound note. Having been treated so fairly in court, I felt more than a twinge of guilt pocketing the money so soon after my case concluded, let alone doing so on the courthouse steps.

$$* \quad * \quad *$$

That night at dinner, a neighbor came calling, holding out her copy of *The Irish Press* newspaper evening edition.

"Bob, that American moon fellow you have staying with you is on the front page of my paper, and my son wants to purchase one of those moon things he's been selling."

They had run the same picture that had accompanied the Sunday story, only this time they cropped it tighter and added my name under the photo. The headline read:

Had no license to sell acres of the moon!

The story started: "A 24-year-old American who said he was a 'student of life' was charged in Dublin District Court today with selling 'lunar certificates' without a street trader's license..."

This was very exciting. I was in court less than 7 hours ago and now I'm reading almost the full transcript of the proceedings.

The article itself was long, taking up almost a third of the page. I especially liked the subheading placed mid-way through the article:

HUGE CROWD.

The next morning there was no debating outside my bedroom door. Breanna knocked once and then burst into the room with her father, mother, and sister following.

"Jesus, Mary and Joseph, you're on the front page again," she said and tossed the *Dublin Times* morning edition on the bed. The headline was all in caps, it shouted:

MOON SALESMAN FACES DUBLIN SNAG

This article began: "Unlike several of his fellow Americans, Barry McArdle has never been to the moon. But his fascination for things lunar landed him in trouble..."

Forgoing my morning tea and toast, I ran to the closest newsstand. As I approached, I could hear the young paperboy shouting out the headline to passing pedestrians, as he waved a copy of the newspaper over his head.

"Paper, get your paper here...moon salesman faces Dublin snag...paper here...read all about it...moon salesman faces Dublin snag...get your paper..."

I was stunned, elated, and mesmerized all at the same time. I bought 15 copies and then sat on a nearby bench just to hear the boy hawking his papers. It was the first and (so far) the only time in my life a story about me was being used to sell newsspapers! I was the moon salesman. I was the one facing the Dublin snag. I sat there until mid-morning and would have stayed longer had he not run out of his supply.

I would end up having two additional stories written about me. One of the papers—reminiscent of our supermarket tabloids—ran this headline:

'MOON SALE' MAN BUMPS BACK TO EARTH.

The article started: "MOONMAN Barry McArdle was brought down to earth with a bump yesterday. For his 'space mission' in Dublin...landed him in court..."

The final bit of press appeared two days later and once again in the largest circulated Dublin paper—*The Irish Press*. It was a follow-up article that ran with the caption:

"Barry the moon seller is back in business..." The story was in answer to a question asked of me on the courthouse steps regarding "future plans." I had jokingly mentioned my intention to start up a mail order business now that I was barred from any further selling on the streets of Dublin.

The article opened: "SUPER salesman Barry McArdle, fined 3 pounds last week for selling chunks of the moon, is planning his comeback. And this time, he claims he will be immune from prosecution..."

In my wildest dreams, I had never imagined I could generate so much press so quickly. Once again, I sent my family, Paula and David my clippings. With so few certificates left and not wanting to risk being arrested again, I was ready to go to Galway Bay.

Driving through the Irish countryside was like looking into a kaleidoscope that contained bits of emeralds—moss covered rocks, lush green grass, mist, fog and surprising sunshine. The fact that it was currently raining did nothing to dampen my excitement, or Breanna's. We were laughing easily, happy just to be in each other's company.

The fact that I was leaving for America the day after we were due to return added the only bittersweet element to our euphoria.

After lunch in the village of Moate, where the pub's Guinness tasted especially appropriate, and the sweet smelling turf fire held its own in keeping the chill out of the room, we made our way to the Lough Ree district, just north of Athlone. Breanna, who was driving, turned off the already narrow main road onto a much smaller country lane.

"I have something you might like to see," she said.

We were gaining altitude as we wound our way up the side of a cone-shaped hill. When we got to the top, I could see a lake glistening in the distance—in the foreground stood the ruins of a castle.

"This place was sacred to the early Druids. More than a thousand years ago great fires were built up here in celebration of the summer equinox. Later, three or four hundred years ago, there were people living up here. It lies in ruins now, thanks to the English. I know it's raining, but do you want to brave a closer look?"

I did.

The wind was blowing in strong sustained gusts. The rain was not so much falling as it was being blown sideways. Running past the

remnants of the outer wall, we came into what she believed had been the courtyard. Taking Breanna's hand, I led her to a corner of the inner perimeter where there was a large section of the wall still standing. It was a vantage point that allowed an unobstructed view of the lake below, and provided us some shelter.

Standing with my back snuggly fitted into the corner of what remained of the towering walls of the castle, I pulled Breanna back against me so we were both facing the same spectacular view.

I wrapped my arms around her waist and gently brought her tight against me. For some minutes, we were content to enjoy the blusterous weather and panoramic view from the relative comfort of our protected position. With both of us still facing forward, I lowered my head until my right cheek was flush against her left one. Lightening was flashing on the other side of the valley, and the wind and rain were increasing it their intensity.

"My God, it's beautiful," I said softly into her ear.

"'Tis," she answered.

It was easy for me to turn my face and nibble at the short hairs on the back of her neck. She slowly turned her head. We kissed softly for just a moment and then with a desire that neither of us were inclined to stop. My hands found their way to the warm skin of her stomach. I felt the gravitational pull inviting them lower. Her chest heaved as she let all her weight fall backward into me. My left hand moved instinctively up her warm torso under the protection of her jacket, sweater, blouse, camisole, and bra. Cupping my hand around the full mound of heavy cream I let my fingers seek out the summit. A soft moan escaped her throat as she sucked in her stomach initiating the freefall of my right hand under the elastic band of her panties. It was now my turn to moan.

Much closer this time, lighting tore across the sky, and seconds later we heard our first thunderclap. Are we to be carried away on the howling wind and lashing rain? Would the last of my resolve evaporate as quickly as the lightening flashes and the reverberation of thunder rolling over the Irish moor?

CHAPTER 23

NEW MOON

I FELT A HAND ON MY SHOULDER.

"Sorry to wake you, but you'll need to buckle your seatbelt. We're starting our descent into San Francisco."

Paula. My first conscious thought. She would be waiting.

I had spent three nights with Breanna. We had slept in the same bed. And remarkably, I had, we had, somehow resisted temptation—not all temptation but the one that mattered most. Maybe this time Paula and I will last. Maybe I *have* become more of a man.

As I retrieved my carry-on items from the overhead bin, I realized the notion of where I considered home to be had changed. Home, for me, no longer meant the house where my mother, father and four younger sisters still lived. I may have come back to America, to California, but I had come home to Paula.

I stopped in the men's room and did what I could to avoid looking and feeling like I had spent the night in a Laundromat. After washing up, I put on a clean "peasant shirt" I had bought in Greece. It didn't make any sense to go halfway around the world and come back looking like you had just made a quick run to the local 7-11 for Cheetos and a Slurpee.

I Sold *the* Moon!

By the time I had cleared Customs it was almost midnight. In seven minutes, it would be a new day. I knew Paula was waiting on the other side of the opaque double doors. As much as I wanted to run out and take her in my arms, I decided to wait and let my old life—the person I used to be—fade away with the last few minutes of December 3rd, 1973. After such a long separation, seeing Paula at the dawn of a new day rather than in the closing minutes of this one somehow felt like the right thing to do.

At five seconds past midnight, I pushed through the double doors and walked into the main terminal. I saw her instantly. In her hand was a bouquet of wildflowers, tied together with a light blue ribbon. She wore a blue-black 1940's crepe dress with padded shoulders and tulip sleeves. It was form fitting at the bust and waist, the length allowing just her delicate ankles and a bit of her lower calf to be seen. Her hair had grown out, and she had curled it—perhaps remembering I liked it best that way. Her green eyes were welcoming.

We threw our arms around each other and I melted into the familiar contours of her voluptuous body. I felt Paula's right hand slide down my left arm stopping at my wrist. She found what she was looking for. Her index finger hooked under the well-worn bands of leather. Lifting her head off my shoulder, she looked into my eyes.

"I'm happy you're still wearing these."

"It never occurred to me to take them off."

I leaned in to kiss her.

"Don't you think we should talk first before we start, I mean...?"

I interrupted her.

"No, I don't."

I put my hands into her curls. Our lips tenderly, questioningly, met. The room fell away. I vaguely remember the flowers brushing the back of my head. I have never been one to kiss in public without part of my awareness attuned to the surroundings and the uneasy feeling that people might be watching. This time, at least temporarily, nothing and no one existed outside of our embrace.

The quaint cottage we would be living in was every bit as charming as she had described in her letters. Once we had a fire going in the hearth, and a dozen or more candles lit, it felt as cozy as it looked. It felt like home.

Paula had homemade soup, scones and cookies waiting for me. After eating, we poured tea, and settled in for a long, honest discussion.

Kissing was one thing, making love was another. She wanted to know everything. And over the next few hours, I obliged. I especially wanted her to know about Breanna and the fact that we had stayed platonic.

Paula was poking at the fire sending new heat, and the golden light that carried it, spreading across the room. She turned and faced me. The light from the fire told me her floor length silk nightgown covered her otherwise naked body. With her ringlet curls now framing her face, she reminded me of a grown up Shirley Temple. I had to resist the temptation to fall on my knees in front of her, lift her nightgown over my head, hold the back of her thighs tightly in my hands and lose myself in her taste.

"Barry?" Paula was drawing me back to the moment. "You asked if we're back together again? No, certainly not in the way we were before you left. You're different and so am I. It's true what they say about not being able to step into the same river twice. So, yes, we are together, but, no, we are not together—again."

It must be the jet lag, I thought. Paula could sometimes get "out there" faster than I could follow, although I thought I understood the metaphor about the river. We both had changed, and once again we're stepping back into each other's lives—same river, but with different and unpredictable currents.

"Let's take a bath, Paula. It was a long flight."

After a rejuvenating, candle-lit bubble bath, we returned to the bedroom. I put two more logs on the fire, and now with single mindedness turned back the clean sheets to greet my friend and lover, and be welcomed home in return. Early morning light filtered gently into the room.

An overwhelming feeling of happiness and contentment enveloped me. Golden dust mites floated weightlessly in a shaft of diffused sunlight. The faint smell of smoke from the fire, mixed

with the coconut smell of our bath soap, and the dancing shadows created by the ring of candles still burning, were imprinted on my mind forever as I turned to admire Paula's moist, naked body. She was lying on her back, waiting, willing.

Looking without touching was painfully pleasurable. Every movement, whether deliberate or not, increased my excitement. Watching her exquisite breasts rise and fall with the accelerating tempo of her breathing was mesmerizing. I sensed, rather than saw, her hips swell.

"Paula, you're more beautiful than I remember, more beautiful than I deserve."

"Love me, then," she whispered.

Taking my hand, she pulled me down into her softness, her center, and her rhythm.

CHAPTER 24

BERSERKELEY

M Y MOTHER MADE MY FAVORITE MEALS, AND THE FAMILY STAYED UP late listening to my travel stories—working for the queen of England, the "Night of the Vampires," and especially my TV appearance, newspaper coverage, and court case.

Although my father was supportive of my intention to continue selling the moon, he was troubled by my current living situation. The fact that I was now "shacking up" with Paula did not please either of my parents. This "living in sin" was one more affront that my long-hair, pot-smoking, Rock & Roll generation was imposing on the sensibilities of moms and dads throughout the country. Although my parents rejected my lifestyle, I never felt rejected as their son.

I returned to Berkeley armed with 5000 Moon Acre certificates and my new costume. From day one, in Berkeley, there was no question as to where Moon Man would call headquarters. It would be Telegraph Avenue. If you were new to The Ave, one of the first things you might notice was the abundance of hair. Except for some of the jocks, fraternity boys, Hare Krishnas, cops, and the real crazies, everyone had long hair. More individualistic than the length, dreadlocks, or

I Sold *the* Moon!

Mohawk cut, was the choice of color some of these first-time-away-from-home students were now dyeing their tresses. They seemed to come in all shades. My favorites were orange, pink (especially on Asian girls) and neon lime-green. I liked the idea that Moon Man would add aluminum to The Ave's hair color palate.

Mixed in with the people who looked like they'd just walked off a Fellini film set or out of a Salvador Dali painting were dogs wearing bandanas, or sunglasses, or both, many with well-chewed Frisbees in their mouths. There were high school kids wanting to get high, trying to pass themselves off as college students. There were college professors trying to look like high school students and street corner preachers ranting about hell and eternal damnation. These preachers railed primarily against sins of the flesh—no doubt because they weren't touching any of it (other than their own).

These self-proclaimed messengers from God were themselves in competition with any number of heavenly-connected organizations represented on the street. The apostles of Korean-born Reverend Sun Myung Moon—referred to as "Moonies"—would invite you to a free dinner and the next thing you knew, you were at the airport selling flowers, one flower at a time, and oh, yeah, no further contact with anyone outside the "family" was permitted. L. Ron Hubbard's aggressive—pay now, be saved later—Scientologists were competing with each other to fill their quotas of new converts. Even the Jehovah's Witnesses trolled the street—forgoing being at your door at 7 AM on Saturday morning.

The Buddhists, Muslims, Seventh Day Adventists, Jews for Jesus, followers of Edgar Casey, those claiming to be Born Again, and everybody else, including mainstream Baptists, Protestants, Methodists, Lutherans, and the hip-leaning Newman Center of the Catholic Church, were relegated to picking up the scraps left behind by all the New Wave proselytizers who promised shortcuts to salvation and free food, as well. Also struggling to expand the flock were the two Mormon boys, in matching white shirts and black ties, riding twin bikes, bibles in their baskets, up and down The Ave at all hours of the day and night.

This was the Mother Lode, a modern day Sodom and Gomorrah. There was no shortage of those needing to be saved. The problem was, these groups needed to convince the lost sheep that deliverance was worth the price they were charging.

I would come to appreciate the shaven-headed, mostly barefooted, Hare Krishnas. You would hear them coming before you saw them. The melodious, repetitive chant this group sang was pleasingly hypnotic. These one-time accountants, out of work beauticians, and former altar boys would materialize in their head-to-toe burnt-orange, plain cotton garments. Handing out flower petals, they would chant and twirl in circles with expressions of bliss on their face, all the while keeping time with the small brass cymbals they wore on their thumbs and middle fingers. Over and over again, they would chant in one harmonious voice:

"Hare Krishna, Hare Krishna
Krishna, Krishna
Hare, Hare
Hare Rama, Hare Rama
Rama, Rama
Hare, Hare."

Telegraph Avenue would come to rival the notoriety of San Francisco's Haight/Ashbury, the street corner synonymous with Hippies, drugs, and the 1968 Summer of Love. One reason for The Ave's ascendance to icon status was the number of street characters that called the avenue home. Moon Man would join their ranks, and from his first appearance would draw bigger crowds, and make more money than any of the other human oddities that swarmed the carnival-like freak show that was Telegraph Avenue.

One notable character was the former Harvard professor who went by the name of X Swami X. When not talking about the benefits of LSD, he would share his revelations on subjects both scientific and philosophical.

"Are you all aware that the human body is comprised of more space, more nothingness, than it is solid matter? It is also true that when you consider the distance between the atoms that make up our molecules, relative to their size, that this distance is no less than that which separates one planet from another or one galaxy from another relative to their respective size. Just as one could travel outward for an infinite amount of time and distance, so, too, could one travel inward into the sub-atomic realm. I'm merely suggesting that no matter how

small something is, it stands to reason that it can be halved. I also believe at the moment of ejaculation, man comes as close as he will ever get to understanding the Big Bang theory. Now, if any of you women listening are thinking the obvious extension to that metaphor is that your vagina represents the eternal void waiting to be filled with the explosive seed of cosmic creation—you're right!"

Yeah, that X Swami X knew how to keep a crowd. He would prove be my toughest competition whenever the two of us were pontificating at the same time.

The "Bubble Lady's" real name is Julia Vinograd. She would walk The Ave daily waving her wand, and in the process create thousands of delicate bubbles that drifted on carbon monoxide rich air, providing a stark and welcome contrast to the grit, grime, and vacant stares of the lost innocents huddled against the graffiti-marked walls of Rasputin's new and used record and black-light poster store. Always in her long black dress and signature yellow and black beret, she would sell her books of revolutionary street poetry from her reserved table at the oldest and most authentic coffeehouse in Berkeley—Café Mediterranean or The Med.

One of the many panhandlers on the street was known as Rubber Man. He combined just a touch of showmanship with his request for spare change. No matter what the weather he would wear a complete wet suit including swim fins, snorkel and mask. It was hard not to drop a quarter into his beach pail, especially when his face became completely obscured by the condensation on the inside of the mask. Hearing a coin land, Rubber Man would respond with, "Thank you... whoever you are."

Brother Hubert was not the only preacher called to take his message to the streets, but he was the most entertaining. He was fun to watch even though he had no sense of humor about anything —especially what he thought to be sinful—which as far as I could tell was just about everything. He wore a three-piece white suit that was in desperate need of dry cleaning. His Old Testament fire and brimstone evangelizing was made almost comical by his use of a cheap combination amplifier/speaker "squawk-box." Pounding on his bible, he would raise his voice to fever pitch, and, lifting his eyes skyward, he would implore the Almighty to unleash righteous vengeance and smite the fornicators, the blasphemers, and especially

the sodomites. He seemed to especially enjoy quoting those passages in scripture where someone, or better yet entire nations, were on the receiving end of God's all-powerful wrath. As long as he could rant about pestilence, floods, droughts, swarms of locusts, scorched earth, plagues, or people getting turned into pillars of salt, Brother Hubert had no trouble allowing the spirit to move him.

One person was unfortunately *really* crazy. Not funny crazy or eccentrically crazy, but downright scary crazy. It came as no surprise that everyone just referred to him as "The Crazy Guy." The first time I saw him, he was wearing a green hospital smock with the name "Dave" handwritten on the breast pocket. From that moment on, I always addressed him as Dr. Dave.

On more than one occasion, I saw Dr. Dave throw a wine bottle against a wall or into the street. Saying that he was unkempt would be like saying Nixon probably knew something about Watergate. Dr. Dave should have been institutionalized for his own safety and that of everyone he took notice of. His scraggily, dirty hair failed to cover patches of bald spots. His food-encrusted beard obscured few of the open sores and scabs on his face. It was obvious that he urinated on himself, which added to the foul odor that pervaded the air space around him.

Scavenging for food in garbage cans, he would eat and drink what he found immediately, sometimes digging deeper with one hand while he ate with the other.

Whenever he started yelling obscenities at the demon voices in his mind, people would scatter, creating distance between themselves and the unpredictability that was heading their way. The problem was if you didn't see him coming, his filthy mildewed blanket trailing after him, he could, without warning, suddenly be in your face. His phlegm-hacking, sour-smelling, Night-Train-wine breath could paralyze you where you stood. He would grab hold of your arm with a surprising strength that seems to be given to people who have lost touch with reality. If there was no cop around, forget it, you were on your own. You were trapped, up close and way too personal with "The Crazy Guy."

"Asshole what you staring at? You're fucked up man. I mean fuuuuuuuuuucked up. This is bullshit man, yeah, total bummer, but I say fuck it. No shit man, if you want to meet Aldatron from planet

I Sold *the* Moon!

Zord I know how, man. I shit my pants the first time man, fuckin-A. Not now. Fuck off, fuck off, I said. OK, OK, be nice. Shit, man, I need some wine. Wine makes me pee, but fuck it. What makes you pee? Haaaaaaaaaa... Hey, asshole, where you going? No, you gotta gimme some fucking money prick. OK, OK shhhhhhhhit it's all fucked up. Yeah, I gotta get me fucked up. You and me are friends. I like you... you're nice, fuck it..."

Over time, I developed my own coping technique in dealing with the good Doctor. As he stumbled in my direction, I would call out to him (trusting that the best defense really is a good offense).

"Dr. Dave! I've been looking everywhere for you, man...glad I found you...I got your money, so be cool. Here's that dollar I promised you, but no more until tomorrow. Aldatron wants me back on Zord, but, hey, I gotta tell you man, wine makes me pee...but fuck it."

Moon Man was easy to find, and not only for Dr. Dave. Early on, I made it my policy to give fifty cents to anyone who asked for money. If I didn't have the change, and sometimes even when I did, I would give the person asking for spare change a dollar bill, with the understanding that they were to get it changed and bring me back fifty cents. I'd tell them I realized it would be easy to walk away with the dollar and not come back, but if they did that, it would be the last time I would ever give them anything. Once they promised me they would come back, I handed over the George Washington.

"OK, I have your word of honor. You know where to find me," I'd say, as I turned my attention back to selling Moon Acres.

Rarely did someone fail to return with the change. It might be hours later, and in a few cases days later, but virtually everyone who gave his or her word to return kept it. I was not concerned about losing the half-dollar as much as I was in giving these homeless, mostly sad street people a chance to demonstrate—not to me, but to themselves— that they could be trusted. Some would come running back, and often I would hear statements like, "I guess you never thought you'd see me again, did you?" or, "You thought I wasn't coming back, right?"

"You gave me your word, and I believed you," I'd answer. They may have been on the streets, but most of them were not of the streets, at least not yet.

Exactly why Dr. Dave was the only person I regularly gave a dollar to, I'm not sure. Maybe I just had a soft spot for "The Crazy Guy."

DAY AT THE OFFICE

THE CHRISTMAS BUYING SEASON WAS GATHERING MOMENTUM. I was ready to go to work.

Paula and I called the city newspaper and the campus rag, *The Daily Cal*. We asked for the editor's desk and reported that we had just seen a person in a silver space suit selling land on the moon to a huge crowd.

"He's on the corner of Telegraph and Bancroft and we want to know: Is this person legitimate?"

In less than an hour, both papers sent over a reporter and cameraman. From then on, wherever Moon Man appeared, I would call the local newspapers and television stations beforehand, pretending to be an amazed citizen with a possible scoop about some space guy, a large crowd of people, and something about selling the moon. In this way, my moon book rapidly started to fill up with press clippings.

* * *

As it turned out, Berkeley would be one of Moon Man's most lucrative and accommodating locations. On and off for the next ten years, I would consider the corner of Telegraph and Bancroft

I Sold *the* Moon!

"Moon Base One." During all that time, not once did Campus Security or the Berkeley police bother me—except occasionally when a member of the force would stop to purchase a certificate or two. Of course, this was no bother at all.

With so many people on the street, it was easy to draw a crowd of a hundred or more in just a few minutes. My recent performances in Ireland gave me confidence as I looked out over the bustling throng of potential land speculators. How many of them were looking back at me wondering who was this oddity, standing out in a menagerie of oddities?

With the blustery December wind unfurling my cape behind me, it was time to let the land rush begin.

"Ladies and gentlemen, thank God for Berkeley, California! Where else will you find someone selling land on the moon? That's right, sir, you heard right. I'm selling property on the moon! Don't be alarmed; every precaution has been taken to insure your safety. Now, one may ask, who gave me the right to do this? My answer is, who has the authority to issue me that right? Just because I'm the first person in history to officially claim the moon should that necessarily invalidate my claim? I warn you, however, that our government does not, I repeat does not, recognize my claim nor have they authorized the sale of these deeds. Only in Berkeley! Land on the moon! One dollar an acre! You won't find these certificates on sale in bookstores, in poster shops, on television... or on the back of a box of Fruit Loops."

The crowd, most of whom wore bemused expressions, was now about 80 strong and growing. Knowing that Christmas was less than a month away, I felt no reluctance in pandering to the commercialization of the holiday.

"If you can find a better, more original stocking stuffer for one dollar, please let me know. Give the gift that keeps on giving—one acre one dollar. Maybe you know someone who loves the ridiculous. Maybe you know someone who would appreciate the collector's value inherent in this document, or maybe you know someone in real estate who knows the value of buying property when the market is low. Or you just might have a few people on your list that you don't want to spend...two dollars on. Give an acre of land on the moon this year and you can feel fairly confident that the person won't already have one. Yes, it's crazy. Yes, it's ridiculous. Yes, it's preposterous but the most unbelievable thing about

what I'm offering is that it's actually happening. And don't forget every acre I sell comes with a terrific view...of earth."

Someone yelled from the back of the crowd: "What area of the moon are you selling?"

"The gentleman asks, what area of the moon am I selling? Sir, is your concern the type of neighborhood you might be moving into?"

This line got the crowd laughing.

"The truth is the property you get is on a first come first serve basis. Once arriving on lunar surface, you simply stake out your acre parcel. Think Oklahoma Land Rush. However, be advised, the rumor circulating that my company is providing transportation to the property is not true. I mean, your toll to cross the Bay Bridge is fifty cents. You can't expect to go to the moon for a dollar."

Someone else yelled: "You're nothing but a phony con man."

I yelled back: "Sir, I take exception to that. What do you mean... *phony*?"

I heard what I loved hearing—laughter. The audience seemed to be having fun and so was I. There were people in the crowd ready to buy but I wanted more than just a few sales. I would provide some credibility, then go for the close. Picking up my "Moon Book," I opened it to the first newspaper clipping.

"Front page of the Scrotumento Bee, uh...*Sacramento Bee*, reports quote: 'Young college grads try novelty market.' Yes, my friends I am a living example of what a college degree can do for you. Of course, the Bee's motto is: 'If news is happening...it's news to us.' In Ireland, this story was on the front page of *The Irish Press*, I quote: 'Thirty buy plots at a pound an acre.' That's twice what you're paying today. Then again on the front page..."

Someone cut in and shouted, "So if we're paying half, does that mean property value on the moon just fell by 50%?"

"The gentleman obviously is in real estate. No, moon property value has not fallen. That is a scandalous lie started by the guy who's trying to sell Mars. I choose to believe the value's up over 100% in Ireland and simply just on sale here in America."

More laughter.

"But as you can read in this front-page headline, 'Had no license to sell land on the moon,' not all was trouble free in Ireland. However, once the Irish courts realized that giving me a license to sell land

on the moon was a wee bit out of their jurisdiction—I was back in business."

More laughter.

Dramatically pulling a certificate out of my "moon bag," I continued.

"For those of you in the back who want to take a closer look at the document, please feel free to come on up and read this over. No magnifying glasses, please. Pay no attention to the fine print. It just clearly says this and that about the legal back and forth, regarding more or less the ins and outs of the pros and cons."

The most critical phase in the presentation cycle had arrived. I had gathered a crowd and had them both laughing and considering. Now I needed someone to step forward and be seen buying an acre. It was time to ask for the sale. The danger, I had discovered, was that if it took too long for that brave person to come forward it would start to get embarrassing. The audience would begin to feel uncomfortable and melt away.

There were people in the audience who wanted to buy one, but no one wanted to be first. On occasion, someone would buy during the middle of the presentation, reducing the criticality of this moment. I just needed that first confident soul to step forward. I brought out a fistful of dollar bills, and raised them over my head. The moment of truth had arrived.

"Ladies and gentlemen, some of you have been listening to me for more than 15 minutes. If nothing else, I believe you've gotten a dollar's worth of entertainment. This show is free, of course, but obviously, I would not be able to continue doing this if no one supports me. So, I ask you to keep the American spirit of individuality alive and support your local Moon Man. Remember these certificates are 8 ½" by 11" and suitable for framing. The conversational value alone inherent in this document will pay for itself in...20 to 30 years. Yes, I do accept personal checks—no ID required. If you're going to write me a bum check for a dollar, you've got to be in worse shape than I am. Take a chance on lunacy."

I would usually wait until I saw someone bring out a dollar before I would say; "Moon Acres are now on sale." Once someone had a bill in his or her hand, I felt secure enough to take the plunge and ask for the sale. Pointing to the person with the money in hand, I would

announce, "Congratulations on being the trailblazer of this group. Come on up and claim your Moon Acre."

Holding the moon certificate out at full arm's length in their direction was almost always enough to overcome their inertia. The first wave of buyers was on its way in....

I found I could perform between 8 and 12 shows a day. If I averaged just $40.00 per show, I had a good chance of making $400.00 a day.

In Berkeley, as the sun went down and the crowds thinned out, I simply walked to the curb on Bancroft Avenue to catch the bus that would drop me off a few feet from my new bungalow. After a few days, the regulars on the bus would clap as I climbed aboard. I found I could sometimes sell as many 15 acres before I arrived at my stop. Because I had a limited amount of time, my pitch needed to be shortened considerably. Standing in the aisle, I would hold on to the overhead rail with one hand and immediately bring out a certificate and a few dollar bills and hold them in the other.

"Ladies and gentlemen, please don't be alarmed. I sell land on the moon for one dollar an acre. This certificate I'm holding is the deed for one acre of lunar surface. Should you want to buy one, I would be happy to make the transaction as you leave the bus, just please have your dollar ready. I know some of you must be thinking, what right do I have to sell the moon? Believe me, that question is asked many times every day. My answer is always different, I mean, the same. It's really all about fun. Who has the sense of humor to take a chance on lunacy? It's not every bus ride someone offers you a piece of the moon."

The bus would stop every few blocks, letting some people off and picking up new riders. Everyone who stayed on the bus seemed to enjoy the surprise and momentary confusion visible on the faces of the new passengers as they boarded.

"Welcome on board folks, nothing to be worried about. I was just explaining to your fellow riders that I sell the moon for a dollar an acre and I'm open for business until I get off at Sacramento Street. Unfortunately, for those considering buying one, there is not a lot of time to decide. But then this is not a decision I want you to think too much about anyway. The truth is, these Moon Acres

make great stocking stuffers. Put this in a frame and you have the best conversational item ever created. Just think, when you get home you can ask, 'Guess what I bought on my bus ride home tonight?' Moon Acres, they're just a dollar. One dollar one acre. Who would like to read one over?"

It would go like this until I had to get off—usually to more applause. I was never sure if the clapping was in appreciation for the free entertainment or that the riders were glad to be rid of me. Either way, I made a few extra bucks and no doubt provided my fellow passengers with something to talk about—whether they bought a Moon Acre or not.

"Sweetheart, I'm home from the office," I'd announce as I entered our cottage.

I felt like the Great White Hunter returning to the cave with the kill. Paula would surprise me with a new and wonderful meal and I would surprise her with the amount of money I would dump on the bed. After taking a bath and washing all the silver color out of my hair, I would return to the counting room where Paula had organized bills, checks, change, food stamps, and joints (I often traded acres for joints). The first stack of bills I would look for would be the 20's. A nice stack of Andrew Jacksons usually meant a successful day.

Paula would have already counted, and now it was my turn to guess. I would start low just to hear her say "more." I would continue guessing higher amounts until she said "less," and then she would announce the exact figure for the day. As Freud said "To be happy one needs love and work." I had both. I was happy.

MOONSHINE

MONEY WAS GROWING IN OUR NEWLY OPENED CHECKING ACCOUNT, we had two months rent saved, there was "Crazy Cash" in the cookie jar, my wallet bulged with bills, quarters were filling up a big coffee can, and the kitchen was well stocked. We felt rich. However, even though taking the bus might have been good for business, it was bad for my self-esteem. I wanted a car. Money also had to be put aside for the next run of 5000 acres. But the most immediate expense was buying the expensive material Paula had picked out for her moon costume. I had suggested and she had agreed that selling the moon was once again going to be a team effort. She had already decided on her name. Paula would be known as Ms. Honey Moon.

Exactly how Ms. Honey Moon would fit into the moon act was still to be determined. Paula did make one thing clear. She would not engage in any of the overt selling—the "barking" as she called it. She intended to roam through the crowd showing the newspaper articles and Moon Acres to individuals who were reluctant to come forward. More than that, she was intent on getting the moon act off the streets and into the comedy clubs. With her degree in drama, I understood her desire for a more legitimate stage.

"We need to have the act rehearsed. It's way too free form now. You could get so many more laughs if you stuck to the lines that consistently get a good reaction and stop using all that filler. You've got a good act as it is, but why not have a great one?"

Her makeover of the moon act would start to be implemented in the New Year, but for now I was making too much money and having too much fun to want to change anything. Besides, Paula was busy putting the finishing touches on her Honey Moon costume. For reasons known only to her, she felt she needed three different silver tops to choose from. The lower half of her body would be covered with a black and silver satin skirt or pants that looked like space age bloomers. These were sewn from thick quilted royal blue cotton. Her cape was fashioned out of expensive diaphanous fabric. It was translucent black with sparkles of silver thread running throughout. On her feet, she wore black tap shoes with laces whose ends sported silver glittered stars. I especially liked the fluorescent ribbons she tied in her hair, along with my favorite accessory, her fairy princess rhinestone tiara.

After just a few days working with Ms. Honey Moon, both Paula and I recognized that we were underutilizing her talents. Not willing to address the crowd, she had been relegated to picking up the occasional sale on the fringes of the audience. I also knew she was unhappy playing second banana. She had, after all, been accustomed to performing lead roles to packed theatres both in High School and at the University. I was unsure of what we should do. She wasn't.

"I've been working on *Moonshine* for the last three weeks, and just finished it," she said laying a 22-page script down on the table. "It's a combination of your best moon rap monologue, a couple of comic scenes between us, three original songs, with choreography, and one finishing song and dance routine that we do together. It's going to take a lot of rehearsal, but once we get it down, we can take it to the clubs and get paid for entertaining. If we're going to be professional, we have to start acting like it."

Her script was written as a play within a play. Paula and I would act out the story of two struggling street performers who finally make it to the big time. The final scene, complete with song and dance, took place "opening night" on Broadway.

"Paula, this is really good, but I'm not sure we can make it work on the sidewalk. This is better suited for a controlled environment. We're on the streets."

"And that's exactly where we're going to stay unless we start thinking how to get off the streets. You know how cold I get out there. It's not your little nips that freeze up. I'm just asking that you give it a try. We don't have to perform the whole thing right away. We can start by adding one scene at a time. I already have my lines memorized."

She changed into her tap shoes and then to the tune of *Moon River*, she started singing and tap dancing to a song she had written called *Moon Acres*.

Moon Acres further than a mile...
I'll be seeing you in style someday...
All you land takers, you groundbreakers...
Wherever you're going I'm going your way...

Two moon sellers, off to see the moon...
There's such a lot of moon to see...
We're after the same moonbow's end...
Waiting round the bend...
My lunar speculating friends...
Moon Acres...and me...

I applauded enthusiastically when she finished. She had obviously rehearsed the routine. Her talent as a dramatically trained actor came shining through. Her singing voice and dancing ability were more professional than I would have thought. I was starting to appreciate her desire to revamp the moon act. As it stood now, she was on the outside. For her to be happy, and the moon couple successful, she would need to feel like a full partner.

"OK, Paula, I'll give it a try. But you know I can't sing, and there is no way I tap dance. I do think I should check on those frozen nips, though. I know I would enjoy thawing them out."

For the next two weeks, Paula acted as director, voice coach and choreographer. I did make progress, but slowly and painfully. For the

first time the moon act became work. Even selling door-to-door had been less demanding. The spontaneity and the energy of my usual performance was being replaced with rehearsed lines, songs and soft-shoe shuffle ball changes.

Paula was buoyant while I felt depressed. I told myself to reserve final judgment until we tried it out in front of a live audience. Near the end of the third week of rehearsals, I was growing impatient and the once robust cash flow had come to a complete stop. Ready or not, we needed to bring the curtain up.

Thinking it best if we "opened" out of town, we headed for Sacramento in "Slug," my newly acquired, 1962 Ford Fairlane. My sister Shelley had clearly gotten the better of the $175.00 transaction. With a top speed of 41 miles an hour (on level ground), Slug more than lived up to its name.

When our road show opened, I was as ready as I'd ever be. My lines were memorized, and my singing voice had been transformed from unbearable to simply irritating.

"You have such great volume nobody will care that you're off key. Remember, this is a comedy skit," Paula encouraged me.

"There's a big difference between people laughing with you or having them laugh at you," I reminded her.

Unlike me, Paula was in her element. She was invigorated and focused now that she was playing a character in need of dramatic expression. I, on the other hand, felt drained of energy and, for the first time, self-conscious.

The plan was that once our 20-minute performance was over, I would try and sell Moon Acres. It just didn't work. One of the problems may have been the length of time it took from the start of our play until I asked for the sale. Not everyone has 35 or 40 minutes to spend listening to two spaced out realtors—no matter how weird they look. There was also more than a little confusion as to just what we were doing. Consequently, the crowds were smaller, the laughs were fewer, and polite applause took the place of people lining up to buy certificates. Except for the press we got, our big opening was a bust. The headline, in the *Sacramento State Hornet*, February 26, 1974 read:

"You Too Can Be A Lunatic Buy A Piece Of The Moon"
The article continued:

"The word "lunatic" has been used throughout the ages to describe an individual whose mental capacity had been affected by the moon. A new dimension has been given to the word by two people who are attempting to make a living by selling land on the moon."

I liked the last paragraph:

"Although it is not the best buy in town, one must admit the deed hung upon a living room wall would make a heck of a conversation piece. All in all it's a very creative improvement over the old Brooklyn Bridge routine."

A few days later, we were slowly making our way north to my alma mater, Chico State College.

"You can't expect everything to work perfectly right away. We're going to need more time. The act will come together, have a little faith," Paula was telling me.

"Sweetheart, I'm not throwing in the towel yet, but we made a total of $56.00 for the two days in Sac Town. We could have made $300.00 or more."

"Barry, it's not about the money. We may have to give up the quick easy scores now for the potentially big paydays later. It's all about polishing and perfecting our act. Once we're good enough, selling Moon Acres won't be necessary. Think Burns and Allen, think Desi and Lucy."

The realization that Paula and I had two very different views of the future and how we wanted to get there had me feeling confused and more than a little scared. Let's see what tomorrow's performance brings, I thought. Right now, I had enough to worry about trying to keep Slug moving along at a 28-mph clip.

Our two-day run in Chico felt a little more polished and professional than our initial performances a few days earlier. The comedic timing was better, I forgot fewer lines, we got more laughs, but the students at Chico State were no more inclined to buy Moon Acres, in any greater numbers, than had their counterparts at Sac State. Once again, we had to settle for some nice press. The school paper, *The Wildcat*, ran a front-page story with photograph, the headline shouted:

"Moon People Invade Chico"

The last paragraph read:

"Brouhaha, charlatanism, or Seventies idealism—if you paid a dollar for a deed, who knows—one day you may be on your way for a visit to Moon Park to relax, unwind, from the world and everyday tensions—wherever and whenever it comes together."

✳ ✳ ✳

Making little more than gas money in Chico, we headed east to UNR—the University of Nevada Reno. The crawl over the Sierra Nevada mountain range took four hours longer than it should have. UNR, home of the Wolf Pack, was a very conservative campus. The student body had a completely different look than we were used to. Some of the guys were wearing Stetson hats and almost everybody had cowboy boots on. I was not real excited thinking about doing my new soft-shoe routine. Why hadn't I learned calf roping or bull riding?

"Paula, maybe we should rethink putting on our show here tomorrow. Did you see that guy? He had spurs on. Look, they're making sparks on the cement. Hey, maybe Dr. Dave is not so bad after all."

"Chill out, it's going to be fine. Besides, these guys need entertainment just as much, if not more, than they do in Chico or Berkeley."

Yeah, but did that include seeing a bad song and dance man dressed in tinfoil hawking bogus property on the moon?

Evidently not. Besides getting whistled and catcalled to as much as Paula did, the only good news was *The Reno Gazette* headline:

"Caped Couple Sells Loony Land"

Under a flattering photograph of the two of us, ran this caption: "Gainfully Employed"

"Moon Man and Moon Maiden show off a sample deed to an acre of "land" on the moon. What started out as "more or less" a hoax has kept them employed and off welfare... "

✳ ✳ ✳

It was true we were off the dole, but if things didn't change, we would be singing and dancing our way onto the welfare rolls very soon.

As we headed back to Berkeley, I told Paula I was unhappy with the way the moon act was going and why I wanted to stop performing *Moonshine*.

Back in front of our fireplace, Paula remained unconvinced. "The problem is not with the act itself. The problem is one of perception. If the audience had to pay something to see us or if we were in a club, we would have legitimacy. We need someone to promote us. We need management," she concluded.

Something deep inside—maybe a vision of the future—convinced me that Paula was right. I might make more money in the short term selling the moon the way I wanted to, but she was challenging me to perfect our act into something that people would to pay to see. Maybe this could still work.

"I know of a San Francisco promoter. He handles stage acts and rock bands. I'll give him a call first thing tomorrow," I said with more enthusiasm than I felt.

CHAPTER 27

MOON MADNESS

O NE WEEK LATER, WITH THE MOON BOOK IN HAND, WE ARRIVED at the North Beach offices of Mario Luciano & Sid Goldberg. As we climbed the stairs to their San Francisco office, it was impossible not to notice the gold records lining the walls. Between each framed album were pictures of Luciano and Goldberg hobnobbing with different celebrities: on stage with Bill Graham, The Who, the Rolling Stones, and backstage with Bob Dylan. In one poster-sized image, the two men were standing with a half naked woman I recognized as Carol Doda. Carol, who was blessed, or, depending on how you looked at it, cursed, with enormous breasts, was the main attraction at the Broadway strip club "The Condor," owned by the two men we were about to meet. The poster read: "See Carol Doda and two of the three most famous landmarks in San Francisco." This should be interesting, I thought, as Paula pushed me up the stairs, breaking the hypnotic effect Carol's two landmarks were having on me.

I don't remember much from that first meeting with Mario and Sid partly because I was distracted by the decor. The walls of their office were covered with photographs of nude women. Mario, who did most of the talking, wore a solid gold earring that spelled out the word F-U-C-K. Yes, they would take us on as clients, but not before we paid them $500.00.

"When we set up a publicity event we need to know you'll be there. The $500.00 retainer is our insurance that you two aren't flakes. I'm sure you understand. We have our reputation to protect," Sid, the quiet one, explained.

"Everybody knows you gotta spend money to make money," Mario added. "And before we can do anything, you'll both need to get professional costumes. Call Tissa Duke Smith," he said, handing me a business card. "She makes most of the outfits my girls wear."

Looking at the framed pictures of scantily-clad "girls," it was hard to evaluate exactly what Tissa's costume-making ability was. As we left the office $500.00 lighter, I noticed that Mario wore a similar gold earring in his opposite lobe. It spelled out the word Y-O-U.

"I don't like or trust those two," Paula stated unequivocally once we were back in Slug and making the return trip to Berkeley.

"I guess you noticed the earrings Mario was wearing?"

"I can't believe you gave them $500.00."

"Hey, you wanted management. We got management. I guess I was swayed by all the nice photography," I joked.

Paula was not laughing.

"Lordy be, now don't tell me. You must be an Aquarius," Tissa accurately concluded in a soft southern drawl, after opening her front door and taking one look at Paula.

Our 20-something seamstress was short of stature and wide of girth. Her curly black hair tumbled down past her waist. Just the toes of her bare feet were visible under her floor length yellow and black hoop skirt, which clashed in both color and style with her intricately designed Chinese silk housecoat. The only complementary fashion element was her bright orange lipstick which matched the bright orange pincushion she wore on her wrist.

Her tiny workshop/apartment was strewn with exotic fabrics. Bolts of material lay helter-skelter on the bed and floor. Sparkling sequin, rickrack, and sewing patterns were draped

over open cabinets and drawers. Various saucers held pins, glass stars, beads, buttons, all manner of costume jewelry and eye-catching baubles. Before we had time to clear a place to sit, Tissa passed me a perfectly rolled joint.

Paula and Tissa talked astrology for an hour. They were both excited about Pluto's imminent return from retrograde. Once this happened, it would trine with Mars and Saturn and for anybody who had Mercury near the horizon in their seventh house, it sounded like things were about to get very intense. I finally had to interrupt and explained why we were there.

"Oh, Lordy be, you're not going to get Paula involved with those two creeps are you? They're bad vibes. They owe me money. Take my advice, sugar, and stay away, far away from them."

"Tissa that's going to be hard to do. We've already paid them," I explained.

"You'll need to pay me, too. I hope you understand, but their credit ran out a long time ago."

To show our good faith I gave her a check for $300.00. It would cost us another $800.00 before we each had our new "summer moon suits," and a custom-covered Moon Book to match. When finished, they were spectacular and worth every cent.

The brilliant reflection of sunlight off my new suit, mirrored glasses and moon jewelry actually hurt the eyes if a viewer stared too long. The entire Mylar outfit interacted with sunlight like a giant crystal prism, spreading multicolored patterns of light out before me in a dazzling arc of iridescent brilliance. If I'd felt confident in the suit Breanna had made me in Ireland, I now felt invincible.

Paula's costume was as elegant as it was beautiful.

Over her "princess dress," she would wear five different-colored diaphanous skirts with small glass stars sewn into the fabric. The translucent hues of these garments came in aqua, lavender, silver, and pink. Her platform tap shoes had been sprayed metallic glitter, and tied above the ankle with Silver Star laces. Ms. Honey Moon would wear a new, larger, tiara on her silver-dusted curls.

The next few months were spent mostly calling on, and waiting for our "managers" to start managing—they never did. And although the new

costumes contributed in helping to draw bigger crowds, they were not the panacea for dramatically increasing sales.

"Paula, we may have to shelve performing *Moonshine* and go back to selling acres the way I...the way we used to."

The look on her face told me she was hurt by my repeated suggestion that we change our artistic direction.

"Barry, I can't believe you want to abandon what we're just now starting to perfect. We're making progress. The way it is now we actually get paid to rehearse. Maybe not enough for your liking, but income nevertheless. And if we stay at it, when we do get the call, we'll be ready."

"Sweetheart, you may be right, but we both know Mario and Sid will never do anything for us. It's been three months and not a single call. We got taken, plain and simple. But now I'm more concerned about not having rent money in twelve days and food in five. If you haven't noticed, we're out of firewood, the gas tank is on empty, our coffee can is down to pennies and nickels, and we... "

Paula interrupted and in a baby's voice said, "I spent all the nickels yesterday."

I didn't want to laugh but couldn't help myself.

We fell into bed mentally exhausted, with neither of us willing to compromise enough to satisfy the other. For the first time since I'd returned, our lovemaking felt less than complete.

Two days later, we were a hundred and fifty miles north, staying in a quaint Mendocino bed and breakfast. We could hear the thunderous waves of the Pacific Ocean crashing into the rock outcroppings outside our window.

Paula had surprised me by insisting I open a gift she had been keeping from me until, as she said, "...the stars aligned."

Four months earlier, she had prepaid for two nights lodging, breakfast and dinner included, at our current seaside getaway. It no longer surprised me that Paula would choose now to go on this extravagant weekend, when we were, for all practical purposes, broke. In her mind, it was my Virgo practicality in opposition to her Aquarian trust in cosmic inevitability.

"It's going to be fine. Besides, it's all paid for, and you said we now have enough for next month's rent. So can we just mellow out? Anyway, the real reason I brought us up here now is to talk to you, well, to ask you something."

"OK, we're here. What's the question?"

"Let's go down to the beach."

Neither of us said anything on the short walk to the rugged piece of shoreline that fronted our romantic accommodations. Why would she feel she needed to wait until we were up here to ask whatever it was she wanted? It would have to be something unusual, something heavy. Maybe she wanted a separation again? Maybe she was tired of the whole moon thing? No, it had to be a separation. She wanted to break up. No question about it, that has to be it, I concluded.

We had our shoes off. We were holding hands. I could feel the salt mist on my face and could smell it in the air. The sea was turbulent, dark, and timeless. It was near dusk and getting cold. The few people who were still on the beach were far away. They reminded me of how people looked in silent movies.

"Sweetheart," Paula started in a somber voice, as she made sure I was looking into her eyes. "We've been through a lot together. You are my first real love, and I believe you when you tell me I'm your first. You say you love me and I say I love you. We've been saying this since high school. I think it's time our relationship moves beyond what we've known, what we've grown comfortable with. I know what I'm about to say will come as a surprise, but it really shouldn't."

No, Paula, it won't come as a surprise, I thought. I've known for days now. We're over. Sometimes I wished I were less perceptive, less attuned.

She pulled me close and, staring deeper into my eyes, said, "Barry, will you marry me?"

Maybe my powers of perception were not as razor sharp as I'd thought. Surprised? I had to admit I was dumbfounded. I was scared. I was speechless. Did I want to marry Paula? Yes, I did, but.... But what? Say yes. I need some time to think about it. You've had six years to think about it.

The roar of the ocean faded away as the screaming in my mind got louder. What I did, what I said in the next few seconds would affect us for the rest of our lives. Say something. I realized that every passing

second of silence was its own answer. Paula's eyes started to fill with tears. I knew the only thing I could say to make it better, to make us whole again, was the one word that was caught in my throat, and nothing I could do would free it.

I didn't realize it then, but I had been right. We were over.

Paula made plans to leave for Los Angeles by the end of the month.

During our last bittersweet weeks, Paula and I continued to perform together, in Ghirardelli Square and at the Cannery in San Francisco. Even though her heart wasn't in it, the audience never knew. And although content to let me do my solo act, she refused to accept any of the money I made during that part of our program.

Two days before she was due to leave for Los Angeles, I knew what I had to do. Surprising Paula I took her to the beach in San Francisco, just at the foot of the famous Cliff House. With my hand in hers, we walked down to the water's edge.

"Paula, I've had time to think. I don't want to lose you. I love you. I'm asking you now. Paula, will you marry me?"

Unlike me, she had no trouble answering.

"No, Barry, I won't marry you. You talked yourself into this. Getting married now would seem like accepting the consolation prize. Marriage is the grand prize. Loving you has not always been painless, but I'm not sure I had a choice. For both our sakes, I'm making the right choice now, just as you did. I can never be wholly free of you any more than you will or can be completely free of me. In that sense, we are already married. I can't stop loving you even if I wanted to, but I can and will stop living with you. You can't give what you don't feel, and I can no longer pretend that what you do give is enough."

She was right. She knew me better than I was willing or able to know myself. My tears, now mixed with hers, fell silently, dissolving into the wet sand.

For the next few years, we would stay together occasionaly— sometimes for as long as two months. But never again would we believe our futures were inseparable. Our new relatedness would never seem as fluid, as effortless, as we both remembered it once was. Our

lovemaking would have a disconnected quality to it. Lingering hurt, born of loss and potential unrealized, was too close to the surface to stay buried beneath our longing for remembered passion.

And yet, for years to come, neither of us was willing to abandon all hope that someday we might yet fulfill the promise glimpsed in that first transcendent kiss, when worlds collided, time stopped, and dreams took flight.

HAWAII'S CONTEMPORARY WEEKLY

After Dark

FEBRUARY 25 — MARCH 3, 1979

AFTER DARK:
REDD FOXX INTERVIEW

BEFORE DARK:
MARATHON DISCO DUEL

ISLAND LIFE:
WHO IS THE MOON MAN?

SPORTS & LEISURE
Stereo Section INSIDE

free

FULL MOON

AFTER TWO WEEKS OF FEELING SORRY FOR MYSELF, I MADE MY OWN plans. I would travel to colleges and universities around the country, performing my solo moon act, and sell as many Moon Acres as I could. Paula and I were always splitting up, and we always found a way to get back together. Why should this time be any different? Besides, my leather wristbands hadn't worn off and I had no intention of taking them off.

* * *

Over the next four years, I crisscrossed America with suitcases crammed full of Moon Acres. As I entertained on campuses from California to New York, my moon act would evolve into a polished, funny, and lucrative form of street theater. My Moon Book began to bulge with press clippings. A sampling of headlines (in bold) and article excerpts follow: (All but two of these stories appeared on the front page with one or more pictures included.)

(Berkeley, CA: *The Daily Californian*—January 29, 1974)
"Land Boom on the Moon?"
"LUNACY...? Gullible buyers, may discover that their land lies on the bottom of a crater, or is inaccessible."

I Sold *the* Moon!

(San Francisco, CA: *San Francisco Examiner*—1974)
"He's all spaced out in a loony business"
"In one hand he holds an inch stack of one dollar bills and in the other a stack of certificates… "

(Riverside, CA: *Daily Enterprise*—December 12, 1974)
Laughter 'a legitimate business'
"Moon Man's dollar-an-acre sale of lunar lots interrupted by police"
"The Riverside Police dispatcher sent word of a "5150" (psycho)…
"I assume they're looking for me," McArdle remarked as the officers strolled into the quad area…"

After taking my name, the officer asked, "Barry McArdle, from Redlands? So you're a Moon Man now?"

I saw his nametag: R. Garcia, and suddenly realized I knew him. "Ralph Garcia. What, are you a cop now?"

After a bit of reminiscing—we hadn't seen each other in seven years—Garcia told the other officer that it would be alright to let me go, adding, "He's always been a little crazy, but he's harmless."

I was not arrested. The police cleared the incident as: "psycho unfounded."

(Redlands, CA: *The Daily Facts*—1974)
Former Redlands youth will gladly oblige
"Wanna buy a piece of the moon?"
"If I can make people laugh, that's important," he said. "If they laugh, they tend to support the person who makes them do it."

(San Luis Obispo CA: *Telegram/Tribune*—January 28, 1975)
"Selling pie in the sky"
"After each half-hour sales pitch, which drew laughter and loud applause from hundreds of students…dozens of them flocked, dollar-in hand, to buy a piece of the moon…"

(University of California Long Beach: *The Forty-Niner*—February 20, 1975)

"The man who sold the moon"
"McArdle explained that part of the reason for his selling of moon lots was an attempt to get lunacy into the open..."

And a year later, (March 18, 1976) I was back on the front page of the school paper generating this headline:

"Moon Man still selling lunar land"
"A spaceship slowly descends on the moon...and hundreds of property owners rush out to stake claims on the Hartland Crater they bought from the Moon Man..."

My appearances at UCLB were memorable for two reasons. First, I sold almost 500 moon acres on each of the days I appeared. Second and more compelling was that someone standing further back than the far edge of the crowd, someone too shy, too self-conscious, to come forward and buy a Moon Acre (even though she wanted one) was watching me. She had been drawn by the excitement, the laughter, and the energy generated by the guy dressed in silver, standing on a bench, surrounded by hundreds of her fellow students. Half hidden by the tree she was leaning against, she felt safe from being noticed or, worse yet, being asked to participate in some way by this ranting, charismatic, space realtor. For two days, she would spend her lunch hour by the tree, unobserved, but intently observing.

She had every reason to be apprehensive. Had I noticed this statuesque, sensitive-looking, young woman with long blond hair, intelligent blue eyes, and lips that said "kiss me" in any language, I absolutely would have attempted to draw her into conversation. That conversation would have to wait for a couple of years, but once started, it would be ongoing for the rest of our lives....

(California Polytechnic State University, San Luis Obispo: *Mustang Daily*—January 28, 1975)

"Moon salesman invades campus"
"Astronaut Neil Armstrong's small step for man, but large step for mankind, also might have been a crime: trespassing..."

I Sold *the* Moon!

(*The Cincinnati Enquirer*—May 16, 1975)
"Buying A 'Moon Acre?' Say Cheese"
"Buyers know it's a joke," he laughed, "but if any of the deed holders make it to the moon they can grab any acre they like..."

(*San Francisco Chronicle* (AP)—May 19, 1975
"Land Sales on the Moon—$1 an Acre"
"Barry McArdle is selling pieces of The Rock, but the rock he's got up for sale is the moon..."

(University of Cincinnati: *The Newsrecord*—May 20, 1975)
"Moon Man: lunar con or sale of laughter?"
"Each lot, comes with a fantastic view and is prime acreage around Moon River...."

(*The Sacramento Bee*—June 25, 1975)
"Loony Real Estate" 'Reach For The Moon' Is His Pitch
"A buck doesn't go far these days, but at least it can get you a piece of the moon—on paper, that is..."

(Madison, Wisconsin: *The Capital Times*—August 13, 1975)
"Buy a Piece Of Moon: $1 an Acre"
"Barry McArdle landed in Madison Tuesday and hawked deeds to the moon.... I found out that all the jobs had been taken by dropouts..." he said.

(University of Wisconsin—Milwaukee: *The UWM Post*—September 25, 1975)
"Moon monger makes money"
"He's been punched out, beaten up, bombarded by water balloons, pelted with tomatoes and eggs—but Barry McArdle continues to sell pieces of the moon with a few laughs thrown in for free..."

(Milwaukee, Wisconsin: *Marquette Tribune*—October 3, 1975)
"Get a piece of the moon, lunar—tic urges students"
"Marquette was thrown into near hysteria Tuesday when the world's 32nd marvel, the mysterious, caped, hooded, speckled Moon Man materialized..."

(The Milwaukee Journal (*Green Sheet*)—October 9, 1975)
"The man in the moon business"
"…beguiling hundreds with a delightful "sales" routine and proving that lunacy still lives…"

(San Bernardino, CA: *San Bernardino News*—December 15, 1975)
"Caped crusader selling little pieces of lunacy"
"The moon man is back!" The cape-crusading salesman shouted into the wind from the trunk of a Toyota…"

(University of Southern California: *Daily Trojan*—February 12, 1976)
"No cheese, just $1 for a plot of land on the moon"
"… He said he wanted to discredit the rumor that the certificate can be ground down and smoked in order to get high…"

(California State University, Northridge: *Daily Sundial*—February 25, 1976)
"Moon man sells 'moon acres' to CSUN students"
"Once, for example," Moon man said "a man yelled out to me, 'You phony con man!' I take exception to that," I said to him. "What do you mean 'phony'?"

(Los Angeles City College: *Los Angeles Collegian*—February 27, 1976)
'Moon Man' Stirs Lunar Land Craze
"Described by some as a "confidence man" and by others as a "peddler of dreams," "I'm a living example of why not to take LSD…"

(California State University, Fullerton: *Daily Titan*—March 24, 1976)
"Man appears at CSUF to sell shares of moon"
"People who buy the deeds are buying entertainment," he said. "Who knows, at some point in history these acres might be worth more than a dollar bill."

Traveling up and down the state of California, I would often make a return appearance at my more lucrative venues. In almost all cases, my encore would result in more sales than I'd made during my debut. Many of the students who had previously purchased wanted another,

and those that had missed seeing but had somehow heard about the Moon Man, now needed far less encouragement than they otherwise would have.

(USC: *Daily Trojan*—May 5, 1977)
"GALAXY REAL ESTATE"
"The Moonman returned to campus Wednesday to offer students another chance to buy one of the few remaining choice plots of land on the moon..."

(San Jose State University, CA: *Spartan Daily*—October 28, 1977)
"Invader peddling lunar acreage"
"... 'Even if one doesn't want an acre, maybe a friend who has just had a "frontal lobotomy" will,'" McArdle said.

(Chico, CA: Chico Enterprise-*Record*—November 10, 1977)
"Own a Chunk of Moon!"
"With one hand full of dollar bills and the other full of bogus deeds to land on the moon, Barry McArdle fires a rapid series of jokes at his gathering audience..."

(Redlands, CA: *Daily Facts* (UPI)—December 7, 1977)
"Moon property all in fun"
McArdle sells real estate 240,000 miles from anyone
"... I've found Americans have not lost their sense of humor..."

(Los Angeles, CA: *Los Angeles Times*—December 11, 1977)
"30,000 SALES IN SIX YEARS"
Real Estate Man Promises the Moon
Land for sale: Exclusive, reasonable, comes with hour's worth of laughs.
"Barry McArdle sells real estate that is 240,000 miles away from the nearest supermarket or school. And yet he has made at least 30,000 sales in the last six years..."

(University California Davis: *The California Aggie*—February 10, 1978)
"Invasion On Quad"
"... McArdle, who told the crowd that he simply wanted to trade paper

for paper. 'Look at the value of my paper,' he said, 'its been stable since 1971, you can't say that about your paper...'"

(Stanford, CA: *The Stanford Daily*—February 16, 1978)
"Moon Man fell to Earth..."
"... Moon Man promised buyers better grades on exams, because buying a moon acre 'relieves pressure on the brain...'"

(*The San Francisco Progress*—May 5, 1978)
"MOONIE LAND DEAL"
"Not all Moonies peddle flowers...combining the old tradition of the medicine man spiel with the new fashion of silver lame space age garb..."

After one of my appearances at Chico State College, my mother got a call from her father, who lived near Chico in the dairy community of Willows, California. My Grandfather, John Leonardo, spoke very little English. His rare use of the telephone was prompted by a story he had just seen on his local TV news. The segment had opened with a rocket ship blasting off and then "landing on the moon." It then cut to me in my moon costume with the lunar surface superimposed behind me. The announcer's information was not fully understood by my Grandfather, but he did recognize the words: Barry McArdle, moon, and United States.

"No one tells me anything. Someone should have told me that my Grandson had gone to the moon! I didn't even know he was an astronaut," my Grandfather lamented.

With my mother's fluency in Portuguese not what it used to be, it took a little while for her to explain to her father that I hadn't gone to the moon—I was just selling it.

✳ ✳ ✳

Whenever I was performing in Northern California, my father made an effort to come and watch me. One afternoon in Washington Square Park in San Francisco, I was thankful he was in the audience and not just because he gave me moral support. On this day, he saved my life.

The person pushing his way through the crowd was big, very scary and looked like he'd slept in an oilcan. His oversized black

leather jacket had a big number 13 sewn on the front. I knew that number stood for the letter M—the thirteenth letter of the alphabet—and symbolized the advocacy of marijuana. His torn and filthy black t-shirt hung out over his oil-stained black jeans. The pants were tucked into heavy motorcycle boots, the kind that advertised a steel plate in the toe. A loop of bicycle chain hung from his belt and on his nicotine-stained hands were two primitive looking tattoos. Across the top of four fingers on his right hand were the block letters: **L O V E**. On his left: **H A T E**.

In *The Night of the Hunter*, Robert Mitchum, playing the part of a psycho preacher, had worn these same monograms. The fellow standing before me was not an actor playing a deranged killer, but what looked like the real thing.

"Gimme some of that money I know you got," he snarled.

Being asked for a handout was nothing new, and I responded as I had been doing for years whenever faced with this situation.

"Ladies and gentlemen," I announced to the crowd surrounding me, "this gentleman has asked me for money. The Moon Man's policy has always been to accommodate these requests with a donation of fifty cents."

I felt some degree of protection by letting the crowd know of any solicitation. Finding two quarters in my moon bag, I handed them over. When he closed his fist around the coins I could clearly read the blue-black letters **H A T E** carved into his skin.

"This is a one time withdrawal. I don't give more than this," I softly mentioned as he glared up at me, eventually turning away and shuffling off.

I saw his back for the first time. Between two demonic looking red faces, with horns sprouting from their heads and fangs for teeth, were the words: "DEVIL'S REJECTS."

The encounter had gone as well as could be expected, considering I was dealing with someone that even Satan found unacceptable. I returned to the business at hand and tried not to think about the creep in the black leather jacket who now sat on a garbage can staring at me. Half an hour later, he left his perch and once again bullied his way through the crowd, coming straight towards me.

"Hey man, I want some money. And none of that quarter

bullshit. I seen you getting lots of paper money. Now you gotta gimme some."

"Ladies and gentlemen, for those of you who were not here earlier, I gave this person fifty cents when he asked for money last time. Now he tells me he wants more but none of that quarter bullshit. I ask you, should I give him more?"

A number of people responded with shouts of "No!"

"I'm sorry, sir. I'm trying to make a living here. I gave you money once, and that's all I'm going to give you."

"Don't fuck with me," he hissed.

"The gentleman says not to fuck with him," I reported back to the crowd, eliciting some nervous laughter.

Growling and with blazing eyes he said, "Fuck you, man."

I was scared. I took off my glasses in preparation for what I thought he might do. Thankfully, he turned and left.

"For those of you considering going into my line of work, you can see it's not all glamour and beautiful people. But let's get back to what I was talking about and what you, hopefully, were thinking about— speculating on some moon property."

As I continued my spiel, I noticed my father, who had been looking past me for a while, suddenly bolted through the crowd. I turned in time to see my father push the Devil's Reject onto his butt. It took a few seconds to comprehend what was going on. Behind me on the ground was a can of lighter fluid. The back of my cape had been soaked with the liquid. The psycho had a box of matches in his hand and had been moments away from setting me on fire. I jumped off my bench and stood in-between my 65-year-old dad and the Devil's Reject who was getting back to his feet. For the first and only time in my Moon Man experience, I started yelling for the police.

"Help! Police! Police, help!" I shouted—sounding like a real lunatic.

I also ripped off my cape as fast as I could. A few of the men in the crowd, having realized what might have happened, now came and stood by me. The pyromaniac, his face filled with hate and now fear ran off. After a few sympathy sales were transacted, I was more than ready to pack it in.

An hour later, sitting at the counter of the Oyster Bar restaurant on Polk Street, my father paused over his white clam chowder and fresh sourdough bread. "Son, maybe it's time you think about another line of work."

This would not be the only time I was surprised from behind while performing my moon act. On a return visit to Sacramento State College, in front of a large crowd, I would be the recipient of two oversized cream pies to the face. I didn't see them coming, and was embarrassed more than hurt. I could hear the audience start to boo whoever my unseen assailant was. After wiping the sticky white froth from my face and moon glasses, and pretending to have regained my dignity, the fat grinning face of my old associate and one time manager, Big Eddie Fergus, came into focus.

"Hey, now, don't be mad." Fergus was talking fast, "Only a real friend would have the guts to do that. Every great performer should experience a pie or two in the face at least once in their career. It puts things in perspective. You'll thank me for this in a few years. Consider it a badge of honor, trial by fire, that kind of thing."

I hadn't seen Fergus in almost three years, and realized I hadn't missed him much. I had heard through mutual acquaintances that he and Woody were again deeply in debt. Their new scheme included constructing a huge geodesic dome. It was to be the home of their new business—the creation and marketing of Kirlian photography. Taking pictures of the light or aura around one's body was a niche opportunity in the growing marketplace of new age enlightenment. And Fergus, with Woody's money, was hoping to capitalize.

The cream had splattered over my moon suit. I was mad and getting madder. As much as I wanted to leave and clean up, I decided to stay. I didn't want to give Fergus any further satisfaction.

"Ladies and gentlemen, if that was not worth a dollar bill...what is? It's not every day you see a Moon Man take a couple of pies in the face for your entertainment. The show is free. The Moon Acres are just a dollar. Land on the moon is now on sale. Who will be the first to help me with my dry cleaning bill and buy a certificate?"

I had barely finished my last sentence before the crowd started surging forward with dollars in their outstretched hands. The last glimpse I had of Fergus was watching him push his way through the throng of students all intent on buying a little piece of lunacy.

THE DAILY
FORTY-NIN

California State
University, Long Beach
Volume Twenty-seven
Number One hundred

THURSDAY, MARCH 18, 1976

Moon Man still selling lunar land

By Jonathan Muench
F-N Staff Writer

A spaceship slowly descends on the moon. The earth is a small forgotten blue ball over the horizon. A metal door slides open and hundreds of property owners rush out to stake claims on the Hartland crater they bought from the Moon Man.

The Moon Man was a real estate salesman during the 20th century who was thrown in jail, sued for fraud and heckled for his profession—selling bogus property on the moon.

Yesterday, the Moon Man landed at Cal State Long Beach.

Clad in a silver "Moon suit," embellished with shiny jewelry, the Moon Man shouts out to a crowd that is gathering.

"Buy a piece of the rock!"

Everyone laughs as the Moon Man continues a 20 minute sales pitch on why you should buy an acre of moon property.

"Take a chance on insanity," he says and receives a round of applause.

And people did. Moon Man probably made over a hundred dollars in one afternoon. He also made a hundred others

Who's the lunatic?

Students crowd around "Moon Man" to buy acres of the moon as others look on in won[...] will be on campus again today from 10 a.m. to 2 p.m.

Former Redlands youth will gladly oblige

Wanna buy a piece of the moon?

By BETTYE WELLS

The moon may not be made of green cheese, but the sale of land in a mythical crater on its surface is producing enough green stuff to provide Barry McArdle, a former Redlands resident for 12 years, a comfortable and unusual living.

"I'm not a lunatic (pardon the pun)," he insisted as he strolled through the University of Redlands campus yesterday in his Moon Man costume, selling one-acre sections of lunar surface in the Hartland crater, a territory that exists only in his imagination.

"There's still some good property left on Moon River," he quipped.

McArdle, who attended Redlands schools and lived at 109 W. Olive before his family moved to Carmichael in 1966, is one of the first to "claim" the moon and has been selling one-acre plots since his [...]

California college campuses.

McArdle said there is nothing illegal about his activities and told a group of puzzled university students, "You're investing in insanity."

McArdle's escapades have landed him in jail in Ireland, seen him suffer a hail of tomatoes at one campus, and have made him the subject of more than one government controversy.

"I'm being sued in San Francisco as a fraud, but another small claims court judge said that what I'm doing is legal," he said.

Undaunted, he has filed a countersuit against the government for trespassing and littering on private property.

"They didn't ask my permission to go up there and leave all that stuff there," he said.

Purchasers of McArdle's "property" receive a certificate of ownership from [...]

Commons. "With the energy cri[...] provide transportation, an[...] guarantee water, mineral right[...]

McArdle, who admits that [...] doing may "look a little weird," [...] is "a method to my madness."

Namely, the promotion of in[...] and creativity, "keeping lunac[...] making people laugh, surviva[...] credibility back into real estate[...] establishment of Moon Park [...] undetermined date in the futur[...]

"If I can make people lau[...] important," he said. "If they l[...] tend to support the person w[...] them do it."

McArdle, who said that sel[...] real estate keeps him employe[...] of rising unemployment, said t[...] is a Moon Park in his future.

"It will be a non-pollutan[...]

CHAPTER 29

AS TIME GOES BY

A YEAR OR SO AFTER I WAS ALMOST SET AFLAME, MY FATHER WAS witness to another of my more unpleasant days at the office. We were in New York seeing relatives and visiting the neighborhoods of my father's youth. As always, I brought my moon suit and certificates. Getting a crowd to gather in New York was much more difficult than anywhere I'd been. It was almost as if I were invisible. People would barely look in my direction. And yet, once a small outline of an audience started to form, it would grow into a huge crowd very quickly. I performed at Washington Square Park, Columbia University and City College.

It was at City College that I was attacked from behind by a belt-slapping maniac. The first strike hit me across the shoulders and back. I turned around and took a misplaced lash on my legs. Not only was this bad for business, it hurt like hell. I was facing a large black woman, with feral eyes, who was re-coiling her leather strap, intent on continuing the whipping. She also continued her verbal abuse.

"Ain't no mother-fuckin white-ass CIA bullshit FBI agent gonna sell us no fuckin land on no fuckin moon. This is the biggest fuckin bullshit CIA fuckin conspiracy I ever fuckin..."

When she went to whip me for the third time, I was ready. I caught the belt in mid-air and yanked it out of her hand.

245

"I am not with the CIA or the FBI. Does this outfit look like Government Issue?"

"She's crazy," someone yelled from the crowd.

"That's a relief," I responded. "I thought she was someone unhappy with her moon property."

This line got a laugh from the audience, but enraged my assailant. Now she charged me, intent on wrestling the belt out of my hand.

I was saved the indignity of having to fight off this woman by a man in the front, who was also black. He reached up and literally lifted her off her feet and held her in the air over his head.

Looking up at her, he said, "Now sister, you just be makin' a damn fool of yourself. This man ain't no CIA and he ain't no FBI neither. He's just a capitalist, and a funny one at that. Now you just let the man be. He ain't hurtin' you none." Then he slowly lowered her to her feet.

I thanked him and asked him to take the belt for safekeeping. Once again, my humiliation was good for sales, but not the method I preferred.

My father, having been present at my near death by fire, and now my cat-o-nine-tails whipping, was more convinced than ever that I should pursue a different occupation.

✳ ✳ ✳

Before we left New York, dad took me to "Hell's Kitchen", the neighborhood he grew up in.

"This was home plate," he told me as we stood over a manhole cover in the middle of the street. "These letters used to have gold paint on them. Look, there's flakes of it still left around the inside edge. This is where I played most of my stickball. It's gone now, but one day I hit a home run with the ball landing on the top of Murphy's warehouse. It used to be at the end of the block, on that corner over there. It had never been done before. I had to wait until dark to go up and get the ball. What a shot! I think Mickey Sullivan and his brother, what was his name...yeah, we called him Hacker, he was always coughing, I think they were on base at the time. It was a three run dinger. A couple of the boys could hit the side of the place, Red O'Shanlin was good at that, but no one but me ever blasted one onto the roof. What I'd give for one more game..."

I could see him gazing down the street and into the past.

"Around the corner is where I lived for 6 years."

He sat on one of the wide stone slabs that framed the stairs leading up to the building's entrance. Pointing up, he identified a window on the fourth floor of the old brownstone. Growing up, my sisters and I had heard stories of how he would fill small brown paper bags with water and drop them on the unsuspecting pedestrians below. It was strangely wonderful to actually be looking at the window I had imagined for so many years.

He had me sit in front of him on the wide stone banister.

"Put your fingers under the lip. Can you feel that little ledge?" he asked. "That's where I would hide my pennies and sometimes even a nickel. I don't think I would have taken a chance leaving a dime there. And of course, I never got my hands on a quarter. I would sit right where I am now and count my pennies without any of the gang knowing. When the boys wanted to get some candy, I didn't need to go up and ask my mother for money. I would just secretly slide my fingers along this ledge until I touched a coin. It's hard to believe the last time I sat here was almost 60 years ago."

He grew silent for a minute or so.

"And yet that same seven-year-old kid is still with me, still in me. My God, where has the time gone? Where are all people I thought would never age? I wonder what happened to the McLaughlin's...they had that little deaf girl with the most beautiful curly red hair. I can't remember when I've thought of her last..."

The only time I had ever heard my father's voice carry this particular wistful tone was when he'd talked about his boyhood dog Mittsy, and the day he came home and discovered his dog had died.

"Hey, Dad! Look what I found!" I exclaimed, as I pulled out the penny I had just placed on the secret ledge of my father's childhood memory.

Fortunately, my dad would not be with me when I got arrested in New Orleans. I had never been to Mardi Gras, and wondered if Moon Man would even be noticed amidst the wild party atmosphere that I'd heard so much about. After arriving, I called all the television stations and explained who I was and what I did. One station invited me in for an interview, and two days later aired a short piece with me in full Moon Man costume.

I Sold *the* Moon!

I had been told that after the last parade, on Fat Tuesday, anybody who wanted could walk the route whether in costume or not. This ragtag group of marchers was referred to as "Krewe of the People." There must have been three or four hundred of us. As we surged along, many in the group threw candies or strings of colored beads to the thousands of spectators jammed together on the sidewalks. The shouts of "Throw me something, mister," came from young and old alike.

I positioned myself at the very end of the marchers, so people on both sides of the street could see me. Every few steps someone would shout out of the crowd that they had seen me on TV or, better yet, would run out from the curb with a dollar in hand to buy an acre. I was having a great time holding the Moon Acre up above my head and repeating my very short sales pitch:

"You saw me on television. Now is your chance to buy land on the moon—one dollar, one acre. Only in New Orleans, land on the moon one dollar. You saw me on television..."

I had been walking about 20 minutes and had sold more than 30 acres. Knowing that the parade route would take over 90 minutes to complete, I had a good chance of this turning into a very profitable day. Additionally, the exposure I was getting would help me tremendously in the days to come as I planned on appearing on Bourbon Street, in the heart of the French Quarter.

Two more people came out of the crowd ready with their dollars. Before the two buyers reached me, I was grabbed from behind, shoved through the throng, and unceremoniously forced to the ground face down. With a knee in my back, my arms were brought together behind me, and I was tightly handcuffed.

"Party's over, asshole," one of my uniformed assailants gleefully informed me.

I had no idea what I'd done wrong or why I was being apprehended. It had all happened without a word of explanation. Sitting up, I noticed my moon glasses lying a few feet from me.

"Officer, my glasses fell off. Could I ask you to please put them in my bag here?"

"Oh, the asshole wants his glasses? I don't see them. Do you, Del?"

As he said this, he walked over and crushed them under his boot. He made a special point of grinding his foot in slow motion pulverizing the mirrored glass and frames.

"No, I sure don't see them," his partner replied.

While waiting for a patrol car, I realized my hands and especially my right thumb were throbbing, but after the glasses incident I was afraid to say anything. By the time the car arrived, I had no feeling whatsoever in my right hand, and knew I needed some relief. I hesitated before I got into the back seat.

"Excuse me, sir, I can no longer feel my hands. Would it be possible to loosen these cuffs a little?"

The three cops looked at each other and I knew I'd made another mistake.

"Yeah, sure, I can adjust them for you," the driver said, as he squeezed the cuffs tighter by another notch. "There, that should be better."

They all had a good laugh over this and then I was shoved into the car. Riding to the station with me were two other guys who claimed to have no idea why they were being busted.

The station house was bedlam. A mob of people, most of them drunk, were in the process of being fingerprinted and having a mug shot taken. This completed, they would stand in line for one of three pay phones in the hope of arranging bail. When the handcuffs were finally removed, my hands were ice cold, swollen to twice their size, and dark purple in color. It would be days before I got feeling back to all my fingers and over a year before my right thumb felt normal.

Jail is no place I ever wanted to be, and certainly not dressed as I was. In a situation where I would have preferred to be invisible, I was the center of attention. At four in the morning, I was finally released. I left New Orleans the following day.

A few weeks later I got a notice informing me that my court date had been set some five months in the future. I would not need to appear, but in that case, I would be found guilty of the misdemeanor charge of disorderly conduct and my bail of $200.00 would be forfeited. The bail money would pay the fine and the case would be closed.

I usually have trouble deciding where I'll be going tomorrow or next week, but I knew exactly where I would be in five months time. It would cost me more than $200.00 to make the trip back to the Big Easy, but I wanted to tell my side of the story. Besides, my thumb still throbbed.

On the appointed day, I listened most of the morning as the judge called one name after another. Each person was being charged with disorderly conduct, and each person, by his or her absence, forfeited their $200.00 bail. When my name was called and I answered, "present," there was a moment of confusion in the near empty courtroom.

Looking through some papers the judge asked, "Is Officer Del LeFrenz here?"

When no one answered, the judge simply said, "Return bail," and continued to the next name on the list. I would be given no chance to say anything. What a racket. Tens of thousands of dollars were being generated in what looked to be an orchestrated, systematic bilking of anyone the New Orleans police decided to single out. In my case, I must have looked like a red cape waving in front of a snorting, sadistic bull.

Not all towns were as inhospitable to the Moon Man as New Orleans. Madison, Wisconsin, or "Mad Town", as the students called it, was wonderful, welcoming, and very profitable. State Street ran from the state capitol rotunda to the University of Wisconsin campus and was the closest thing to Berkeley's Telegraph Avenue that I'd found. I was definitely in the Midwest, but the liberal politics and general ambiance of Madison had me feeling right at home.

On Moon Man's first day on the street, a local celebrity (of sorts) by the name of Edward Ben Elson, who claimed to be the Messiah of the Odd Infinitum Church, traded me a ticket for travel on the Kohoutek Comet for an acre on the moon. On the face of the ticket it read (in part): "Admit One on an Intergalactic Spaceship—Leaving Earth December 24th Nineteen hundred and seventy-three. Reserved For The Chosen Few." And at the bottom in small print: "Retain Stub for Proof of Purchase." Although I had missed the departure date by two years, I knew I was going to like this place.

I had planned to stay only three or four days and ended up staying four months. I was appearing, almost daily, at the end of State Street at the entrance to Capitol Square, and both the *Wisconsin*

State Journal and *The Capital Times* had run favorable front-page stories about me. This exposure would help me in averaging $100.00 every time I put on the moon suit. And there was Paula. Even though I had not seen her for six months, she was never far from my mind. And now she was coming. All the old excitement and anticipation came rushing back. I reminded myself that we had finally let each other go. Yet it was equally true that this intellectual conclusion could not deny how just the thought of seeing her made me ache with anticipation.

This reunion, although lasting longer than most, would, like all the others, end in separation. Paula had been building a new life for herself in Los Angeles with new friends and mentors. She had been living with a man (platonically, she was quick to point out) who was teaching her to sing and play the guitar. She had written a few original tunes and although tentative, her voice and playing showed promise.

During the past few years, our lovemaking often ended in tears. The realization that what we once had was gone, and nothing would bring it back, became more obvious with each new reunion and subsequent separation. It was as if we were stuck—in love with the memory of us. And that distortion worked to sabotage any chance we may have had to see each other as who we had become rather than always as who we once were. Our belief in our future together was over. Thankfully, the friendship, which had been the foundation of our love, remained unshakable.

Two and a half years later, Paula would be on her way back to California, having hitchhiked across the country with her musical guru Joseph. They had long since passed the platonic stage of their relationship. She wanted to see me on her way through Sacramento, where I was temporarily making my Moon Man headquarters in an apartment I shared with my sister Shelley.

"We have a lot to talk about," she told me over the phone late one night. She was calling from a pay phone outside an all night diner, somewhere in Tennessee.

I didn't say much. I got the feeling she needed to talk. She needed someone to listen.

"I miss you. I'm tired of being on the road, but Joseph says all real artists need to suffer. I heard Dourene won a Halloween costume contest wearing my Honey Moon outfit. That's great. I'm glad it's getting some

use. I'm glad to know you're still selling the moon. I think a lot about when we did that together. Joseph thinks it's too capitalistic, but if he saw the act, I think he might change his mind. Did I tell you we have a magic box where I keep my songs? Whenever we're hitchhiking and really need a car to stop, you know if it's raining or something, I just rub the box between my hands. It really does work. Of course, Joseph can do real magic. He's promised to teach me as soon as I'm ready. But I don't know.... It's hard sometimes. I really want to come home. I want to see you. I've been thinking maybe, just maybe, *this* time we..."

"Overtime charges of $3.00 are now due. Please deposit this amount," a recorded voice interjected.

"I'm out of change. Actually, I'm out of money, but Joseph says money is an illusion, and that love and music will sustain you. I better go. I miss you, Bare."

Just before the line went dead, I thought I heard the sound of an 18-wheeler somewhere in the background, rumbling through the Tennessee night.

Waiting for Paula and Houdini to arrive did not appeal to me. Yes, I wanted to see her, but not on her terms. I didn't want her to think I had nothing better to do than to wait around for her to show up. I felt that the sooner she got out of her current relationship with a guy who had far less grip on reality than she did, the better off she'd be. Maybe if I made it a little less convenient she would see the light. If she wanted to see me, to be with me, she would need to leave Joseph and his "magic box" behind.

My best friend David Barclay, having made good on his promise to bring Katrina back from Germany and marry her, now lived in Hawaii. They had been asking me for years to come visit them. Now would be a good time to take them up on their invitation. There's no need to pack my winter Moon Man costume, my summer one will be just fine, I decided.

I packed for six weeks. I should have brought more. I would stay in the islands for the next 10 years.

HULA MOON

As my plane descended from the clouds into the heart-stopping beauty that was Honolulu, it was easy to understand why David and Katrina wanted to live nowhere else. I had been to Hawaii one time before. After High School graduation, David and I had spent a "coming of age" summer on Oahu. During that time, we had talked about one day living in the islands, and now, 11 years later, David was doing it. As I waited for my luggage, I didn't know it yet, but I, too, had moved to Hawaii.

David greeted me with a fragrant plumeria lei, and on the ride through town, my first joint of volcanically enhanced "Maui Wowie."

"When they talk about 'one hit shit' this is what they're referring to," David was saying as he exhaled the sweet, pungent smoke.

We drove towards Diamond Head in David's VW convertible, with the lush green mountains on one side, and rolling aqua waves on the other.

I smelled the lei while appreciating its fragile elegance. What a charming and soulful custom, I thought. To arrive at a place and be immediately surrounded by a ring of flowers said something good about the people and the place that continued such a practice.

"This lei is wonderful. I was hoping I might get one."

"Hey brah, everyone should get laid in Hawaii. Old joke, but you can thank Katrina. She made it from the blossoms off the tree in our front yard."

They were renting a small one-bedroom place attached to a million-dollar property, in an exclusive neighborhood one block from the ocean. Although it was not a sandy beach, they did have access to their enclave's private pier. The water off the pier was calm, deep, and perfect for swimming. About 300 yards out, past the coral reef, was the hypnotic and endless surf break. The white foam created by the tumbling waves looked like liquid marshmallows appearing momentarily and sporadically across the dazzling, rainbow-shaded horizon. With palm trees swaying in the gentle trade winds, and the long dormant volcano crater, Koko Head, in the distance, the pier also served as a fine place for sunbathing and picnicking.

I would always remember this place not for the swimming, not for the sun, and not for the food, but rather as the debarkation point, from which I ended one life, and the place I returned to, ready to begin a new one.

In what seemed like minutes, my six-week visit was up, and I was scheduled to leave the following day. I was packed, my non-refundable return ticket in hand. But I really didn't want to leave. I loved being in the islands hanging with my best friend, and I had recently generated more positive press. The Moon Man had appeared at the University of Hawaii, Manoa Campus, and both of Oahu's major newspapers, *The Honolulu Advertiser* and the *Star-Bulletin* had covered the event with pictures and story. The October 26, 1978 headlines read:

Once in blue moon sale—it's fee simple Simon (*The Honolulu Advertiser*)

"Nearly 100 University of Hawaii students lined up yesterday to buy genuine bogus deeds of ownership to one-acre lots on the moon... 'This is the best real estate buy I've seen in Hawaii...'"

And

He's Selling Moon at a Buck an Acre (*Star-Bulletin*)

"Investors take note: want to buy some land with a spectacular view? At a dollar an acre no less? Boy, does Barry McArdle have a deal for you..."

In addition to the good press, my Portuguese skin had tanned to a dark golden brown and I was just starting to feel less than totally panicked on a surfboard. I could think of lots of reasons why I didn't want to get on that plane. Just because I'd paid for the ticket and would forfeit the fare, was that reason enough to leave when I didn't want to?

Intellectually, I felt I should go back. Emotionally, I wanted to stay. Something told me the decision I made would have a profound effect on the rest of my life. I was right. It did.

David stopped for gas. We were half way to the airport. I was staring at my ticket looking for a sign, hoping for divine intervention.

"Too bad you're leaving. There's a big luau party tomorrow night, should be fun," David was saying as he started the car and pulled back into traffic.

Although David was not my image of divinity, he would have to do.

"Never let it be said I don't like a good party," I dramatically announced. Then, slowly and deliberately, I ripped my ticket into ever-smaller pieces.

It was a birthday party. The Birthday Girl's name was Sheri Lynn. She was turning 21, although she would tell me it was her 22nd. Later I would find out she added a year thinking I would be more attracted to someone not quite so young. She was on summer vacation from school. In the fall, she would return to Long Beach State as a senior, majoring in Speech Pathology.

I was standing behind the food table with my finger having just scraped some of the icing off her birthday cake, when she came in from the patio carrying a tray of barbecued shish-ka-bobs. My frosting-covered index finger froze in mid-air, inches from my lips, as I saw her for the first time. It was as if my life had been spent waiting for this moment. In a room full of people, she was the only one in focus. I had heard of love at first sight, and now I experienced it. Nothing would ever be the same again. If this was half of what

I Sold *the* Moon!

David felt years ago on that ship headed to Greece when first meeting Katrina, I owed him an apology.

Sheri had an advantage. She had seen me before. For two days, she had stood half hidden by a tree on her college campus, fascinated by the man in the silver suit. She had wanted to come forward, to get closer, but was held in place by her natural shyness.

Later that night, when we were alone under the Hawaiian moon, I slipped off my Japanese kimono and dove into the lava rock swimming pool. I invited her to join me. I suppose I thought she would take off the purple silk scarf she had fashioned into a wrap-a-round top, and her long white skirt.

After slipping out of her sandals, she walked step by step, fully clothed, into the water. Wow! I realized she was both refreshingly modest and surprisingly daring. She may have been too shy to remove any clothing, but that would not prevent her from enjoying a moonlight swim. Here was someone unafraid to look foolish, rather than appear prudish. In her willingness to look un-cool, she did the coolest thing imaginable.

Later, we sat on the edge of the pool holding hands, having dried off considerably with the help of the warm trade winds. We talked about what was important in our lives. She laughed easily and our conversation flowed like reminiscences of old friends after a long separation. She was shocked and excited to find out I was the same person she'd watched selling the moon two years earlier. It came as a surprise to discover we both had spent our childhood and most of our adolescence in the small town of Redlands, California. We had shared memories of streets lined with palm trees, parks, the Plunge, soda fountains, High School teachers, and the Fox Movie Theater. Without putting words to how we were feeling, we both knew "something" was happening between us.

"Sheri, may I give you a birthday kiss?"

She nodded.

We kissed.

When our lips parted, applause filled the night air. Everyone at the party had been secretly watching us. Their boisterous approval of our first intimacy felt like a warm embrace.

Leaving the party, I asked Sheri if I could see her the following day.

"I'd like that," she said.

Something was definitely different. It dawned on me that tonight had been the first time I'd kissed a woman and not compared it—as it was happening—to the kiss Paula and I had experienced after seeing "Gone With The Wind." Tonight something had shifted. Maybe the past really could stay in the past.

For the first time in ten years, I truly believed I could be happy without Paula as part of my future. Would I feel this confident in the morning, I wondered? I drifted off to sleep content in knowing I would be spending tomorrow with Sheri.

$$* \quad * \quad *$$

There are some days, just like some memories, that stand out. They're etched forever as part of the retrievable images stored somehow differently in the mind. The next day started with my wondering about nothing more important than what I wanted to wear. Then the mail arrived.

There was a letter for me—from Paula. Just seeing her familiar handwriting had me doubting my newly formed conviction that I could be happy without her. With unsteady hands, I unfolded the single sheet of stationery.

Dearest Barry,

I talked to your mother and she told me where you were. I'm happy knowing that all that beauty surrounds you. Joseph and I are back in California. I was so much hoping to see you. I wanted to be the one to tell you before you found out from someone else. When I talked to you from Tennessee, about two months ago, I didn't know, or would have told you then.

My first true love, I hope you can be happy for me. I'm pregnant. I had always thought we would have a child together. I wanted that from the beginning, but it was not to be. My darling, we all are part of an endless ring of light, but you know that. I'm writing because I'm afraid to hear your voice, afraid of how much I still love you. But now, my heart, at long, long last, must let go.... Our life paths will now finally turn their separate ways. I will always cherish the time we were together. I will always honor the memory of what young love, of what first love, felt like. Nothing can ever take away what we felt for each other. When I close my eyes, I can still taste our first

I Sold *the* Moon!

kiss. We had our time. We were more blessed than we knew. Please be happy for me.
  Paula

I had a sharp pain in my chest, and it was growing. Dizziness and nausea turned the edges of my field of vision black. I could feel madness, like a fast spreading vine, taking hold. It hurt to breathe. I was going to be sick. I needed to be alone.

I grabbed David's surfboard, ran to the pier and got into the water. With the letter between my teeth, I started paddling out to where the waves were breaking. Once through the surf break I kept going. I paddled out for what might have been an hour, stopping only when my arms and back burned enough to make me momentarily forget the knife in my heart. I had never been this far from shore before. I sat up on the board, and had a passing thought to just keep paddling out further and further into that great unknown.

The letter was thoroughly wet, and yet when I unfolded it I could still make out some of what was written. I read again, "first true love...endless ring of light...be happy..."

I sat quietly staring into nothingness, unaware of the passage of time or my relationship to it. Bobbing on the swells, I let the current take me where it would. Then from deep inside I felt an overwhelming need to release. It originated from that hidden place I recognized as having been awakened on the day my golden hand shattered on the sidewalk. It was from that part of the soul that held a child's bliss, having unwrapped a golden handled gun set. It emanated from the area of the heart that safeguards the universal human emotion of both love and loss. It was where the joy of Paula's and my first passionate kiss was sheltered. And so it was from that same repository that I now began to howl, and to weep. Into the great expanse of wind, water and sky, my sorrow over first love, over lost love, my agony over what might have been, poured forth.

Eventually, I felt sanity return. I felt reconnected to my body. Paula had set me free. She must have known. She had always known. I held the letter in my right hand and brought my left

wrist to my mouth. In a few minutes, I had chewed through the last knot holding my leather bands together. I noticed how light in color the undersides of the knots were compared to the rest of the leather.

It was time to set us free. I tied the worn cords around the soggy paper. I kissed the little packet and set it adrift. It floated momentarily, and then slowly descended into the darkening depths until it was lost from sight.

"I loved you as best I could, Paula, and I will be happy for you."

Time passed as I sat meditating, staring at the horizon. I realized I was thankful to be alive. It was time to go back. I turned around and started the long paddle in. As I got inside the break and was making my way through the quiet harbor, I noticed someone standing at the end of the pier watching me, waiting. As I drew closer, I recognized the person. It was Sheri. She was smiling.

EPILOGUE

I︎T'S BEEN 26 YEARS SINCE I CLIMBED UP THE LADDER TO GREET SHERI. We got married a few years later and have been together ever since. We lived in Hawaii for the next ten years. Sheri earned her Masters degree in Speech Pathology from the University of Hawaii and, later, a Ph.D. in Neuropsychology from the California School of Professional Psychology, Berkeley.

While in Hawaii, I got involved in the world of fine art and managed a gallery for some time. On Maui, I worked as a television producer, writing and directing television commercials. When we moved back to the Mainland, facilitating Sheri's doctorate program, I continued my career in media production, working as a television producer for the next 16 years.

Not being blessed with children has been the one deep sorrow of our life. However, my six sisters and Sheri's one sister have all had children. Our 19 nieces and nephews provide us, at least vicariously, with the journey of parenthood. Well, more like Parenthood Lite.

Big Eddie Fergus married and had six children in eight years. He now works as a professional auctioneer, traveling around the state

of California liquidating the earthly belongings of the newly departed. I still see him, but only occasionally. He claims I owe him money.

David Barclay truly did fall in love at first sight and has been with Katrina ever since the day, 35 years ago, when I introduced them on that ship headed to Greece. They still live in Hawaii and run their own travel business—specializing in Bed and Breakfast accommodations. Our friendship continues.

Our dear Paula passed away in 2006, after a courageous and inspirational five year battle with cancer. True to her Aquarian nature, she lived the artist life. She had four children with three partners. Beyond working as a professional astrologer, she was a full time mom and was well on her way to finishing her first novel—the arc of which, she told me, relied heavily on the time in her life she spent selling the moon. As I did with David, I also introduced Paula to the man she married, Skip. He owns a media production company in San Francisco. Together, they had two lovely daughters adding to their clan of four other children—two sons from Paula and a son and daughter from Skip's first marriage. Knowing both Sheri and Paula as I do it was not surprising that they became good friends. Sheri misses Paula as much as I do.

The following is an excerpt taken from the eulogy I gave at Paula's "Celebration of Life" ceremony.

Paula was the most inclusive person I have ever known. She was a true optimist. She looked for and found the best in people. She burned with the love of fairness and aligned herself with those less fortunate than she. She lived at the dawning of the Age of Aquarius and could have easily been the poster child—I was madly in love with her.

It was as if Paula was on loan from a different world, a better world. If our task, in the lives we lead, is to leave this world a little better for us having been here, than I think Paula more than did her part. She lived her life not completely earthbound. More than most of us she lived a good deal of her life in the stars. And if it's true that we are all star-stuff, then it is truer still that Paula never fully severed her ties to her heavenly home during her visit here on Earth. But she is home now, at peace, among the stars.

* ✱ *

Almost immediately after meeting Sheri, I performed my moon act less and less.

Like other Baby Boomers, my life evolved into careers, cappuccinos and a 30-year mortgage.

The day eventually came when the moon suit, the Moon Book—chock-full of news clippings—and the Moon Acres would be put away for the last time, or so I thought.

It's a different world now—especially since the events of September 11, 2001. People everywhere are now in fear for their safety. We live in a Code Orange world, or is today Code Yellow? However, in our desire for safety and security, I wonder if we're not sacrificing public spontaneity and individuality. I'm concerned that the American spirit is being dragged backwards into a culture of anxiety, fear and conformity. It seems as if we're now on a slow slide away from the free and open society that, since our nation's founding, we have come to take for granted. I believe the light of American freedom has dimmed.

And so, the Moon Man is coming back. I'll do this because I want to spin the dial back a few years to a time when personal, public, interactive entertainment was not so rare. I want to show by example that the American birthright, to follow your dreams, in spite of those who may label it lunacy, is still encouraged and possible. Moon Man will once again be a practitioner in the mode of the Traveling Medicine Show performer, which, if nothing else, provided a pre-Madison Avenue form of entertainment and a forum for one-on-one engagement. It was a time unlike today, where even television programs labeled "Reality TV" are contrived and edited. I believe more and more people are starting to confuse these programs with actual reality. "Reality" can't be scripted. Neither can it be sanitized.

Yes, Moon Man will come back, because I believe that as long as people anywhere are free to speak in city squares, on university campuses or on street corners, then people everywhere are reminded that freedom expressed is freedom realized.

There was a time, not so long ago, when public diversity and street humor were encouraged and supported. I know. I made my living

for ten years "selling the moon." And as long as Moon Man, and troubadours like him, are "out there," that time has not vanished completely.

So, don't be surprised if you see a man on a platform, with real silver hair and a brand-new moon suit, sounding a little bit like a lunatic...

"I'm not pickled, stuffed or mummified but alive, yes, alive and on the outside. It's crazy, it's ridiculous, it's preposterous...but the most unbelievable, the most valuable thing about it is, it's actually happening! Take a chance on lunacy! Moon Acres are once again on sale!"

To order Moon Acres or additional copies of
this book, please visit:

www.isoldthemoon.com